William Faulkner Manuscripts

General Editors

Joseph Blotner • Thomas L. McHaney
Michael Millgate • Noel Polk

Senior Consulting Editor

James B. Meriwether

A Garland Series

Contents of the Set

1. *Elmer* [1925]
2. *Father Abraham* [1926], bound with *The Wishing Tree* [1927]
3. *Soldiers' Pay* (1926). Two volumes
4. *Mosquitoes* (1927)
5. *Flags in the Dust* (*Sartoris*, 1929). Two volumes
6. *The Sound and the Fury* (1929). Two volumes
7. *As I Lay Dying* (1930)
8. *Sanctuary* (1931). Two volumes
9. *These 13* (1931)
10. *Light in August* (1932). Two volumes
11. *Doctor Martino and Other Stories* (1934)
12. *Pylon* (1935)
13. *Absalom, Absalom!* (1936)
14. *The Wild Palms* (1939). Two volumes
15. *The Hamlet* (1940). Two volumes
16. *Go Down, Moses* (1942). Two volumes
17. *Intruder in the Dust* (1948)
18. *Knight's Gambit* (1949)
19. *Requiem for a Nun* (1951). Four volumes
20. *A Fable* (1954). Four volumes
21. *The Town* (1957). Two volumes
22. *The Mansion* (1959). Four volumes
23. *The Reivers* (1962). Two volumes
24. Short Stories
25. "Unpublished" Stories

William Faulkner Manuscripts 8

Volume II

Sanctuary

The Carbon Typescript
and Miscellaneous Pages

Arranged by
Noel Polk

Garland Publishing, Inc.
New York and London 1987

Library of Congress Cataloging-in-Publication Data

Faulkner, William, 1897–1962.
Sanctuary.

(William Faulkner manuscripts ; 8)
Includes bibliographies.
Contents: v. The holograph manuscript and miscellaneous pages—v. 2. The carbon typescript.
1. Faulkner, William, 1897–1962—Manuscripts—Facsimiles. 2. Manuscripts, American—Facsimiles.
I. Polk, Noel. II. Series: Faulkner, William, 1897–1962. Works. 1987.
PS3511.A86 vol. 8 813′.52 86-25622
ISBN 0-8240-6810-6 (v. 1 : alk. paper)
ISBN 0-8240-6811-4 (v. 2 : alk. paper)

The volumes in this series have been printed on acid-free, 250-year-life paper.

Printed in the United States of America

Contents

SANCTUARY

Oxford, Miss.
January - May, 1929

I.

Each time he passed the jail he would look up at the barred window, usually to see a small, pale, patient, tragic blob lying in one of the grimy interstices, or perhaps a blue wisp of tobacco smoke combing raggedly away along the spring sunshine. At first there had been a negro murderer there, who had killed his wife; slashed her throat with a razor so that, her whole head tossing further and further backward from the bloody regurgitation of her bubbling throat, she ran out the cabin door and for six or seven steps up the quiet moonlit lane. He would lean in the window in the evening and sing. After supper a few negroes gathered along the fence below---natty, shoddy suits and sweat-stained overalls shoulder to shoulder---and in chorus with the murderer, they sang spirituals while white people slowed and stopped in the leafed darkness that was almost summer, to listen to those who were sure to die and him who was already dead singing about heaven and being tired; or perhaps in the interval between songs a rich, sourceless voice coming out of the high darkness where the ragged shadow of the heaven-tree which snooded the street lamp at the corner fretted and mourned: "Fo days mo! Den dey ghy stroy de bes ba'ytone singer in nawth Mississippi!"

Sometimes during the day he would lean there, singing

alone then, though after a while one or two ragamuffin boys or negroes with delivery baskets like as not, would halt at the fence, and the white men sitting in tilted chairs along the oil-foul wall of the garage across the street would listen above their steady jaws. "One day mo! Den Ise a gawn po sonnen bitch. Say, Aint no place fer you in heavum! Say, Aint no place ffer you in hell! Say, Aint no place fer you in jail!"

"Damn that fellow," Goodwin said, jerking up his black head, his gaunt, brown, faintly harried face. "I aint in any position to wish any man that sort of luck, but I'll be damned.........." One day more, and he was gone. Then Goodwin could sit all day in his cell, waiting for Popeye to come and shoot him with an automatic pistol through a window not much larger than a sabre-slash. Horace said:

"Which will disappoint you most? To not be shot through that window, or to get out of this with me for your lawyer?"

"If you'll just promise to get that kid a good newspaper grift when he's big enough to walk and make change," Goodwin said. "Ruby'll be all right. Wont you, old gal?" he said, putting his hand on the woman's head, scouring her hair with his hard, lean hand. She sat on the narrow cot beside him, holding the child on her lap. It lay in a sort of drugged immobility day after day, its pinched face slick with faint moisture, its hair a damp whisper of shadow across its gaunt, veined alone then, though after a while one or two ragamuffin boys or negroes with delivery baskets like as not, would halt at the fence, and the white men sitting in tilted chairs along the oil-foul wall of the garage across the street would listen a-bove their steady jaws. "One day mo! Den Ise a gawn po sonnen bitch. Say, Aint no place fer you in heavum! Say, Aint no place fer you in hell! Say, Aint no place fer you in jail!"

"Damn that fellow," Goodwin said, jerking up his black head, his gaunt, brown, faintly harried face. "I aint in any position to wish any man that sort of luck, but I'll be damned.........." One day more, and he was gone. Then Good-win could sit all day in his cell, waiting for Popeye to come and shoot him with an automatic pistol through a window not much larger than a sabre-slash. Horace said:

"Which will disappoint you most? To not be shot through that window, or to get out of this with me for your lawyer?"

"If you'll just promise to get that kid a good news-paper grift when he's big enough to walk and make change," Goodwin said. "Ruby'll be all right. Wont you, old gal?" he said, putting his hand on the woman's head, scouring her hair with his hard, lean hand. She sat on the narrow cot beside him, holding the child on her lap. It lay in a sort of drugged immo-bility day after day, its pinched face slick with faint mois-ture, its hair a damp whisper of shadow across its gaunt, veined skull, a thin crescent of white showing beneath its lead-colored eyelids.

The woman wore a dress of gray crepe, neatly brushed and skilfully darned by hand. Parallel with each seam was that faint, narrow, glazed imprint which a woman would recognise at a hundred yards with one glance, establishing by the very cunning of the workmanship the hopeless subterfuge. On the shoulder was a purple ornament of the sort that may be bought in ten-cent stores or by mail-order; on the cot beside her lay a gray hat with a brim and a neatly-darned veil, and each time Horace saw it he wondered again when he had last seen a veil. She wore the costume every day. The only other time he had seen her she was wearing a shapeless garment of faded calico, a battered pair of man's unlaced brogans flapping about her naked ankles, and so, although he had seen her daily now for three weeks, it seemed to him at times that he had seen her only twice in his life.

He had not noticed the veil when he first saw her in town. It was only when he returned to town on the evening of Goodwin's arrest, after he had told his sister and Miss Jenny that he had taken the case.

"You're just meddling!" his sister said, her serene face, her voice, furious. "When you took another man's wife and child away from him I thought it was dreadful, but I said At least he will not have the face to ever come back here again.

And when you just walked out of the house like a nigger and left her I thought that was dreadful too, but I would not let myself believe you meant to stay. And then when you insisted without any reason at all on leaving here and opening the house, scrubbing it yourself and all the twwn looking on and living there like a tramp, refusing to stay here where everybody would expect you to stay and think it funny when you wouldn't; and now to deliberately mix yourself up with a woman you said yourself was a street-walker, a murderer's woman."

"I cant help it. She has nothing, no one. In a made-over dress all neatly about five years out of mode, and that child that never has been more than half alive, wrapped in a piece of blanket scrubbed almost cotton-white." She nurses it too much, he thought. "Perhaps you hold it in your arms too much," he told her. "Why not get a nurse for it, so you can leave it at the hotel?" The woman said nothing, immersed immediately and without haste in one of those rapt maternal actions which any mention of the child seemed to evoke in her new surroundings. "Dont be silly," Horace said, watching her. "Dont you see they haven't got any case against him? Marks my words, three days after the trial opens he'll be able to see it as often as he wants to. More, from what I've heard about babies. ------Asking nothing of anyone except to be let alone, trying to make something out of her life at the time when all you sheltered chaste women------"

"Do you mean to say a moonshiner hasn't got the money to hire the best lawyer in the country?" Miss Jenny said.

"It's not that," Horace said. "I'm sure he could get a better lawyer. It's that--------"

"Horace," his sister said. She had been watching him. "Where is that woman?" Miss Jenny was watching him too, sitting a little forward in the wheel chair. "Did you take that woman into my house?"

"It's my house too, honey." She did not know that for ten years he had been ~~paying/interest/on/a/mortgage~~ lying to his wife in order to pay interest on a mortgage on the stucco house he had built for her in Kinston, so that his sister might not rent to strangers that other house in Jefferson which his wife did not know he still owned any share in. "As long as it's vacant, and with that child-----------"

"The house where my father and mother and your father and mother, the house where I---------I wont have it. I wont have it."

"Just for one night, then. I'll take her to the hotel in the morning. Think of her, alone, with that baby.........Suppose it were you and Bory, and your husband accused of a murder you knew he didn't---------"

"I dont want to think about her. I wish I had never heard of the whole thing. To think that my brother------Dont you see that you are always having to clean up after yourself?

It's not that there's litter left; it's that you------that------ But to bring a street-walker, a murderess, into the house where I was born."

"Fiddlesticks," Miss Jenny said. "But, Horace, aint that what the lawyers call collusion? connivance?" Horace looked at her. "It seems to me you've already had a little more to do with these folks than the lawyer in the case should have. You were out there where it happened yourself not long ago. Folks might begin to think you know more than you've told."

"That's so," Horace said, " Mrs Blackstone. And sometimes I have wondered why I haven't got rich at the law. Maybe I will, when I get old enough to attend the same law school you did." Miss Jenny was eighty-nine. Five years ago she had had a mild stroke. Since then she had spent her days in the wheel chair beside a window which looked down into the garden, carried up and down stairs, chair and all, by two negroes. Sometimes she slept in it. "You're going to fall out of that chair some day, doing that," they told her.

"Then I'll get up and get back in it," she said. "I'm going to get up tomorrow, anyway.-------And so, if I were you," she said, "I'd drive in now and take her to the hotel. It's still early."

"And go back home until the whole thing is over," Narcissa said. "These people are not your people. Why must you do such things?"

"I cannot stand idly by and see injustice-------"

"You wont ever catch up with injustice, Horace," Miss Jenny said.

"Well, that irony which lurks in events, then."

"Hmmph," Miss Jenny said. "It must be because she is one woman you know that dont know anything about that shrimp."

"Anyway, I've talked too much, as usual," Horace said. "So I'll have to trust you all--------"

"Fiddlesticks," Miss Jenny said. "Do you think Narcissa'd want anybody to know that any of her folks could know people that would do anything as natural as make love or rob or steal?" There was that quality about her. During all the four days between Kinston and Jefferson he had counted on that imperviousness. He hadn't expected her---any woman---to bother very much over a man she had neither married nor borne when she had one she did bear to cherish and fret over. But he had expected that imperviousness, since she had had it thirty-six years.

When he reached the house a light burned in one room. He entered, crossing floors which he had scrubbed himself, revealing at the time no more skill with a mop than he had expected, than he had with the lost hammer with which he nailed the windows down and the shutters to ten years ago, who could not even learn to drive a motor car. But that was ten years ago, the hammer replaced by the new one with which he had drawn

"I cannot stand idly by and see injustice-------"

"You wont ever catch up with injustice, Horace," Miss Jenny said.

"Well, that irony which lurks in events, then."

"Humph," Miss Jenny said. "It must be because she is one woman you know that dont know anything about that shrimp."

"Anyway, I've talked too much, as usual," Horace said. "So I'll have to trust you all--------"

"Fiddlesticks," Miss Jenny said. "Do you think Narcissa'd want anybody to know that any of her folks could know people that would do anything as natural as make love or rob or steal?" There was that quality about her. During all the four days between Kinston and Jefferson he had counted on that imperviousness. He hadn't expected her---any woman---to bother very much over a man she had neither married nor borne when she had one she did bear to cherish and fret over. But he had expected that imperviousness, since she had had it thirty-six years.

When he reached the house a light burned in one room. He entered, crossing floors which he had scrubbed himself, revealing at the time no more skill with a mop than he had expected, than he had with the lost hammer with which he nailed the windows down and the shutters to ten years ago, who could not even learn to drive a motor car. But that was ten years ago, the hammer replaced by the new one with which he had drawn the clumsy nails, the windows open upon scrubbed floor spaces still as dead pools within the ghostly embrace of hooded furniture.

The woman was still up, dressed save for the hat. It lay on the bed where the child slept. Lying together there, they lent to the room a quality of transience more unmistakable than the makeshift light, the smug paradox of the made bed in a room otherwise redolent of long unoccupation~~,.As/though/the woman/herself~~ It was as though femininity were a current running through a wire along which a certain number of identical bulbs were hung.

"I've got some things in the kitchen," she said. "I wont be but a minute."

The child lay on the bed, beneath the unshaded light, and he wondered why women, in quitting a house, will remove all the lamp shades even though they touch nothing else; looking down at the child, at its bluish eyelids showing a faint crescent of bluish white against its lead-colored cheeks, the moist shadow of hair capping its skull, its hands uplifted, curl-palmed, sweating too, thinking Good God. Good God.

He was thinking of the first time he had seen it, lying in a wooden box behind the stove in that ruined house twelve miles from town; of ~~the/black/pre/~~ Popeye's black presence lying upon the house like the shadow of something no larger than a match falling monstrous and portentuous upon something else otherwise familiar and everyday and twenty times its size; of the two of them---himself and the woman---in the kitchen lighted by a cracked and smutty lamp on a table of clean, spartan dishes and Goodwin and Popeye somewhere in the outer darkness peaceful with insects and frogs yet filled too with Popeye's presence in black and nameless threat. The woman drew the box out from behind the stove and stood above it, her hands still hidden in her shapeless garment. "I have to keep him in this so the rats cant get to him," she said.

"Oh," Horace said, "you have a son." Then she showed him her hands, flung them out in a gesture at once spontaneous and diffident and self-conscious and proud, and told him he might bring her an orange-stick.

She returned, with something wrapped discreetly in a piece of newspaper. He knew that it was a diaper, freshly washed, even before she said: "I made a fire in the stove. I guess I overstepped."

"Of course not," he said. "It's merely a matter of legal precaution, you see," he said. "Better to put everybody to a little temporary discomfort than to jeopardise our case." She did not appaer to be listening. She spread the blanket on the bed and lifted the child onto it. "You understand how it is," Horace said. "If the judge suspected that I knew more about it than the facts would warrant-------I mean, we must try to give everybody the idea that holding Lee for that killing is just------------"

"Do you live in Jefferson?" she said, wrapping the blanket about the child.

"No. I live in Kinston. I used to-----I have practised here, though."

"You have kinfolks here, though. Women. That used to lige in this house." She lifted the child, tucking the blanket about it. Then she looked at him. "It's all right. I know how it is. You've been kind."

"Damn it," he said, " do you think-------Come on. Let's go on to the hotel. You get a good night's rest, and I'll be in early in the morning. Let me take it."

"I've got him," she said. She started to say something else, looking at him quietly for a moment, but she went on. He turned out the light and followed and locked the door. She was already in the car. He got in.

"Hotel, Isom," he said. "I never did learn to drive one," he said. "Sometimes, when I think of all the time I have spent not learning to do things.........."

The street was narrow, quiet. It was paved now, though he could remember when, after a rain, it had been a canal of blacksih substance half earth, half water, with murmuring gutters in which he and Narcissa paddled and splashed with tucked-up garments and muddy bottoms, after the crudest of to give everybody the idea that holding Lee for that killing is just------------"

"Do you live in Jefferson?" she said, wrapping the blanket about the child.

"No. I live in Kinston. I used to-----I have practised here, though."

"You have kinfolks here, though. Women. That used to live in this house." She lifted the child, tucking the blanket about it. Then she looked at him. "It's all right. I know how it is. You've been kind."

"Damn it," he said, " do you think-------Come on. Let's go on to the hotel. You get a good night's rest, and I'll be in early in the morning. Let me take it."

"I've got him," she said. She started to say something else, looking at him quietly for a moment, but she went on. He turned out the light and followed and locked the door. She was already in the car. He got in.

"Hotel, Isom," he said. "I never did learn to drive one," he said. "Sometimes, when I think of all the time I have spent not learning to do things........."

though he could remember when; after the rain, the mal of blackish substance half earth, half water, with ing gutters in which he and Narcissa paddled and splashed with tucked-up garments and muddy bottoms, after the crudest of

10.

whittled boats, or made loblollies by treading and treading in one spot with the intense oblivion of alchemists. He could remember when, innocent of concrete, the street was bordered on either side by paths of red brick tediously and unevenly laid and worn in~~to/a~~ rich, random maroon mosaic into the black earth which the noon sun never reached; at that moment, pressed into the concrete near the entrance of the drive, were the prints of his and his sister's ~~feet~~ naked feet in the artificial stone.

The infrequent lamps mounted to crescendo beneath the arcade of a fillingstation at the corner. The woman leaned suddenly forward. "Stop here, please, boy," she said. Isom put on the brakes. "I'll get out here and walk," she said.

"You'll do nothing of the kind," Horace said. "Go on, Isom."

"No; wait," the woman said. "We'll be passing people that know you. And then the square.

"Nonsense," Horace said. "Go on, Isom."

"You get out and wait, then," she said. "He can come straight back."

"You'll do no such thing," Horace said. "By heaven~~s~~, I-------Drive on, Isom!"

"You'd better," the woman said. She sat back in the seat. Then she leaned forward again. "Listen. You've been kind. You mean all right, but---------"

"You dont think I am lawyer enough, you mean?"

"I guess I've got just what was coming to me. There's no use fighting it."

"Certainly not, if you feel that way about it. But you dont. Or you'd have told Isom to drive you to the railroad station. Wouldn't you?" She was looking down at the child, fretting the blanket about its face. "You get a good night's rest and I'll be in early tomorrow." They passed the jail--- a square building slashed harshly by pale slits of light. Only the central window was wide enough to be called a window, criss-crossed by slender bars. In it the negro murderer leaned; below along the fence a row of heads hatted and bare above work-thickened shoulders, and the blended voices swelled rich and sad into the soft, depthless evening, singing of heaven and being tired. "Dont you worry at all, now. Everybody knows Lee didn't do it."

They drew up to the hotel, where the drummers sat in chairs along the curb, listening to the singing. "I must-----" the woman said. Horace got down and held the door open. She didn't move. "Listen. I've got to tell--------"

"Yes," Horace said, extending his hand. "I know. I'll be in early tomorrow." He helped her down. They entered the hotel, the drummers turning to watch her legs, and went to the desk. The singing followed them dimmed by the walls, the lights.

The woman stood quietly nearby, holding the child, until Horace had done.

"I guess I've got just what was coming to me. There's no use fighting it."

"Certainly not, if you feel that way about it. But you dont. Or you'd have told Isom to drive you to the railroad station. Wouldn't you?" She was looking down at the child, fretting the blanket about its face. "You get a good night's rest and I'll be in early tomorrow." They passed the jail---a square building slashed harshly by pale slits of light. Only the central window was wide enough to be called a window, criss-crossed by slender bars. In it the negro murderer leaned; below along the fence a row of heads hatted and bare above work-thickened shoulders, and the blended voices swelled rich and sad into the soft, depthless evening, singing of heaven and being tired. "Dont you worry at all, now. Everybody knows Lee didn't do it."

They drew up to the hotel, where the drummers sat in chairs along the curb, listening to the singing. "I must-----" the woman said. Horace got down and held the door open. She didn't move. "Listen. I've got to tell--------"

"Yes," Horace said, extending his hand. "I know. I'll be in early tomorrow." He helped her down. They entered the hotel, the drummers turning to watch her legs, and went to the desk. The singing followed them dimmed by the walls, the lights.

~~The woman stood quietly nearby,~~ holding the child, until Horace had done.

[illegible]

12.

[illegible]

"Listen," she said. The porter went on with the key, toward the stairs. Horace touched her arm, turning her that way. "I've got to tell you," she said.

"In the morning," he said. "I'll be in early," he said, guiding her toward the stairs. Still she hung back, looking at him; then she freed her arm by turning to face him.

"All right, then," she said. She said, in a low, level tone, her face bent a little toward the child: "We haven't got any money. I'll tell you now. That last batch Popeye didn't----------"

"Yes, yes," Horace said; "first thing in the morning. I'll be in by the time you finish breakfast. Goodnight." He returned to the car, into the sound of the singing. "Home, Isom," he said. They turned and passed the jail again and the leaning shape beyond the bars and the heads long the fence. Upon the barred and slitted wall the splotched shadow of the heaven-tree shuddered and pulsed monstrously in scarce any wind; rich and sad, the singing fell behind. The car went on, smooth and swift, passing the narrow street. "Here," Horace said, "where are you--------" Isom clapped on the brakes.

"Miss Narcissa say to bring you back out home," he said.

"Oh, she did?" Horace said. "That was kind of her. You can tell her I changed her mind."

Isom backed and turned into the narrow street and

then into the cedar drive, the lights lifting and boring ahead into the unpruned tunnel as though into the most profound blackness of the sea, as though among straying rigid shapes to which not even light could give color. The car stopped at the door and Horace got out. "You might tell her it was not to her I ran," he said. "Can you remember that?"

~~[illegible]~~

and he would be telling them how he had just walked out, coming at last to realize ~~[illegible]~~ begin to Belle, the places

house, those 10 years, as a [illegible] [illegible] a [illegible] [illegible] before [illegible] it [illegible]. It was as though the [illegible] distance had a

women whom he had seen [illegible] before and would see [illegible] again had given him perspective.

And so as he drew nearer and nearer and turned at last into the drive that led up to the ~~white~~ square white house in its [illegible] of locusts and cedars, he felt like a bridegroom, [illegible] ~~[illegible]~~ in its entirety the tawdry shabbiness of that other where a marriage service had not even meant a new emotional experience, since long before that Belle had taught him to believe

II.

At home, from his study window, he could see the grape arbor. Each spring he watched the reaffirmation of the old ferment, the green-snared promise of unease. What blossom the grape has in April and May, that is: that tortured, wax-like bleeding less of bloom than leaf, until in the late twilight of spring Little Belle's voice would seem to be the murmur of the wild and waxing grape itself. She would never say "Horace, this is Louis or Paul or whoever" but "It's just Horace", and the pale whisper of her small white dress moving in the hammock, whispering to the delicate and urgent mammalian rifeness of that curious small flesh which he did not beget. She had just got home that afternoon from school, to spend the week-end. The next morning he said:

"Honey, if you found him on the train, he probably belongs to the railroad company, and we'd better send him back. He might get fired, even. And we'd hate that."

"He's as good as you are. He goes to Tulane."

"But on the train, honey."

"I've found them in lots worse places than on the train."

"I know. So have I. But you dont bring them home, you know. You just step over them or around them and go on. You dont soil your slippers, you know."

"What business is it of yours who comes to see me? You're not my father. You're just------just--------"

"What? Just what?"

"Tell Mother, then! Tell her. That's what you're going to do. Tell her!"

"But on the train, honey. If he'd walked into your room in a hotel, I'd just be enraged. But on the train, I'm disgusted. Let's send him along and start over again."

"You're a fine one to talk about finding things on the train! You're a fine one! Shrimp! Shrimp!" Then she cried "No! No!" flinging herself upon him in a myriad secret softnesses beneath firm young flesh and thin small bones. "I didn't mean that! Horace! Horace!" And he could ~~see~~ smell that delicate odor of dead flowers engendered by tears and scent, and in two mirrors he saw her secret, streaked small face watching the back of his head with pure dissimulation, for getting that there were two mirrors.

When the swift, hard clatter of her heels ceased beyond a slammed door, he stood where she had left him between the two mirrors. In one of them he looked at a thin man in shabby mismatched clothes, with high evaporating temples beneath an untidy mist of fine, thin, unruly hair. It had never suffered ordering, though it was six years now since his wife had given over worrying him about preparations for that end.

In the window the curtains blew in and out of the sunlight in alternate fire and ash; he could smell locust on the breeze, burning along the air almost like that of full summer. It was ten degrees warmer here than in Jefferson, with that vivid, unimpeded heat of flat lands across which roads ran like plumb lines into shimmering mirage, and which lie with a quality of furious suspense even under the cold moon. Belle had chosen Kinston because of that land, the black, rich, foul, unchaste soil which seemed to engender money out of the very embrace of the air which lay flat upon it for five thousand square miles without any hill save a few bumps of earth which Indians had built to stand on when the River overflowed.

Once she had not been so keen about money. That was with Harry Mitchell, who never pretended to offer her anything but money, who had probably learned to believe from her that that was what she wanted and who would have given it to anyone else that asked for it; who had to build pools and tennis courts and buy a new car twice a year to get rid of what Belle had been too inert, too richly bemused in discontent, to spend. Sometimes he`thought it had been because Harry insisted on calling her Little Mother in public, sometimes because it flouted her ego to see a man's emotional life apparently fixed upon a woman of whom he could not desire, let alone gain, physical satisfaction in return.

"Dont talk to me about love," she said, her eyelids

smoldering, lying in a wicker chair while Harry scuttled back and forth across the tennis court, applauding all shots in his harsh jarring voice; "you're in love with your sister. What do the books call it? What sort of complex?"

"Not complex," he said. "Do you think that any relation with her could be complex?" A woman for whom even luck, life, simplified itself. Four months after his return from the war she married a man whom anyone could have known was doomed, who carried his fatality about with him, whom she had known all her life without having said four words to, or thought of ~~it~~ half that many times save with serene and shocked distaste; three months after the wedding she was deserted; eight months later she was a mother and a widow.

"Call it what you like," Belle said. "How did she come to let you go to the war, even in the Y.M.C.A.?"

"I did the next best thing," he said. "I came back."

"Yes," Belle said. "To her. Not to me."

"Isn't one man at a time enough for you?"

"Yes. And that wont be again, Horace. Do you hear? I dont need a lover. Even though it did take a war to show me that."

"Did it last long enough to make you sure of that?"

She looked at him, smoldering, contemplative, relaxed in the chair. "Your impossible hair," she said. She said: "So you hope one man isn enough for her too, do you?" He said nothing. "That is, if you're the man, of course." She watched him from beneath her slow lids. "Horace, what are you going to do when she marries? What will you do the night a man makes------" He rose quickly, catching up his racket.

"I think I'll play a set," he said. "Dont let that worry you. You know nothing about virginity. You've neither ever found it nor lost it."

Two days before her wedding he said to her: "Is there any reason why you are marrying this particular blackguard?" She was reading in bed then; he had fetched her a letter which he had forgotten at noon. She lowered the book and looked at him, her brow beneath her loose hair broader than ever, with a serene placidity like that of heroic statuary. Suddenly he began to speak at her with thin fury, watching the sense of his words accomplish steadily behind her eyes, a half sentence behind, as though he were pouring them from a distance into a vessel. "What are you, anyway? What sort of life have you led for twenty-six years, that you can lie there with the supreme and placid stupidity of a cow being milked, when two nights from now----------" he ceased. She watched him while the final word completed itself behind her eyes and faded. "Narcy," he said, "dont do it, Narcy. We both wont. I'll----Listen: we both wont. You haven't gone too far that you cant, and when I think what we........with this house, and all it-------Dont you see we cant? It's not anything to give up: you dont know, but I do.

Good God, when I think..........."

She watched him while that sentence completed itself. Then she said: "You've got the smell of her all over you. Cant you tell it?"

After her marriage she moved out to the country, to her husband's. Horace did not attend the wedding; he merely saw her walk out of the house in a costume he had never seen before and would never see again; he never saw the two of them together after the wedding.

He saw her once before her husband died. He returned home at noon in the November rain and opened the door and ~~stood~~ they stood looking at one another.

"Narcy," he said, "has that surly blackguard------?"

"You fool! You fool! You haven't even an umbrella!" she said.

In the window the curtains blew faintly upon the smoldering breath of locust. The house was new, of stucco. They had lived in it seven of their ten years of the nineteen years she had been Harry Mitchell's wife. She had been married to Harry nine years, and Horace thought how it had required Harry's wife's promiscuity to render him the affirmation of her chastity.

He walked out of the mirror and crossed the hall quietly and looked into Belle's room. It was pink, the bed piled high with pink pillows frosted with lace. On the night-table beneath a pink shaded lamp lay a box of chocolates and a stack of gaudy magazines. The closet door was ajar, the symmetry of the dressing-table broken where she had paused again to don her hat. He went to the table and looked. In a moment he found what he knew he should: a soiled handkerchief with which she had removed surplus rouge from her mouth and stuffed between the mirror and the wall. He carried it to the closet and put it in a bag for soiled linen and closed the closet and left the room.

He passed the door beyond which Little Belle's heels had ceased. It was blank, still. He went on and entered his study and stood beside the flat desk beside the window. Through it he could see the grape arbor, the green-snared bubbles of the waxing grape, with the sun of May stippling the small murmur of young leaves upon the floor, the light winds talking of dogwood out of the south and west.

On the desk sat a photograph in a silver frame. Within the frame the small, soft face mused in sweet chairoscuso. He looked at it quietly, wondering at what age a man ceases to believe he must support a certain figure before even the women at whose young intimacies he has made one: counsellor, handmaiden, and friend. Upon the silence there still seemed to lie the reverberant finality of the slammed door, and he thought of Little Belle beyond it, lying face-down on the bed probably, in that romantic despair, that dramatic self-pity of the young.

The house was quiet. There was no sound save a clash of metal, a slip-slop of feet on a bare floor where a negro woman in unlaced gymnasium shoes went about hetting dinner, the same dinner he had been eating for ten years: only the cook was different, one of a now anonymous succession who were not Belle's husbands. He crossed to a bookcase and took out a dog-eared volume and put it in hi pocket. From the desk he took a pipe and tobacco pouch. Then he tried to slip the photograph into his inside breast pocket, but the frame was too wide. He worked it free of the frame and it went in. From the closet in his bedroom he took a disreputable hat of brown felt. When he was clear of town he crammed the hat also into his pocket, so that the sun could reach his thinning skull.

That night he was lying in a bed of sawdust at a sawmill sixteen miles away, still telling himself that all he wanted was a hill to lie on for a while. Just a hille, he told himself, toying with that lie, turning and turning it on his tongue until it wore away, like a lozenge, until there wasn't even anything left to swallow. Then he began thinking of the house in Jefferson forty-four miles away; letting himself go into the thought with that profound relaxation of sense which is the precursor of sleep, thinking of the gladioli now in bloom upon the lawn and of the wistaria along the eaves in thick, twisted ropes, thicker than a man's wrist.

Later, though still aware of the black sky cold with stars severed half overhead by a flat roof and two thin joists, he was talking to her. They were talking of their father and mother, then he was telling her that he had been dead ten years.

She did not reply at once. She merely mused above him with that quality of utter and detached finality with which women instinctively sift man's folly down to the infinitesimal kernal of impossible longing and desire. She was so still that he said:

"Oh. Was that what it was?"

"Yes. Reality is just a phenomenon of the senses."

"Oh.......Where have you beenm then?"

"I've been at home." She leaned above him with her broad, serene brow, the slow dark wings of that hair which had never been bobbed.

"How about that Sartoris blackguard? How about him?"

Again she did not answer for a time, seeming to communicate to him by sheer hovering the warmth af a wisdom ~~which he~~ whose substance he himself would never touch. "Death is just a phenomenon of mind. A state in which those that aren't dead."

Four days later he was within twelve miles of Jefferson, in the hills at last, kneeling at a spring, drinking. The night before he told her, "There's no hurry. You cant break into ten years like a footpad in an alley crashing into the fatuous moment of an oblivious pedestrian." It was afternoon. He was walking, the coat over his arm, along an empty road through a a high desolation of pines in which the wind drew in long, sombre sighs and where the fading crises of dogwood glinted in the still sunny vistas, while time, the sunny afternoon, brooded kindly and inscrutably about him. If he got a lift he would

She did not reply at once. She merely mused above him with that quality of utter and detached finality with which women instinctively sift man's folly down to the infinitesimal kernal of impossible longing and desire. She was so still that he said:

"Oh. Was that what it was?"

"Yes. Reality is just a phenomenon of the senses."

"Oh.......Where have you beenm then?"

"I've been at home." She leaned above him with her broad, serene brow, the slow dark wings of that hair which had never been bobbed.

"How about that Sartoris blackguard? How about him?"

Again she did not answer for a time, seeming to communicate to him by sheer hovering the warmth of a wisdom ~~which he~~ whose substance he himself would never touch. "Death is just a phenomenon of mind. A state in which those that aren't dead."

Four days later he was within twelve miles of Jefferson, in the hills at last, kneeling at a spring, drinking. The night before he told her, "There's no hurry. You cant break into ten years like a footpad in an alley crashing into the fatuous moment of an oblivious pedestrian." It was afternoon. He was walking, the coat over his arm, along an empty road through a high desolation of pines in which the wind drew in long, sombre sighs and where the fading crises of dogwood glinted in the still sunny vistas, while time, the sunny afternoon, brooded kindly and inscrutably about him. If he got a lift he would

23.

reach town in time to go out to the house that night, but after not having been passed by a car or passing a house himself in more than an hour, he left the road to seek water.

The spring welled up from the roots of a beech and flowed away upon a bottom of whorled and waved sand, into willows. It was surrounded by a close growth of cane and cypress and gum in which broken sunlight lay sourceless and where, toward the invisible highroad which he had just quitted, a bird sang. He listened to it as he knelt his face into the reflected face in the water, hearing the bird above the cool sound of his swallowing. When he rose, the surface of the water broken into a myriad glints by the dripping aftermath of his drinking, he saw among them the shattered reflection of the straw hat.

The man was standing beyond the spring, his hands in his coat pockets, a cigarette slanted from his pallid chin. His suit was black, with a tight, high-waisted coat, his tight trousers were rolled once and clogged at the bottoms with dried mud above his mudcaked shoes. His face had a queer bloodless color, as though seen by electric light; against the sunshot jungle, in his slanted hat and his slightly akimbo arms he had that vicious depthless quality of stamped tin.

The bird was behind him somewhere. It sang again, three bars in monotonous repetition: a sound meaningless and profound out of a following silence suspirant with the peaceful afternoon, the golden murmur of sunlight in the leaves; the very peacefulness of the sound seemed to isolate the spot, so that when another sound swelled out of the silence and rushed remotely past and died away, Horace did not recognise it: when he thought in a flashing instant of the highroad he had just left, it was as though it ran in another world, another time.

"You've got a pistol in that pocket, I suppose," he said.

Beyond the spring the man appeared to contemplate him with two knobs of soft black rubber. "I'm asking you," he said "What's that in your pocket?"

"Which pocket?" Horace lifted his hand toward the coat.

"Dont show me," the man said. "Tell me."

Horace stopped his hand. "It's a book."

"What book?"

"Just a book. The kind people read. Some people do."

"Do you read books?"

Horace's hand poised in frozen midgesture above the coat. Across the spring they looked at one another. The cigarette wreathed its faint plume across the man's face, one side of his face squinted against the smoke like a mask carved into two simultaneous expressions.

"I'm going to move my hand back like it was," Horace said. "I'm not armed. I just want to move my hand."

"Go on," the man said. His voice was cold and still, without inflection, his face squinted against the smoke. "Move it

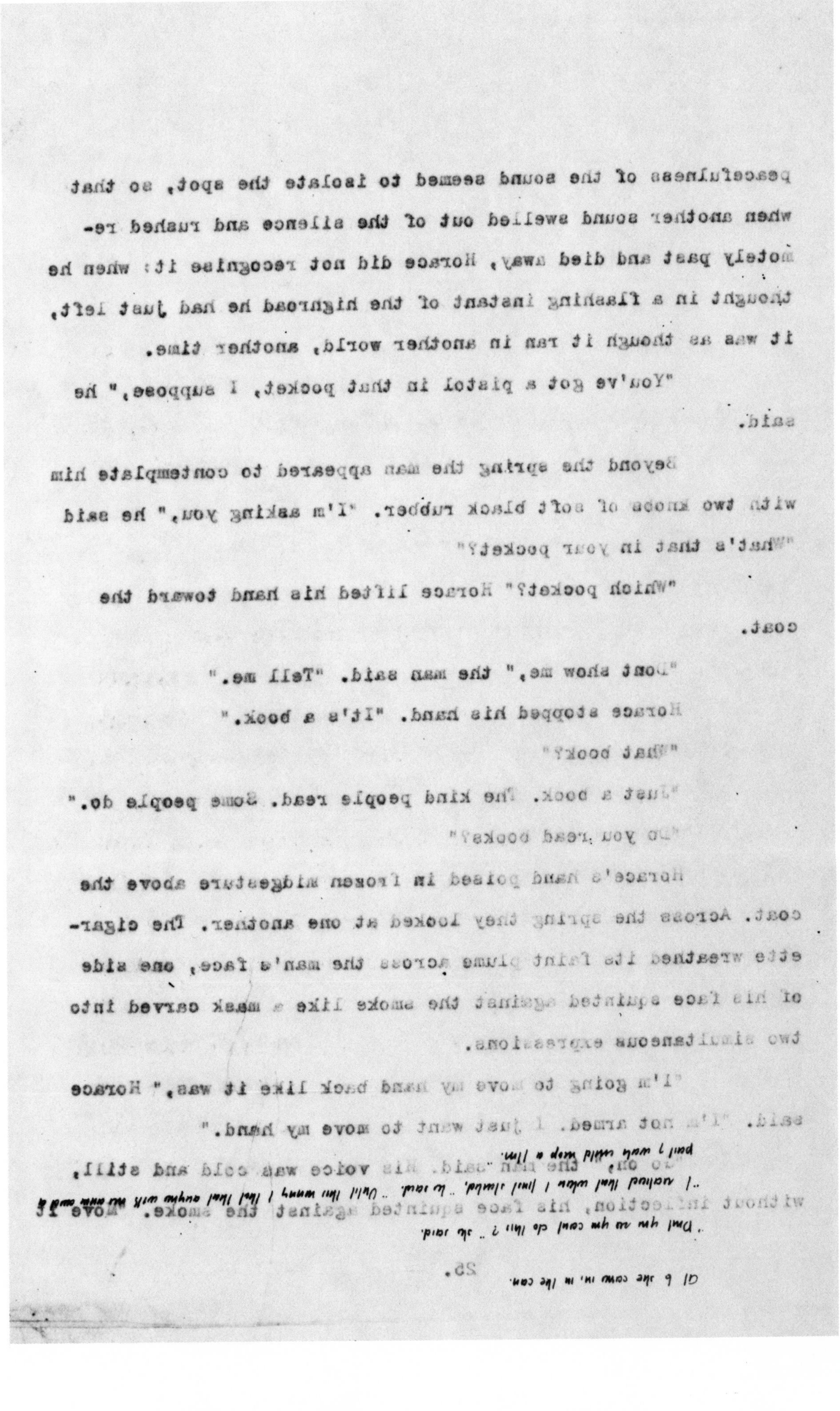

peacefulness of the sound seemed to isolate the spot, so that when another sound swelled out of the silence and rushed remotely past and died away, Horace did not recognise it: when he thought in a flashing instant of the highroad he had just left, it was as though it ran in another world, another time.

"You've got a pistol in that pocket, I suppose," he said.

Beyond the spring the man appeared to contemplate him with two knobs of soft black rubber. "I'm asking you," he said "What's that in your pocket?"

"Which pocket?" Horace lifted his hand toward the coat.

"Dont show me," the man said. "Tell me."

Horace stopped his hand. "It's a book."

"What book?"

"Just a book. The kind people read. Some people do."

"Do you read books?"

Horace's hand poised in frozen midgesture above the coat. Across the spring they looked at one another. The cigarette wreathed its faint plume across the man's face, one side of his face squinted against the smoke like a mask carved into two simultaneous expressions.

"I'm going to move my hand back like it was," Horace said. "I'm not armed. I just want to move my hand."

"Go on," the man said. His voice was cold and still, without inflection, his face squinted against the smoke. "Move it

25.

Later---much later, it was---the woman---she was sitting on the bed in the hotel, beside the child. It had been really sick this time and it lay rigid beneath the blanket, its arms spread in an attitude of utter exhaustion, its eyelids less than half closed, breathing with a thin, whistling sound while Horace looked dwon at it, marvelling at the pertinacity with which it clung to the breath which was destroying it.---the woman said: "If I had my way, I'd ~~have every~~ hang every man that makes whisky or sells it or drinks it, every God's one of them."

And he thought at the time of the two of them---Pope eye and himself--facing one another across the spring. Only the water seemed to move, to have any purpose. It whispered and gurgled and wimpled on, glancing from sunlight to shadow, on and away among the willows to which it communicated a faint unceasing motion in no wind, no breath. Not only the air, but time, sunlight, silence, all appeared to stand still. The spot, the two figures facing one another decorously, were isolated out of all time: he seemed to see time become space: it was as if he looked down a swiftly diminishing tunnel upon that motion which is the world, seeing even places become a part of a rushing panorama which he would never be able to overtake.

He sat looking at the man with impotent and despairing rage. Beyond him, beyond the sunny jungle where the bird was, another car passed along the invisible road. Before lowering his weight to his heels Popeye had spread a soiled handkerchief carefully over them, and he squatted in his tight suit, his right hand pocket sagging compactly against his flank, twisting and pinching cigarettes in his little doll-like hands, spitting into the spring. His nose was faintly acquiline, and he had no chin at all. His face just went away, like a wax doll set too near the fire. Across his vest ran a platinum chain less coarse than a spider's skein. Behind him the bird sang again and Horace listened to it in a kind of rage, trying to remember the name by which country people knew it.

"And of course you dont know it," he said. He said: "Look here. My name is Horace Benbow. I'm a lawyer in Kinston. I used to live in Jefferson. If you know anybody around here, they can tell you I'm harmless. I dont care how much whisky you people make. I just stopped for water. All I want is to get to town."

The man's eyes looked like rubber knobs, like they'd give to the touch and then recover with the whorled smudge of the thumb on them.

"I want to reach Jefferson before dark," Horace said. "You cant keep me here like this."

Without removing the cigarette the man spat past it into the spring.

"You cant stop me like this," Horace said. "Suppose I break and run."

The man put his eyes on Horace, like rubber. "Do you want to run?"

"No," Horace said.

The man removed his eyes. "Well, dont, then."

Horace heard the bird again, trying to recall the local name for it. On the invisible highroad another car passed, died away. Between them and the sound of it the sun was almost gone. From his trousers pocket the man took a dollar watch and looked at it and put it back in his pocket, loose like a coin.

Where the path from the spring joined the sandy by-road a tree had been recently felled, blocking the road. They climbed over the tree and went on, the highroad now behind them. In the sand were two shallow parallel depressions, but no mark of hoof. Where the branch from the spring seeped across it Horace saw the prints of automobile tires. Ahead of him the man walked, his tight suit and stiff hat all angles, like a modernist lampstand, and Horace thought how the man seemed to know that he would not break and run, like there really was an economy of bloodshed, violence. He had never seen the pistol, yet he knew it was there just as he knew the man had a navel, and watching the other's finicking gait he thought how the man should have been a eunuch, serving his ends with a silken cord in a chamber lighted by a ~~scented/in~~ silver lamp of scented oil; a silent shadow high on the secret arras beyond which nightingales were singing.

The sand ceased. The road rose, curving, out of the jungle. It was almost dark. The man looked briefly over his shoulder. "Step out, Jack," he said.

"Why didn't we cut straight across up the hill?" Horace said.

"Through all them trees?" the other said. His hat jerked in a dull, vicious gleam in the twilight as he looked down the hill where the jungle already lay like a lake of ink. "Jesus Christ."

It was almost dark. The man's ~~hat~~ gait had slowed. He walked now beside Horace, and Horace could see the continuous jerking of the hat from side to side as the man looked about with a sort of vicious cringing. The hat just reached Horace's chin.

Then something, a shadow shaped with speed, stooped at them and on, leaving a rush of air upon their very faces, on a soundless feathering of taut wings, and he felt the other's whole body spring against him and his hand clawing at his coat. "It's just an owl," Horace said. "It's nothing but an owl." Then he said: "They call that Carolina wren a fishing-bird. That's what it is. What I couldn't think of back there," with the man crouching against him, clawing at his pocket and hissing through his teeth like a cat. He smells black, Horace thought; he smells like that black stuff that ran out of Bovary's mouth and down upon her bridal veil when they raised her head.

A moment later, above a black, jagged mass of trees, the house lifted its stark square bulk against the failing sky.

It was after midnight when he left the house with the barefooted man. He found that he was drunker than he had thought, as though some quality in the darkness, the silence, the steady motion of walking, had released the alcohol which the woman, her presence, consciousness of her voice, her flesh, had held for the time in abeyance.

Just as they began to descend the hill he looked back at the gaunt ruin of the house rising above the once-formal cedar grove. The trees were massed and matted now with long abandonment; above the jagged mass the ~~house~~ stark shape of the house rose squarely like an imperishable and battered landmark above an extinct world. There was no light in it; he could not think of the three of them---Popeye and Goodwin and the woman---as people preparing peacefully for bed and slumber, but as three figures fixed forever in the attitudes in which he had left them, waiting for him to return with the orange-stick.

The road descended gradually---an eroded scar too deep to be a road and too straight to be a ditch, gutted by winter freshets and choked with fern and bracken, with fallen leaves and branches moldering quietly above scars of ancient wheels. Horace could see broughams and victorias, French or English-made, perhaps, with delicate wheels ~~in/the~~ behind sleek flicking pasterns in the mild dust, bearing women in flowered muslin and chip bonnets, their bodies rising pliant to the motion of deep springs, flanked by riders in broad cloth and wide hats, telling the month-old news of Chapultepec or Sumter across the glittering wheels. By following in his guide's footsteps he walked in a faint path where feet had worn the rotting vegetation down to the clay. Overhead an arching hedgerow thinned against the stars to the ultimate leaf.

The descent increased, curving. It was about here we saw the owl...... felt, Horace thought. It was as though he were feeling Popeye crouched against him, the hand between them clawing at the coat pocket. The earth was beginning to have a tendency to revolve on a horizontal axis just under his feet. It ~~as~~ was as though he were actually walking along a sidehill none too securely fixed; his left foot began to try to rise higher than the other one; presently he would be staggering. He tried to think of his sister, of Belle. But they seemed interchangeable now: two tiny, not distinguishable figures like two china figurines seen backward through a telescope. He concentrated on walking straight, saying "This damn trouble. All this damn trouble."

The branches thickened upon the stars, shutting out the sky; whereupon the road itself began to grow into relief, like an inversion. A moment later his feet whispered off into sand. Against the sand he could now see the guide---a squat, shapeless figure without any sharpness of outline at all---

moving at a shuffling shamble like one accustomed to walking in sand, like a mule, his feet hissing a little in the sand, flinging it behind in thin spurts with each inward flick of his toes.

A low shadow blobbed across the road. It thickened, defined itself: the prone tree. The guide climbed over it and Horace followed with gingerly concentration, hauling himself over and through a shattered mass of foliage not yet withered, through the scent of recently violated wood. "Some mo of------Kin you make hit?" the guide said, looking back and stopping.

"I'm all right now," Horace said, getting his balance again. They went on.

"Some mo of Popeye's doins," the guide said. " 'Twarnt no use blockin this hyer road. Jest fixed hit so's we'd have to walk a mile to the house. I told him folks been comin out hyer for fo years now, and aint nobody bothered Lee yit. Besides gittin that car of hisn outen hyer again. But 'twarnt no stoppin him. I be dawg ef he aint skeered of his own shadow, come dark."

"I'd be scared of it too," Horace said, "if it was my shadow."

The guide guffawed, in cautious undertone. He strode on, chuckling. The road was completely sealed by a mass of growth blacker than darkness---a black tunnel floored by an impalpable defunctive glare of sand. The spring is about there,

Horace thought, trying vainly to distinguish the place where the path notched the wall of tangled cane and brier. But he could feel the water there, beyond the black barrier, welling up from the tree and glinting away among the willows, and Popeye and himself facing one another across the spring while the bird whose name he could not remember sang from its still more secret place toward the ebbing sun.

"Who drives the truck?2 he said. "Some more Memphis fellows?"

"Hit's Popeye's truck," the guide said.

"Why cant those Memphis thugs stay there and let you folks make your liquor in peace?"

"He's payin Lee a good price fer hit," the guide said. "Takes hit offen his hands and gits hit clean outen the county."

"If I was Lee, I'd rather have a deputy sheriff around me than that fellow," Horace said.

The guide guffawed. "Oh, Popeye's all right. He's jest a little cur'us." He strode on, in shapeless relief against the sand, flicking it behind with each stride. "I be dawg ef he aint a case, now, aint he?"

"Yes," Horace said. "He's all of that."

The truck waited where the sand ceased and the road, clay again, began to mount into the lost darkness of higher ground, where the trees thinned again upon the stars of more than midnight. Two men sat on the fender, smoking cigarettes.

"You took your time," one said, "didn't you? I aimed to be half way to town by now. I got a woman waiting on me."

"I bet she's doing it on her back, though," the second said. The first cursed him.

"We come fast as he could," the guide said. "Whyn't you fellers hang out a lantern and be done with hit? Ef me and him'd a been the Law, we'd a had you, sho."

"Ah, go climb a tree, you mat-faced bastard," the first said. They snapped their cigarettes away and got into the truck. The guide guffawed in undertone. Horace turned and extended his hand.

"Well, goodbye. And much obliged, Mister---------"

"My name's Tawmmy," the guide said. His limp, calloused hand fumbled into Horace's and pumped it once, then dropped away. He stood there---a squat, shapeless figure against the glare of sand---while Horace ~~got into the cab~~ lifted his foot for the step. He stumbled, catching himself.

"Watch yourself, Doc," a voice from the cab said. Horace got in. The second man was laying a shotgun along the back of the seat.

The guide was still standing there when the truck roared and lurched into motion. It ground terrifically up the gutted road that joined the highway. The lights swept through the treetops, then sank and levelled away upon the yellow gravel. The wind increased, blowing upon him. He leaned into it, letting it blow upon his face and neck, looking ahead at the dark horizon beyond which Jefferson lay. The last one, he thought. It's already tomorrow.

But he had merely exchanged one reality for another. He thought of his sister, Jefferson, peacefully, with conviction, but still it was like looking backward through a telescope. The whisky inside him was like the glare of a furnace against his skin from within, cooling away into the wind; his skin itself felt cold, detached, like the outer shell of a vacuum bottle. Presently all sense of motion ceased. The truck seemed to be suspended motionless, a motionlessness steadily vibrant against his thighs and the soles of his feet, beneath and beside which time and space rushed in a ywllow band dividing a black strip that fringed delicately off against the motionless stars.

"I've just left my wife," he was saying. "Just took my hat and walked out"; getting himself across to them, with the frogs booming off in the darkness, and an owl---perhaps the same one---and Goodwin tilted in a chair and the halfwit squatting against the wall, passing the jug back and forth, and Popeye coming out now and then to smoke cigarettes svagely beneath his slanted hat, and the woman standing just inside the door and he getting himself across to them, establishing himself: "You see, I've just left my wife."

III

~~IV.~~

As he had expected, he revealed no more skill with the mop than he had with the hammer with which he had nailed the windows down ten years ago; he realised that the reason he was glad his sister had not stayed was not that there was mis-understand between them, but that he did not want her to see how awkward he was, thinking how women control us not by their skill but through our clumsiness.

"You wont stop and look on?" he said.

"I will not. If you must make a spectacle of yourself, I dont intend to see it," she said. She stood in the door, framed by the door against a background of cedar-splashed sunlight. "Horace," she said. He was striking a match to his pipe, the mop leaning against his thigh, splashed to the knees in an island of pale floor surrounded by damp boards, barricaded by drying water. "You're getting the walls all splotched," she said. "Dont you see you cant do this?"

"It wont hurt them. They'll dry again. Have to be done over soon, anyway."

She was watching him. "Horace." He fanned the match out and put it carefully into his overall pocket. "Why dont you come on back home, Horace? Why must you embarass me this way?"

~~What will people think?~~

"What will people think?" she had said last night,

when he told them what he was going to do.

"Who'll take care of him, you mean," Miss Jenny said. "Let him alone. He'll go on back home in a day or two, if Belle just aint fool enough to send for him." She hadn't done that. Only a wire the day after he left: If Horace comes there tell him I have gone home Little Belle follows when school is out. "Just let him alone," Miss Jenny said."He dont want to be free. None of them do. They just run out now and then to make sure the halter is really tied. He wouldn't come this far, even, if you didn't let him keep that suitcase in the house. If you want him to go back, just dont let him come to the table at meal-time. Which you wont do. And I wouldn't, either."

"You think everybody's soul is in his stomach, dont you?" Narcissa said.

"Well, for Lord's sakes," Miss Jenny said.

Anyway, she'll know now that I mean it, Horace thought, sousing the mop into the pail and swoshing it across the floor, What I said about having the walls done over. Nevertheless, as the mop approached the walls he slowed it and caromed it along the baseboard with awkward care, thinking of that quality atrephied in him, that should free itself in what the world called courage; that thing that by its lack had caused him to tell a moonshiner and a thug and a whore ~~that~~ why he had quit his wife and that ~~was/on/the/point~~ he already saw was on the point of sending him back to her.

He was thinking how man's life ravels out into half-measures, like a worn-out sock; how he finishes his days like a refugee on a levee, trying to keep his entrails warm and his feet dry with cast-offs until he becomes aware of himself, then merely furiously trying to cover his nakedness; of the sorry pillar he runs to, the sorry post he leaves. A shadow with an armful of feathers in a gale, on a black plain deader than the beyond side of the moon..

~~On/the/afternoon/of/his/arrival/~~ He was standing at the window beside Miss Jenny's chair, watching his sister and a man strolling in the garden, along the twilit rows of larkspur and sweet william, hollyhocks and tulips, callacanthus and jasmine. Miss Jenny had brough the callacanthus and jasmine from Carolina in 1867. They wefe starred over with pale buds but not yet odorous.

"They cannot have walked there since last October," Horace said, "because he has changed his clothes." Narcissa was in white, the man in flannels and a blue coat.

"Who has?" Miss Jenny said. "You, Saddie."

Saddie rose from a footstool beside the chair and turned the chair to face the window.

"Ah," Miss Jenny said. "Aint the women you leave enough for you?" Horace watched the two people. "You dont expect to bring one woman another woman's leavings, do you?" Miss Jenny said.

"I dont think I expect anything," Horace said, watching the two people. "They are a little........They should stroll along cloisters, marble, dead shapes, not among mutational greenery. They're incongruous. Flowered walks are for young people with shy, writhing, hidden hands, walking a little blind at an interval over-discreet, while they move with the decorous precision of two figures in the frontispiece of a nineteenth-century novel. All he needs is a dyed moustache; she, one of those hermaphroditic dogs peeping above her shoulder where modern women wear artificial flowers. What is his name? the one last fall, the Virginia gentleman one, who told us at supper about how they had taught him to drink like a gentlemen---------"

"Gowan Stevens?"

"I daresay." They watched the two people move toward the front and disappear. "I dont see Bory, though. Or is Wednesday ~~his~~ her afternoon off?........He and his squire were in the pasture when I passed. I waved, but they sat their steeds and regarded my passing genuflection like a couple of equestrain statues, with wreathes. But when I got out of the car they were coming up the drive about fifty yards back, Bory scrabbling along on the pony and Sundy trying to beat that mule into something more than a prolonged and abortive fall. He got down and was coming in with me when Sundy reminded him of some unfinished business somewhere, so he mounted again. But he paused long enough to assure me that someone would prob-

ably show up after a while and that he would see me later, anyway. Then he said 'Come on here, nigger' and cudgelled himself
off with a flat thing like a barrel stave, a pistol strapped
at his waist, and Sundy behind him on the mule. Which is it?
are you older than the mule, or is the mule older than you?"

"That's the pistol Gowan gave him," Miss Jenny said.
"It hasn't got any trigger." She said: "Do you expect her to
worry very much about a man she never bore ~~and wasn't married~~
or was married to, when she's got one of her own to nag and
fret and worry over?"

"I dont expect anything of her," Horace said. "She
has no heart. She never had."

"You may be right," Miss Jenny said. "The folks that
wont do to suit us never have."

"Perhaps I do expect her to do me the constansy of
being fickle," Horace said. "Perhaps she's going to marry a-
gain, after all." Miss Jenny said nothing. She sat so quiet
that Horace spoke again before he realised that she had tricked
him. "Do you think she will?"

She began to laugh, that cold, steady, cruel laughter
of old women, as though they took a revenge on all breath. She
laughed steadily, watching him. "Go on back, Horace," she said.

"No. I'll do Belle that constansy, at least."

"Go on back, Horace," Miss Jenny said, "if that's
all that worries you. If you and Bayard couldn't teach her
she's well off a widow, I dont know what can."

She didn't talk that way last year. It was in the early fall; again the two of them watched Narcissa in the garden below, in a white dress, flanked on one side by a straight-backed little boy and on the other by a broad, fattish man in brown, and he asked Miss Jenny why she had never married again. More than once he had asked himself that question, telling himself she should with that complacent approbation with which you contemplate a course of conduct for another which you know he or she will not follow.

"Now, I ask you," Miss Jenny said. "A young woman like that needs a man. There ought to be a law making them, from twenty on. They're so much pleasanter to live with. I keep on telling her that, so she wont grow into an ill-tempered old woman like me. And that boy will be needing a man, soon, if not already. Nobody but two fool women and a few darkies that let him walk right over them.........Will you look at that back, now?"

"Thanks," Horace said. "I thought it was his back, but I hated to.........and he'll probably look the same from either side. Which is an advantage, I trust........hope." They watched the three people moving along the ordered rows of where the bright, florid, dusty-odored flowers of late summer bloomed.

"Bayard Sartoris' back, to the living life," Miss Jenny said........."Eh? What're you saying?"

"You'd think their mothers........" Horace said.

"Mud-bath," he said; "la figlia della sua mente/. She co-ordinates really too well. But I must say, that back is not familiar."

"Oh, that," Miss Jenny said, "Narcissa's young man. That's-------You, Saddie."

Saddie was sitting on a footstool beside the chair. In a diminutive white cap and apron she looked like a life-size doll, a figure carved of ebony for some ceremonial make-believe. She rose and looked out the window.

"Mist Gown Stevms," she said.

"Oh, yes; Gowan Stevens," Miss Jenny said. "You wouldn't remember him. He was hardly out of diapers when you moved away. He's a nice, well-bred young man."

"He all time sendin Miss Narcissa flouhs," Saddie chanted in treble sing-song.

"And why shouldn't he?" Miss Jenny said.

"No reason," Horace said; "no reason at all. I envy him the privilege. The privilege of not being her brother. I merely thought it was another one."

"Which other one?"

"Ay. I ask you. She seems---------"

"One fo dat name Mist Herschell Jones," Saddie said.

"Thank you," Horace said, "I couldn't------She seems to keep them not only in hand, but she contrives by some means to make them friends with one another. It's like a club. I wonder if there's a grip, password........No: she's like a very mature little girl playing dolls."

They watched the three people vanish beyond the corner of the house. A moment later they heard them approaching up the hall. At the door the man and the boy turned with a simultaneous and automatic deference, like two faintly insolent footmen, and flanked the door for Narcissa to enter.

"Well, Johnny," Miss Jenny said. The boy went to her chair and permitted her to touch his head with her hand. The man in brown followed, with his sleek head and his plump, young, masculine face. Miss Jenny gave him her other hand and he bent fatly and kissed it.

"Getting younger and prettier every day," he said. "I was just telling Narcissa that if you'd just get up from there and be my girl, I'd give her the air so fast she wouldn't know it."

"I'm going to get up tomorrow," Miss Jenny said. "Narcissa, why dont you--------"

"I'm going to, if you'll hush long enough," Narcissa said. "Horace, this is Gowan Stevens. My brother, Gowan."

"How are you, sir?" Stevens said. He gave Horace's hand the quick, high, close grip current in eastern colleges. "Heard of you, but it's been my misfortune........."

"Gowan went to Virginia," the boy said. "Where my father went."

"Ah," Horace said. "I've heard of it."

"Thanks," Stevens said.

"Dont mind Horace," Miss Jenny said. "He's just jealous."

" 'Fraid that's my part," Stevens said. "But everybody cant go to Harvard. Place wouldn't hold them."

"Not Harvard," Horace said; "Oxford."

"He's always telling folks he went to Oxford so they'll think he means the State University and he can tell them different," Miss Jenny said.

"Excuse me again, then," Stevens said. "My mistake again."

"Gowan goes to Oxford a lot," the boy said. "He goes to dances there. He's got a jelly down there. Haven't you, Gowan?"

"Right, bud," Stevens said. "A red-headed one."

"Why, Gowan," Miss Jenny said. "Narcissa, do you permit-------"

"He didn't go to Princeton, though," the boy said.

"Bory," Narcissa said. "How are Belle and Little Belle? You didn't--------"

"Quite well," Horace said. "No. This is just a flying visit. I happened to be passing through town."

"I've been trying all afternoon to find out myself if he has run away again," Miss Jenny said. "You haven't quit Belle in three or four years now, have you?"

"Uncle Johnny went to Princeton," the boy said.

"Benbow," Narcissa said.

"And even Princeton couldn't hold him, could it?" Miss Jenny said.

Across the hall a small bell rang. Stevens, Horace and the boy went to the chair. The boy looked at Stevens, then gave way. "All right," he said, "if you want to."

Horace said to Stevens: "Will you forbear, sir? since I am the guest. As a mark of especial favor, Miss Jenny."

"Why, Horace," Miss Jenny said. "Narcissa, will you send up and get the duelling pistols from the chest in the attic?" She extended her hand. Stevens kissed it again, the boy watching with his bleak, light-colored eyes. "Johnny," Miss Jenny said, "you go on ahead and tell them to strike up the music, and tell Isom to fetch me two roses from the garden."

"What music?" the boy said.

"There are roses on the table," Narcissa said. "Gowan sent them. Come on to supper."

He had not seen her again until that afternoon when he drove up to the house in a hired car, with something of the chaotic emotions of a bridegroom of twenty-one. It seemed to him that he could now see in its entirity the tawdry shabbiness of that other where a marriage ceremony had neither promised nor meant any new emotional experience, since long before that hour Belle had taught him to believe that he was merely temporatily using Happy Mitchell's body, contriving somehow to dampen the rosy ardor of surreptitiousness with a quality turgid, conjugal and outworn; wearing her second husband like a lover, the lover like a garment whose sole charm for her lay in the belief that no other woman had one exactly like it; clinging to a certain emotional inviolation with a determination very like prurience turned upside down. He sat there making no sound until he heard her descend the stairs and saw her cross the parlor door. Still he made no sound until she crossed the door again and paused and looked at him. She stood for a time, in her white dress, with that quality of stupid serenity upon her brow that statues have; that quality that seemed to take him by the shoulders as though he were a little boy and turn him about to face himself.

"Oh, Horace," she said.

"Did you------" he said, knowing already that she did know. "Did Belle---------?"

"Of course. A wire Saturday. And this is Tuesday. Four days. Where have you been?"

He began to tell her about last night, about the woman and the child and Popeye. He could see himself talking against time, as children do, while she watched him with that expression which he realised now he had known all the time he would find. Well, I cant expect.........He said, leaning in the failing window above the garden, hearing the two people come down the hall. What did I expect of her? he asked himself.

"Go on home, Horace," Miss Jenny said. "You can save your face, anyway."

When they came in, it was the boy instead of Stevens.

"He wouldn't stay," Narcissa said. "He's going to Oxford. There's to be a danse at the university Friday night. He has an engagement with a young lady."

"He'll find an ample field for gentlemanly drinking there," Horace said. "I suppose that's why he's going ahead of time."

"He kept on talking about drinking," the boy said, "until Mother said 'Are you going to drink any., Gowan?' and he said 'Do you want me hot to?' and Mother said 'I dont think I would if I were you' and he kind of---------"

"Bory," Narcissa said.

"Go on, Johnny," Miss Jenny said. "What did he say?"

"He kind of ~~halled~~ looked at her, like he does---you know; kind of walling his eyes and breathing like this-------"

"Yes, I know. I've seen him. And then what?"

"Benbow," Narcissa said.

"And he said 'But do <u>you</u> want me not to' until Mother said said she didn't, and he said he wouldn't, and he----"

"Benbbw!" Narcissa said.

"Taking an old girl to a dance," the boy said. "He's going to Starkville to the ball game Saturday. He said he'd take me, but you wont let me go."

Horace soused the mop into the pail and swoshed it onto the floor, watching the water cream darkly away across the bare boards, crested with dust so long undisturbed as to be impervious at first even to water, cresting the curled edge of the miniature flood with pale, lace-like drifts. He was thinking how even at forty-three a man still believes that his frustrations should make him romantic in the eyes of other people, and how even at a hundred he will probably still believe that the fact that he has quit one woman should enhance his value in the eyes of another---certainly in those of her enemy.

After supper the two negroes returned and lifted the chair down from the platform. It was of wood, low, with two slots in the surface, into which the wheels of the chair fitted, and they lifted it down and bore it up stairs.

Miss Jenny still had a fire in the evenings. The chair faced it. Beside the chair Saddie sat on the footstool. The boy leaned against the mantel, his face bold in the firelight, a little sullen.

On the wall beside the bed, where one lying in the bed could look at them by turning the head, were a number of portraits arranged in a certain order. The first was a faded tintype in an oval frame. A bearded face stared haughtily across the neck-cloth of the '50's, buttoned into a frock coat. The man was in the full flush of maturity's early summer; the whiskers virile, the nose high-bridged, the eyes quick-tempered and overbearing, and turning his head Horace saw a delicate replica of it above Miss Jenny's shawl, beneath the silver coronet of her hair, serenely profiled by the fire, and a shadowy, faintly sullen promise of it leaning against the mantel. He looked at the portrait again. Beside it hung a second and more hasty one, made in the field: the same man in a long gray tunic with the awry shoulder-straps of a Confederate colonel. His trousers were thrust into dusty boots, his gauntleted hands rested upon the hilt of a sabre, the bearded face shadowed by a broken plume.

"What are you doing?" Miss Jenny said. "Looking at the Rogues' Gallery?"

The boy said moodily: "Gowan said he'd take me, but she wouldn't let me go."

"Why, you wouldn't leave your mother and me alone, without a man in the house, would you?" Miss Jenny said.

"Horace is here," the boy said. "Who stayed with you before I was born?"

Next was a conventional photograph dated fifteen years ago. The man was about sixty, going bald, the mouth shaded by a thick moustache, the chin clean-shaven, a little heavy. The quick temper was ~~still~~ there too, but blurred, as though by a film, ~~something/~~ a bafflement, something.

The next was alos light-stained, faintly archaic. The face was thin, dark, with dark hair above a high brow. The face above the broad collar, the puffed cravat and the high lapels of the early 1900's was that of a sick man. It was clean-shaven, haughty, young and proud.

Next was a photograph of two boys with long curls, in identical velvet suits. They were not long definitely out of babyhood, yet there was already upon the infantile chubbiness of their faces a shadow as though from the propinquity of the faces above them; a quality that utterly relegated the curls and the velvet, and already there was a distinction between them, although they were obviously twins.

The next three were in a row. The middle one was a painted miniature, the face that of a boy of seven or so.

At the fire Miss Jenny spoke. She had not moved. Her head lay back, her hands lay on the arms of the chair, the firelight rosy upon her. "Saddie. What are you doing?"

"Aint doin nothin, Miss Jenny."

"What does the devil find for idle hands?"

"Mischuf, Miss Jenny."

"Then what are you going to do about it?"

Horace watched Saddie go to the table and lift down a sewing basket. Squatting on the floor above it she delved into it with that intense gravity of a monkey or a coon. She replaced it and returned to the stool with a piece of coarse needlework and a dependent needle, and sat again and began to ply the needle by firelight, her head bent, tongue in cheek, her still-babyish hands moving like ink upon the white cloth, with the terrific awkwardness of a monkey or a coon.

"Yes, sir," Miss Jenny said, "I cant have any idle folks around me. If you want to be a house-nigger, that is. Or maybe you dont? maybe you want to be a field-hand and wear shoes and stockings only on Sunday?"

Saddie giggled. Bent over the work, she continued to chuckle. "Nome, Miss Jenny," she said, her voice going on in rich, dying chuckles, as though of its own accord.

"She oughtn't to try to sew in that light," Horace said. "I can hardly see her hands on the cloth, even."

"Fiddlesticks. They're part owl, anyway. Aint you, gal?"

Saddie chuckled, without looking up. "Nome, Miss Jenny. I aint no owl."

"What are you then?" Saddie bent over her slow, terrific hands, the cap crisp upon her neat pigtails. "Who made you, then?" Miss Jenny said.

"God made me. Ise a child of God." She said it in a fainting, rapturous voice; immediately she was about to chuckle again.

"You, nigger gal! Why did He make you?" Saddie hung her head above her unceasing hands. "You, nigger! Talk out!"

"For His greater glory," Saddie said.

"And what are you after that?"

"Ise a Sarto'is han'-maiden."

"Why couldn't you say so, then?" Miss Jenny turned and looked at Horace's back. "What do you think of that?"

"Habet, O most eminent republican," he said. He was looking at the miniature. The curls were still there, the eyes bold and merry, the mouth sweet. It was flanked on one side by a hasty snapshot. Both operator and subject appeared to have been moving when the camera was snapped, for the picture was both lop-sided and blurred as well as out of focus. The subject's head emerged from an elliptical manhole in a tubular affair on the side of which the effigy of a rabbit projected its painted ears into the picture. To the front arc of the pit a narrow screen curved tightly, and two struts slanted upward into a flat surface at right angles in horizontal perspective, from which the pistol-grip of a machine gun tilted. The face, beneath a wild thatch, was in the act of turning when the camera snapped. It was full of movement, travesties by the dead celluloid, the eyes squinted and the mouth open, as though he were either shouting or laughing.

On the other side of the miniature was another conventional photograph. In uniform, with orderly hair, he lounged in a deep chair placed cleverly to bring the subdued light onto his bleak, humorless face, and again Horace looked toward the fire, at the boy leaning there, at the brooding face, the mouth emerging sullenly from childhood, then back to the bleak eyes and the sullen mouth in the photograph.

"Did you see the last one?" Miss Jenny said. "Gowan snapped it."

"He went to Virginia, too," the boy said. "But he wasn't an aviator like my father was."

The next row consisted of nine photographs of the boy, one for each of his years, ranging from that in which he sprawled naked on a fur rug, through his various avatars ~~as~~ in rompers, velvet; as an Indian, a cowboy, a soldier, a groomsman in a diminutive tailcoat, to the final one in which he sat the pony, erect, hand on hip, a salvaged revolver-frame in his waist-band, a small negro perched like a monkey on the withers of a gaunt mule in the background. This was Sundy, sadie's twin; Saturday and Sunday. Horace had named them: two minute creatures with still, shiny eyes like four shoebuttons, born to Elnora the cook, a tall woman in middle life who was unmarried at the time.

Narcissa entered, with a newspaper. She drew a chair up and opened the paper and began to read aloud, lurid accounts of arson and adultery and homicide, in her grave contralto voice. Miss Jenny listened, her head lying back and her eyes closed, her thin profile rosy and serene in the firelight. Her husband had been killed in 1862, on the second anniversary of her wedding-day. She had not spoken his name in sixty-seven years.

Narcissa read on. To Horace, listening, it seemed that

they had never been so far asunder, so completely functioning in separate worlds, not even last night when she and Belle had seemed for the time interchangeable. He watched her quietly, wondering what he had expected of her. He could recapture none of it, not even the ~~desire, yes, alone~~ the glib words, let alone the desire.

Saddie moved quietly about, preparing the bed. Beside it was the iron cot on which she slept. The boy leaned against the mantel, gazing moodily into the fire, kicking his heel slowly with the other toe.

"Uncle Johnny was an aviator too," he said. "They were goddam good ones."

Narcissa raised her head, her voice stopping in mid-sentence, in shocked and grave consternation. "Benbow! Who told you such a thing?"

"Aunt Jenny did," the boy said. "He said he'd take me, but you wouldn't let me go." He ~~brooded, staring at the~~ while his mother continued to look at him across the suspended page. "Taking an old girl to a dance."

At eight oclock Narcissa took him off to bed. Miss Jenny stirred, looked at Horace.

"Go back home, Horace."

"Not home. It wasn't her I ran to. I haven't gone to the trouble of quitting one woman to run to the skirts of another."

"If you keep on telling yourself that, you'll be believing it," Miss Jenny said. "Then what'll you do?"

"That'll be time to go back home," Horace said. ~~He said~~ When Narcissa returned she said:

"What're you going to do, Horace?"

"I dont know. Stay here a while, I think. In Jefferson, I mean."

"What I want to know is, why he left," Miss Jenny said. "I cant get him to tell me. Did you ~~//////~~ find a man under the bed at last, Horace?"

"No such luck. It was Friday, and all of a sudden I remembered how I'd have ~~to go to the~~ station and get that-----"

"But you have been doing that for ten years," Narcissa said.

"I know. But, like I told her, I still do not like to smell shrimp."

"Was that why you left her?" Miss Jenny said. "Because you had to walk to the station once a week and carry home a box of shrimp? I always wondered why Belle never sent you back to Harry Mitchell for an automobile too, like she did for that child after she had agreed to give it up. Then you wouldn't have to walk every time you quit her........It took you a long time to learn that if a woman dont make a good wife for one man, she aint very likely to for another, didn't it?"

"But to walk out just like a nigger," Narcissa said. "And then to mix yourself up with moonshiners and street-walkers. Why do you do such things, Horace?"

"Well, he's gone and left that one, too," Miss Jenny said. "Unless you're going to walk the streets with that orange-stick in your pocket until she comes to town. Are you?"

"Yes," Horace said, "out there with that gorilla in his tight suit and his straw hat, smoking his cigarettes in that ruined hall, and that filthy old man sitting in whatever chair they have put him in, waitbng for them to do whatever they are going to do with him, with that immobility of the blind, like it was the backs of their eyeballs you looked at while they were listening to music you couldn't hear."

"Well, he's gone and left that one, too," Miss Jenny said. "Unless you're going to walk the streets with that orange-stick in your pocket until she comes to town. Are you?"

"Yes," Horace said, "out there with that gorilla in his tight suit and his straw hat, smoking his cigarettes in that ruined hall, and that filthy old man sitting in whatever chair they have put him in, waiting for them to do whatever they are going to do with him, with that immobility of the blind, like it was the backs of their eyeballs you looked at while they were listening to music you couldn't hear."

the man that ain't dead."

Two days later he was within 20 miles of Jefferson. That night he told her: "There's no hurry. You can't break into 10 years as a footpad in an alley breaks into the fortunes instead of an oblivious pedestrian." Next afternoon he was within 12 miles, walking again, his coat upon his arm. It was afternoon; he was thirsty, yet he did not want to leave the road, since a lift would get him to town before dark. But he did not pass a house in an hour, so at last he left the road and descended into a valley where cypress and willow grew, left an old road, and then a path which turned off where a tree had been recently felled, along the road, and came to the spring. It welled from the roots of a beech and flowed away upon a bottom of wavering sand, into willows. It was surrounded by a close growth of cane and cypress and gum, in which the broken sunlight hung motionless and where, beyond the sun, a bird was singing.

He listened to the bird as he knelt, drinking, kneeling his face into the reflected face in the water, hearing the bird above the cool sound of his swallowing.

IV

~~III.~~

The man had no eyelashes. At last Horace decided what it was. At first he was trying to remember the name by which country people knew the joree-bird, and it wasn't until they sat down to the supper-table, where the lamp was, that he really saw the man. Then the woman entered and he was looking at her, at her hands.

Later, when he reached the hotel, he could not go to sleep, even with all the whisky he had drunk. He was thinking about the woman. Now and then he would think about the other three, the two men in muddy overalls and week-old beards, or the slim black one without any chin, with his querulous adolescent's voice, who didn't even drink because he said it made him sick to his stomach like a dog and who was always trying to get someone to light a lantern and go some where with him, then he would be thinking of the woman again, of her hands putting platters of fried food on the table, showing him her hands in that gesture half modesty, half pride and coquetry, telling him he might bring her an orange stick when he returned.

When she first came into the room he thought she was just another hill-woman, just another of those hopeless, malaria-ridden women he could see, barefoot, with a snuff-stick in her mouth and half a dozen children peeping around her skirts, in any cabin door. But there was something about her, something of that abject arrogance, that misture of arrogance and cringing beneath all the lace and scent which he had felt when the inmates of brothels entered the parlor in the formal parade of shrill identical smiles through which the old lusts and the old despairs peeped; something that so definitely postulated her femaleness, as though from long and weary habit. Not the fact that she belonged to that nagging disturbing inescapable half of the race, but that she was a vessel about which lingered an aura of past pleasures and a reaffirmation of future pleasures of superior, if automatic, sort.

It was like that sense of muscular co-ordination he got from watching an acrobat light a cigarette or lift a fork, emphasised by the fact that she appeared so calmly oblivious of them all save as so many mouths to fetch food for, with the exception of Goodwin himself, even when Horace could hear the thug talking to her in the dark hall while ~~they other~~ they were drinking on the porch. That was just after he noticed her hands, before she showed him the baby in the box behind the stove. They had washtub, stove, all the unending drudgery which country women appear to accept as a part of their mammalian heritage, grained into them, yet there was something else; something in their gestures evocative of glitter---silks, money, jewels--- and she standing at the moment in a garment of shapeless faded calico, a pair of unlaced man's brogan's flapping about her naked ankles. Then she went away and Horace found the thug watching him across the table, and he saw that the man had no eyelashes at all.

The thug would be back there in the hall, talking to the woman. Horace could hear the murmur of their voices: another reason why he believed that the woman had once been of that half-world which had bred the man, since she was the only one of them who appeared able to meet him on any mutual human ground: that trivial contact of similar experiences which produces conversation. Then he returned to the porch and tried again to ~~get~~ persuade the halfwit to get the lantern and take him somewhere and the halfwit refused and the thug stood there and cursed him in a cold, savage voice and the halfwit guffawed and Horace could hear his bare feet scuffing slowly on the boards. The thug lit a cigarette, his face coming out of the match, and his hooked little nose and no chin and his slanted hat which he had not even removed at supper, and he leaned against the wall for a while, listening to the talk with a kind of savage moroseness. Sulling, like a child that's mad and stays around to show it's mad. There was something childlike about him: his slenderness, smallness; an air of petulant bewilderment. But the other quality, the thing Horace couldn't place while they were at the spring, he didn't get until the halfwit pointed it out. When they reached the house the thug didn't stop. He went on into the hall, and the halfwit said "Whut you let him run around hyer in them clo'se fer? He ought to have a pair of over-halls. Everbody'll know he haint no business hyer. He looks jest like a durn preacher or somethin."

Whatever it was, whatever qualities he had, they were thoroughly co-ordinated. Horace happened to say---he'd had sèveral drinks by then: they had been drinking steadily since supper, passing the jug back and forth: Horace in a chair beside the door, Goodwin in another tilted against a post, the halfwit squatting against the wall. They hd got Horace a tumbler and set a bucket of water nearby, but Goodwin and the halfwit drank from the jug. Horace could see Goodwin's head tilted and the shape of the jug against the sky and his long throat moving, and he could hear the halfwit swallowing and his bare feet scuffing slowly. Then the jug would go thud! lightly on the floor, the liquor sploshing up the sides in a thick, faint sigh, and he was talking about courage, telling them that after all it was no more than a congenital inability to see more than one side of any situation at one time, telling how he ~~had~~ seemed to have lacked it for forty-three years, through a war and all, without knowing it; and they listening in that way country people have, as though they wouldn't directly put their eyes or their ears on you, lest they seem rude. The thug came out again and lit a cigarette, the match yellow in his hands and on his face, and Horace talked on about courage, trying to establish himself with them, and suddenly he heard his voice saying "You see, I've just left my wife. Just took my hat and walked out." He was watching the thug while he talked, as though he were the one he must establish himself with, and he saw that the man was really listening, as if he had forgot even himself for a minute. Horace could see his head turned and the cigarette coal in his hand where his mouth had been, and he continued to tell how he had left his wife, just walked out of the house because he couldn't stand it any longer. He believed that he had postulated himself and they sat for a while in the darkness, with the owls and frogs booming away down ther in the bottom. Then the thug moved, toward the door. "Jesus Christ" he said. He said it in a tone of utter and savage weariness and went back into the house, with his cigarette and his pistol and his dollar watch loose in his pocket like a coin, with the platinum chain across his vest and a turnip-shaped silver watch which wouldn't run on the end of it, which he had inherited from his grandfather, with a lock of his mother's hair in the back of the case. ~~He had shown it to~~

He showed the watch to Horace at the spring, before they came to the house. Darkness had almost come when they reached the house---a gutted ruin of a place set in a cedar grove. It had been a landmark for years. Horace had seen it before: the ruined monument to its builder whose name was lost with the lost dust of his anonymous bones among his neighbors ---an illiterate race which had croached onto his broad domain and who for sisty years had been pulling the house down piecemeal for firewood or digging sporadically about the grounds and stables for the gold he was rumored to have buried when Grant passed thraugh the land on his Vicksburg campaign.

Three men were sitting on the porch. The woman wasn't there. It never occurred to Horace that there would be a woman there; there was that about the bleak ruin which precluded femininity. It was like coming upon one of those antediluvian thighbones or ribcages which flout credulity by its very fragmentary majesty and from which they reconstruct an organization too grandly executed to have housed such trivial things as comfort and happiness and nagging and affection. As though whatever women had ever dwelled there had been no more than a part of the vanished pageantry of a dream; in their hoops and crinoline but the lost puppets of someone's pomp and pride, moldering peacefully now in a closet somewhere, surrounded by a faint shattering of dried and odorless petals, leaving no so much as the print of a slipper on the dusty stage. Since he had last seen it they had chopped down two of the pillars on the portico with axes, and there was a walnut newel post six feet tall and a balustrade without a single spindle left. It went half way up the wall, then it just ceased. Vanished, steps and all, leaving a faded imprint of stairs mounting the wall in ghostly progression, and in one room was a marble fireplace with the scrolled frame of an eight foot pier glass, with a few ~~glasses of~~ fragments of blackened mirror in the corners of the frame.

~~It/never/occurred/~~ They were sitting on the ~~door/~~ porch, on the remaining end. It was almost dark; he could only tell that three people sat there. There was a light back in the hall. It was open straight through the house and he could see the roof of a barn against the sky, and then he saw the man's car. It was parked beside the house, in the weeds---a long, thick, squatting car without a top; the kind you look at with a sort of respectful awe, like one of those shells that shoot once and cost two thousand dollars. The thug mounted the broken steps. "Here's the professor," he said, and went on into the hall, toward the light. Horace could see his head in silhouette above the broken roofline of the barn, then the light came upon him and he turned and vanished through a door, the door beyond which the woman was cooking supper, with the baby in the box behind the stove. But he hadn't seen her then. He didn't even wonder who would be cooking the meal until she brought it in to the table and he saw her hands in the lamplight. And while he was watching her hands he felt the thug looking at him and he raia/ed his eyes and saw that the man had no eyelashes at all, and when he blinked something seemed to move laterally across his eyeballs, like an owl's, and Horace thought, Fancy being killed by a man you didn't know had no eyelashes, feeling the man's naked-looking eyes upon him dead as bits of soft rubber, thinking fretfully, You'd think there'd have to be a kinship between two people who looked on death at the same time, even though it was from opposite sides.

He hadn't actually seen any of them until then. He knew about what Goodwin would look like from his voice, and he had seen the second one, the halfwit, when he came up the hall with the jug just before supper. He had a beautiful face, with pale eyes and a soft young beard like dirty gold. Like Christ he looked: a sort of rapt, furious face. Horace thought of form without substance, like the jet of a plumber's torch under a spell, reft of all motion and heat. He was barefoot. Horace could hear his feet on the floor, hissing a little, and whenever he drank from the jug Horace could hear them scouring slowly in an innocent and prolonged orgasm, and when the thug would quit talking to the woman in the hall---she never came out to the porch. She just stood inside the door until after a while Horace was talking only ~~to/her~~ at her---; when the ~~go~~ thug came out and cursed the halfwit because he wouldn't light the lantern, Horace could hear his feet rubbing on the floor while he chortled. He never would address the thug directly; he'd talk to him in the third person. "I be dawg ef he aint the skeeriest durn <u>white</u> man I ever see," he said. "Hyer he was comin up the path ther and that ere dawg come out from under the house and went up and sniffed his heels, like air dawg will, and I be dawg ef he didn't flinch off like hit was a moccasin and him barefoot, and whupped out that artermatic and shot hit dead as a do'-nail. I be durn ef he didn't." And he'd rub his feet on the floor and laugh while the thug cursed him. "Whose dog was it?" Horace said. "Hit uz mine," the halfwit said, "a old dawg that couldn't hurt a flea ef hit would" and he would laugh a-gain, scouring his feet on the floor until the thug snarled at him and went back into the hall where the woman was.

The third man Horace did not see at all until Goodwin came into the dining-room , leading him by the arm. He set him in a chair---an old man with a short, stained white beard, who took a filthy rag from his pocket and held it to his mouth and regurgitated something that looked like a wad of damp excelsior, and wadded the rag into his pocket again. The woman brought his plate. She set it before him, and then Horace saw that he was blind. The others went on eating, but he just sat there, his beard moving above his hidden mouth. He fumbled at his plate with an abashed, diffident air and found a small piece of ham and began to suck it. He mouthed at it until the woman came and rapped his knuckles, then he put it back on the plate and she cut it up for him. She cut up all his food, bread and all, and poured sorghum over it. Then Horace quit looking, but later he saw the old man open the rag again and put the object back into his mouth. After that Horace didN8t see him again. He never learned who he was nor where he went. He didn't look like any of the others; he was just there, then he was gone, leaving no gap, no hole in the pattern.

They returned to the porch, where the jug was, with the thug coming out from time to time and going back, and after a while Horace could feel the woman standing just inside the door behind him, listening, leaning against the door, her hands still raw with the harsh removal of grease, listening to what he was saying. He had had a lot more drinks by then and he was talking ~~about love~~ again, glibly, about love and death and how a man's soul is the scoriation of his individual disasters upon the primary putty. He had had a lot of drinks, and the owls hooting and the frogs booming down there in the bottom, and the halfwit scouring his feet slowly on the floor and the thug coming out now and then. He ~~didn't~~ wouldn't drink, wouldn't sit down, wouldn't anything: he just lurked sullenly and savagely about, like a sick and ill-natured child.

Goodwin sat so still in his tilted chair that after a while his immobility acquired a sort of personality. If Horace had not seen him by the lamp on the supper-table he could have told exactly how he looked, even to his brown eyes and his black head. He looked like a centaur in overalls and a blue shirt, Horace thought; like the sort of centurion who would have had a shot at the purple and probably made it go. He had been a cavalry sergeant in the Philippines and on the Border and in France. That was after he loosened up a little, talking, about Manila and Mexican girls, and the halfwit guffawing and chortling and glugging at the jug and passing it and~~s~~ saying "Take some mo" and the woman listening inside the door and Horace thinking, Where were you then? ~~what~~ when did he meet you and what could he have said to you to fetch you out here to live like a nigger, doing your own work, waiting for that inevitable day when he'll be caught or killed, and she'll have to start over again. They were not married: he felt that; she'd not have been standing there inside the door, in the dark, just to be near him while they talked. Then he realised that it was not to be near Goodwin, but it was to listen to Horace talking about love with a glibness which even then could not quite obscure the fundamental truth and tragedy which the word evoked, understanding, since it had to do with love, what he was talking about without hearing the words at all.

So when they told him to wait and went to see about the truck, when he entered the door he could feel the shock of antagonism, awareness, coming from her in waves. He could see the still blur of her face, motionless, like a swordsman on guard, her back touching the wall lightly for balance, her hands on either side, against the wall. He said:

"Do you like living like this? Why do you do it? You are young yet; you could go back to the cities and better yourself without lifting more than an eyelid." She didn't move. He could feel the awareness surrounding him, backing up behind him like a wall, like soon he'd not be able to move, escape, and Goodwin and the thug coming around the house and onto the porch. "You see," he said, "I lack courage: that was left out of me. The machinery is here, but it wont run" and he said: "You are young yet" and he put his hand on her face. Still she didn't move, and he touching her face, learning the firm flesh. "You have your whole life before you, practically," he said. "How old are you? You're not past thirty yet." He was saying all this in a rushing whisper, like when there is something that must be said and there isn't time, but when she spoke she didn't lower her voice at all. It wasn't loud, but she didn't whisper.

"Why did you leave your wife?" she said.

"Because she ate shrimp," Horace said. "I couldn't----- You see, it was Friday, and I thought how at noon I'd go to the station and get the box off the train and walk home with it, counting a hundred steps and changing hands with it, and it------"

"Did you do that every day?" she said.

"No. Just on Friday. But I have done it for ten years. And I still do not like to smell shrimp. But I wouldn't mind that so much; I could stand that: it's because the package drips. All the way home it drips and drips, until after a while I follow myself to the station, stand aside and watch Horace Benbow take that box off the car and start home with it, changing hands every hundred steps, and I following him, thinking Here lies Horace Benbow in a fading series of small stinking spots on a Mississippi sidewalk."

"Oh," the woman said. He could hear the deep, slow movement of her bosom, her face still a blur against the dark wall. Then she turned. He followed her down the hall and across the back porch and into the kitchen, where the lamp sat on the table. "You'll have to excuse the way I look," she said, as though he had never seen her before. She went to the stove and into the shadowed corner behind it. He didn't know what she was about until she drew out a wooden box and stood looking down at it, her hands hidden in her dress. "I have to keep him in this so the rats cant get to him," she said.

"What is it?" Horace said, approaching; then he saw that it was a child, not a year old, and he looked down at it without surprise or pity or anything. "Oh," he said, "you have a son." Then he found her watching him with that baffling, enveloping, secret look of women, princess or drab. From the darkness beyond the door came voices; a moment later the men stepped onto the porch. The woman shoved the box back with her knee, her hands still hidden. Goodwin looked in the door.

"All right," he said. "Tommy'll show you the way if you're ready."

"All right," Horace said, "I'm ready." Goodwin went on into the house. Horace turned back to the woman. "Thanks for the supper," he said. "Some day, perhaps........Or maybe I can do something for you in town? Send you something by the......."

For a moment she looked at him with thet baffling, contemplative look. Then she flung her hands out for an instant and jerked them hidden again.

"You might bring me an orange-stick," she said.

V.

He stayed at his sister's two days. After that first evening she did not mention Belle, Kinston, made no reference to any future, yet as he watched the familiar motions of her hands and body and listened to the familiar sound of her voice as they talked of trivial things, of their childhood, their sùr-roundings, it seemed to him that they had never been so far a-sunder. He was watching a stranger, a usurper wearing the gar-ments of someone that had died. There was no strife, antagonism, conflict. There was nothing. The gestures she made, the words she spoke, had no significance. They were not spoken to him, had no relation to his past or present.

He wondered if deserting Belle had altered him, had inculcated him with some quality of falseness which made false all whom he approached. He thought of returning to her and found that he could contemplate it without any emotion whatever save that of a faint reluctance toward the effort of overcoming a primary inertia. He thought of the woman in the calico dress, of the evening he had spent there, wondering if perhaps that had changed him; if perhaps he had become leavened with a real-ity which had completely destroyed a world of illusion which he had thought for forty-three years was real.

In the forenoons he read, or talked with Miss Jenny

or his sister, in the afternoons he rambled about the farm with the boy and Sundy; after supper Narcissa read the Memphis paper aloud in Miss Jenny's room. Then he would go to his room, where the suitcase stayed in the locked closet, where Little Belle's photograph was propped against a book on the table. He stood for a while before it, looking at the soft, sweet, vage face, thinking quietly how even at forty-three a man .... that incomprehensible conviction of aging flesh that respect is due that commonest phenomenon in life: an accumulation of hours, breaths, temporarily in a single impermanent clot. Then he would go to bed, to lie in the darkness while the scents from the garden came up from below upon the soft, dark, blowing air, not thinking of anything at all.

He seemed to have expected her to be impervious not only to marriage, but to Sartorises as well. Yet even as the carentered the drive that led up to the square white house in its park of locusts and oaks, entering that atmosphere with which four generations of cold-blooded men clinging violently to their outword traditions of human behavior had imbued the very soil on which they had lived, he was saying Damn that brute. Damn that brute. And later, pushing the mop back and forth with an awkward and ludicrous escapement of approximately enough energy to gin a bale of cotton, he thought of his sister as a figure enchanted out of all time between a bed-ridden old woman eighty-nine years old who summed in her person the ultimate frustration of all the furious folly of that race, and a nine-year-old boy emerging full-fledged from the soft haze of childhood into a tradition that had violently slain three men in four generations while in the throes of its own rigor-mortis. He had expected a woman to follow a man whom she had neither married nor borne, into that region of truth divorced from all reality which no woman is fool enough to assay; to follow the very man who had just repudiated that region of reality divorced from truth which women accept and make liveable.

On the second night he dreamed that he was a boy again and waked himself crying in a paroxysm of homesickness like that of a child away from home at night, alone in a strange room. It seemed to him that not only the past two days, but the last thirty-five years had been a dream, and he waked himself calling his mother's name in a paroxysm of terror and grief.

He was afraid to turn on the light. Sitting there in the bed in the dark, he believed that he had irrevocably lost something, but he believed that if he turned on the light, he would lose even the sense, the knowlege of his loss. So he sat there, hugging his knees, not ~~crying~~ crying any longer.

After a while he could not tell whether he were awake or not. He could still sense a faint motion of curtains in the dark window and the garden smells, but he was talking to his mother too, who had been dead thirty years..She had been an invalid, but now she was well; she seemed to emanate that abounding serenity as of earth which his sister had done since her marriage and the birth of her child, and she sat on the side of the bed, talking to him. With her hands, her touch, because he realised that she had not opened her mouth. Then he saw that she wore a shapeless garment of faded calico and that Belle's rich, full mouth burned sullenly out of the halflight, and he knew that she was about to open her mouth and he tried to scream at her, to clap his hand to her mouth. But it was too late. He saw her mouth open; a thick, black liquid welled in a bursting bubble that splayed out upon her fading chin and the sun was shining on his face and he was thinking He smells black. He smells like that black stuff that ran out of Bovary's mouth when they raised her head.

He rose and dressed and went down. For an hour he walked up and down the porch before the breakfast bell rang. Narcissa and the boy were at the table.

"I'm going home," he said. "I want the key."

"I knew you would have......." He watched the sentence, the sense, take shape behind her eyes, a half-sentence late, as usual. "They key?"

"To the house," he said. "I'm going home."

The house was of red brick, set above a sloping lawn where gladioli bloomed at random in the uncut grass that year after year had gone rankly and lustily to seed. You entered a wrought-iron gate in a fence massed with honeysuckle, from which the cedar-bordered drive rose and curved in a half-moon. The cedars needed pruning too, their dark tips a jagged mass like a black wave breaking without foam upon the May sky, breaking on against the house itself in a fixed whelming surge.

Along the once white eaves thick, twisted ropes of wistaria grew. Beneath the vine a lilac snow of petals lay upon the dark earth of an unturned flower bed where a few sere canna stalks rose from a blanket of anonymous mold. The gutter were choked with molded vegetation alos, in which grass seed and even acorns had sprouted, sagging beneath the accumulated weight and in two places broken, staining the bricks with dark streaks.

He and his sister had been born in it, seven years apart. It had been closed for tan years, since his sister's marriage and since the day he had moved away to live with Belle in a rented house in Kinston until they built the stucco bungalow, yet as he moved about the tight and inscrutable desolation on a ~~profound/org~~ prolonged orgasm of sentimental loneliness, he seemed to hurdle time and surprise his sister and himself in a thousand forgotten pictures out of the serene fury of their childhood as though it had been no longer ago than yesterday, evoked sometimes by no more than a bracelet of rotting rope, a scarce-distinguishable knot healed into a limb and become one with the living wood.

The windows were as he had nailed them up ten years ago. The nails were clumsily driven, since he had had no more skill with that lost hammer than he expected to reveal with the mop and broom which, with a feeling of humility, immolation, he had ordered. Rusted, mute, the warped and battered heads emerged from the wood or lay hammered flat into it by clumsy blows. From each one depended a small rusty stain, like a dried tear or a drop of blood; he touched them, drawing his finger across the abrasions. "I crucified more than me, then," he said aloud.

At ten oclock a light truck whirled in the gate and rushed up the drive and slewed to a halt at the front door. A hatless white youth began to hurl packages onto the porch. He took a cigarette from behind his ear and borrowed a match from Horace and snatched the truck about and rushed away.

The parcels lay helter-skelter along the porch. Horace gathered them up and opened them until he came upon a small bottle of oil. He oiled the lock and the rusted key and opened the door. He carried the things in---a broom, a mop; pails; a suit of overalls; a hammer. He donned the overalls and ~~went from room to room opening doors upon peaceful dust~~ opened the doors upon peaceful dust. With the hammer he drew the nails in the shutters and opened the windows and let in the bright air, going from room to room. It seemed to him that he came upon himself and his sister, upon their father and mother, who had been an invalid so long that the one picture of her he retained was two frail arms rising from a soft falling of lace, moving delicately to an interminable manipulation of colored silk, in fading familiar gestures in the instant between darkness and sunlight. Then he filled the pail and began to scrub the floors, finding that awkwardness which he had anticipated, stopping now and then to stretch his muscles, falling to work again.

At noon he removed the overalls and went down town. A bell was ringing inside the hotel, and the drummers were quitting the chairs along the locust-shaded curb and moving toward the door, but he didn't stop. In a delicatessen he bought tinned meat and crackers, in the soda-fountain a bottle of milk. He purchased a pair of sheets and a blanket and returned home and ate his lunch from a newspaper on the kitchen table. The newspaper was brown and faded, dated Memphis, Tenn., Aug. 27, 1919. He turned it over, munching the final cracker. His sister's face looked back at him, the print blurred and discolored. In the corner of the picture a smaller photograph, a reproduction of the one on Miss Jenny's wall, was inset. Above was a decorous caption: Mississippi Bride, and beneath: ....<u>of Jefferson, to Captain Bayard Sartoris</u>. He looked at the picture, chewing slowly, asking himself what he had expected of her. When he remembered word for word their talks during the four nights between Kinston and Jefferson, it seemed to him that she had lied to him deliberately, leaning above him with that serene and constant dullness which could not even have assimilated, let alone phrased, the very thoughts which she had voiced. Telling him that reality is just a phenomenon of the senses. Maybe it's because women are wise enough to be moved only by the evocation of the words, while only men insist upon the sense.

At six she returned, in the car.

"Come on home, Horace. Dont you see you cant do this?"

"I realised that when I started," he said. "Until this morning I thought that anyone with one arm and a pail of water could mop a floor."

"Horace."

"I'm going to stay here. I have covers." Suddenly he said: "I'm the oldest, remember."

He went to the hotel for supper and returned in the twilight. In the center of the lawn, equidistant from either wing of the drive, between house and fence, was an oak. It was old and thick and squat, impenetrable to sun or rain. It was circled by a crude wooden bench, onto the planks of which the bole, like breasts of that pneumatic constansy so remote from lungs at to be untroubles by breath, had croached and overbosomed until supporting trestles were no longer ~~needed~~ necessary. He sat on the bench, smoking, his back against the tree, remembering how on summer afternoons all four of them would sit there while the spent summer rain murmured among the leaves and the thick breath of the honeysuckle bore up the slope in rich gusts, and usually a mockingbird somewhere in the peaceful twilight-colored rain already broken to the westward by a yellow wash of dying sunlight.

He was thinking how women seem ~~to be i impervious~~ not to have associations at all. Perhaps it is because she lives here and can see it everyday, he thought. But then he remembered how Belle not only would not return to Jefferson, but spoke of it and the people with a sort of vindictiveness, as a victim of outrage, which she could somehow make quite personal and foist upon him as though he had created the twon and its inhabitants. Perhaps it's trees that affect her so, he thought, thinking of the stucco bungalow set in its treeless lawn, of Belle on the porch watching him with brooding impatience as he watered the maple and cottonwood seedlings which he had set out. Perhaps she lived among too many trees before; thinking of the house where she had lived with Harry Mitchell. It was two streets away from where he sat---a horrible travesty in scrolled and tortured wood and metal, set in a lwn of regal proportions, among oaks under which Grant's infantry had bivouacked, and he remembered that quality passionate and strange with which she had invested it, gargoyles and ~~all~~ scrolls and all, as she moved there in a series of pictures rich with sullen promise; thinking of that aura of voluptuous promise with which sheer discontent can invest another's wife.

At eight oclock Isom drove in. He had a big bundle. "Miss Narcissa say fer you to use them," he said. It was bedclothing. He put it carefully away and made the bed with those which he had bought.

Just before he went to sleep he was thinking of the woman in the calico garment, of himself and Goodwin and the halfwit sitting with the jug on the porch; of how, having blundered into that reality which he thought he was so hot for, his efforts to establish himself as a factor in it had been like those of a boy watching other boys do things he cannot or dare not attempt, and who performs the dwarfed mimicry of their skill or daring with a sort of raging importunity: Look at me! Look at me! Telling one man who had roughly brushed aside all the triviata of registered vows to carry the woman into what was practically a state of servitude, and another man who appeared to have dispensed even with love with a savage finality, that he had left his wife, who couldn't stay married even in that ultimate apotheosis of vegetable comfort which keeps us good from habit: a stucco bungalow. Talking glibly to a woman who had run the gamut of love between galley-bench and calvary, of love, who knew it only as a dead parade of words across dead paper in which was tombed, as though it were a new and terrible thing, ~~the final baffled and bitter plaint against~~ some anonymous one's final baffled and bitter plaint against ~~the injustice~~ time and death and the springing blood and sweat.

"You see, I left my wife," he said, trying to establish himself, get himself across to them, and the woman standing there in the dark hall, just inside the door, listening. As soon as he said it he was wondering if he were trying to establish himself with them or with himself; if he were not trying to complete the gesture of desertion by telling another woman of it as soon as possible; if that were not necessary always, since ascetic man never seems to quit his wife: thinking that if there were no other women in the world a man would not quit his wife for more reasons than one. It was marriage they were trying to quit, since any woman makes a better better mistress than she does a wife. And for the man who marries his mistress there is but one excuse: she was the woman of the two.

"I've just left my wife," he said; "just took my hat and walked out"; and the frogs booming away in the bottom, and Goodwin in his tilted chair and the halfwit squatting against the wall with that timeless patience of country people or crucifixes, and Popeye coming out from time to time to smoke cigarettes savagely under the vicious slant of his hat. Just inside the door the woman stood; he could feel her there: a steady postulate of female flesh with which he was trying to establish that dumb spark of the universal truth which each man carries inside the slowly hardening shell of his secret breath, into a solitary grave.

Next day at noon, eating his cold food at the kitchen table, he saw through the window a wagon stop in the street. Three women got down and standing on the curb they made unabashed toilets, smoothing skirts and stockings, brushing one another's back, opening parcels and donning various finery. The wagon had gone on. They followed, on foot, and he remembered that it was Saturday. He removed the overalls and dressed and left the house.

The street opened into a broader one. To the left it went on to the square, the opening between two buildings black with a slow, continuous throng, like two streams of ants, above which the cupola of the courthouse rose from a clump of oaks and of locusts covered with ragged snow.

Across the street and some distance away, a frame house stood in a lawn of big oaks. It was in need of paint, covered with intricate scrolls of tortured wood and iron. The lawn was cut by wheel-marks and almost grassless, the earthen space between street and house a series of ruts filled with ashes and broken bricks. Along the curb stood a line of cars. Three others stood on the lawn, clay-splashed, bearing mud-crusted, transient license-plates. Along the veranda-railing a row of boot-soles faced the street. Nailed to a tree near the street was a weathered sign: Rooms & Meals. Horace stood across the street, looking at it, the anonymous cars, the feet, the air of furious and transient promiscuity which now invested it; thinking of Little Belle with her round, soft head, in a small colored dress, upon the lawn; of Belle's unseen presence already felt as he would enter the gate; thinking of Harry with his harsh, jarring voice, his scuttling, short-legged gait, his boy-like innocent pride in his possessions---the new car or gun or tennis racket which he would give you if you asked for it, regarding your gratitude or not gratitude with that sad, baffled thing in his eyes ~~you see~~ that bulldogs have; give you his wife, his child.

Big Boy, I'll say---I'll have to say Big Boy---It's like this: I thought I wanted your wife, but I seem to have been mistaken. So I8ve got to find someone I know will be good to her, you see. So I said, Big Boy here will be the man, the man in a thousand, ten thousand........ I'll have to say Big Boy, he thought, walking swiftly toward the square. Empty wagons still passed him and he passed still more women on foot, black and white, unmistakable by the unease of their garments as well as by their method of walking, believing that twon dwellers would take them for town dwellers too, not even fooling one another.

The adjacent alleys were choked with tethered wagons, t the teams reversed and nuzzling gnawed corn-ears over the tail-boards. The square was lined two-deep with ranked cars, while the woners of them and of the wagons thronged in slow overalls and khaki, ~~in and out~~ in mail-order scarves and parasols, in and out of the stores, blocking the pavement with fruit- and peanut-hulls. Slow as sheep they moved, tranquil, impassable, filling the passages, contemplating the fretful hurrying of those in urban shirts and collars with the large, mild inscrutability of cattle or of gods, functioning outside of time, having left time lying upon the slow and imponderable land green with corn and cotton in the yellow afternoon.

Horace moved among them, swept here and there by the deliberate current, without impatience. Some of them he knew; most of the merchants and professional men remembered him as a boy, a youth, a brother lawyer---beyond a foamy screen of locust branches he could see the dingy second-story windows where he and his father had practised, the glass still innocent of water and soap as then---and he stopped now and then and talked with them in unhurried backwaters.

The sunny air was filled with competitive radios and phonographs in the doors of drug- and music-stores. Before these doors a throng stood all day, listening. The pieces ~~they~~ which moved them were ballads simple in melody and theme, of bereavement and retribution and repentance metalically sung, blurred, ~~by static o~~ emphasised by static or needle---disembodied voices blaring from imitation wood cabinets or pebble-grain horn-mouths above the rapt faces, the gnarled slow hands long shaped to the imperious earth, lugubrious, harsh, and sad.

That was Saturday, in May: no time to leave the land. Yet on Monday they were back again, most of them, in clumps about the courthouse and the square, and trading a littàe in the stores since they were ~~th~~ here, in their khaki and overalls and collarless shirts. All day long a knot of them stood about the door to the undertaker's parlor, and boys and youths with and without schoolbooks leaned with flattened noses against the glass, and the bolder ones and the younger men of the town entered in two's and three's to look at the man called Tommy. He lay on a wooden table, barefoot, in overalls, the sun-bleached curls on the back of his head matted with dried blood and singed with powder, while the coroner sat over him, trying to ascertain his last name. But none knew it, not even those who had known him for fifteen years about the countryside, nor the merchants who on infrequent Saturdays had seen him in town, barefoot, hatless, with his rapt, empty gaze and his cheek bulged innocently by a peppermint jawbreaker. For all general knowlege, he had none.

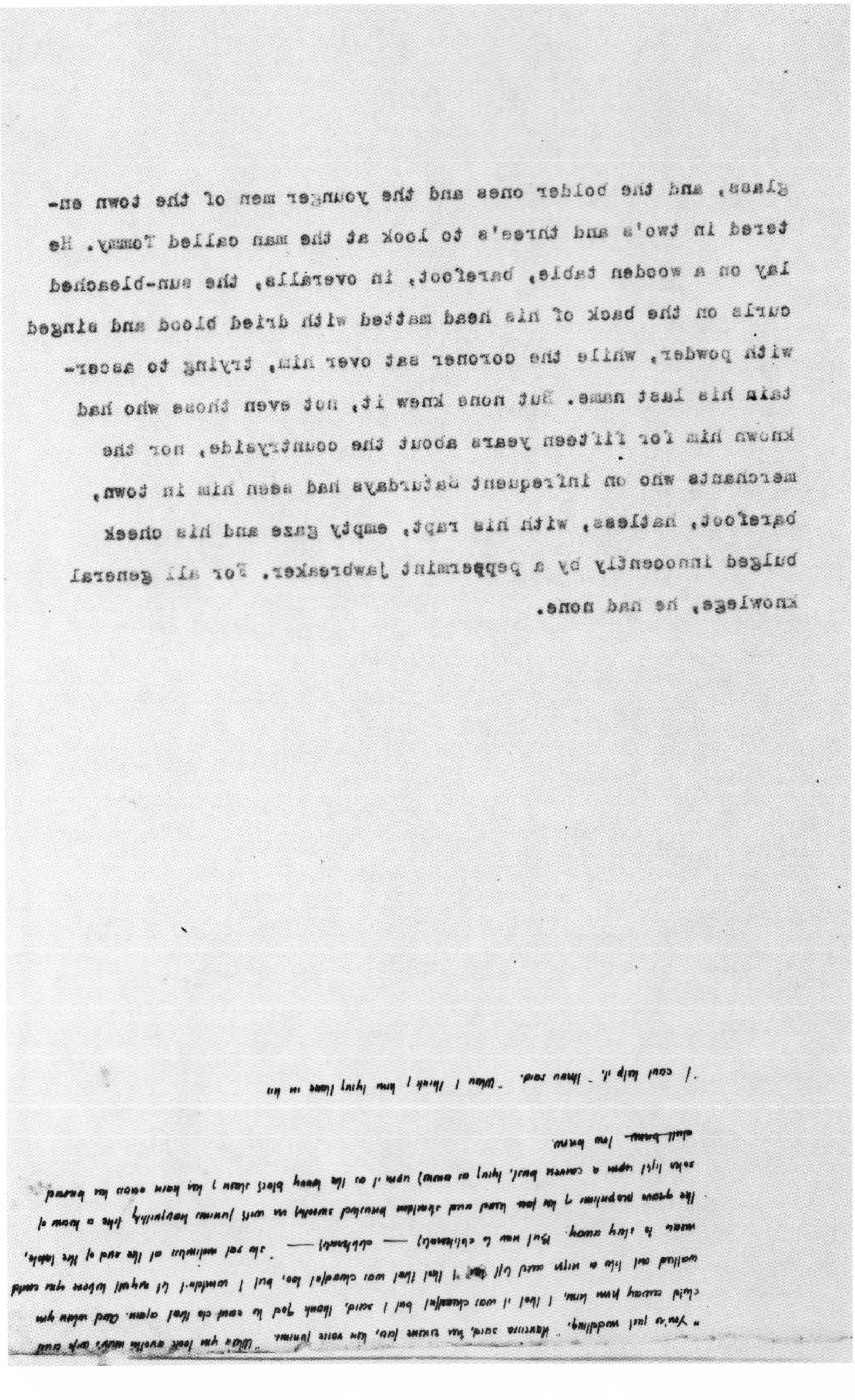

glass, and the bolder ones and the younger men of the town entered in two's and three's to look at the man called Tommy. He lay on a wooden table, barefoot, in overalls, the sun-bleached curls on the back of his head matted with dried blood and singed with powder, while the coroner sat over him, trying to ascertain his last name. But none knew it, not even those who had known him for fifteen years about the countryside, nor the merchants who on infrequent Saturdays had seen him in town, barefoot, hatless, with his rapt, empty gaze and his cheek bulged innocently by a peppermint jawbreaker. For all general knowlege, he had none.

VI.

The last trumpet-shaped bloom had fallen from the heaven-tree at the corner of the jail yard. They lay thick, viscid underfoot, sweet and oversweet ~~upon/the/air~~ in the nostrils with a sweetness surfeitive and moribund, and at night now the ragged shadow of full-fledged leaves pulsed upon the barred window in shabby rise and fall. The window was in the general room, the white-washed walls of which were stained with dirty hands, scribbled and scratched over with names and dates and blasphemous and obscene doggerel in pencil or nail or knife-blade. Nightlily the negro murderer leaned there, his face checkered by the shadow of the grating in the restless interstices of leaves, singing in chorus with these along the fence below.

Sometimes during the day he sang also, alone then save for the slowing passerby~~s~~ and ragamuffin boys and the garage men across the way. "One day mo! Aint no place fer you in heavum! Aint no place fer you in hell! Aint no place fer you in whitefolks' jail! Nigger, whar you gwine to? Whar you gwine to, nigger?"

"Damn that fellow!" Goodwin said, jerking his head up restively, rolling a cigarette from the cloth sack between his teeth. Beside him the woman sat on the cot, the child on her lap. Beside her the gray hat lay, set carefully aside. Heretofore the child had lain in a drugged-like apathy, its eyelide closed to a thin crescent, but today it moved now and then in frail, galvanic jerks, whimpering.

"Hush," the woman said, rocking it on her knees, "shhhhhhhhhhh."

"I tell you, they've got nothing on me," Goodwin said. "They've got no more on me than they have on her, on that kid."

He had waived bond. "He said he was better off there," Horace told Miss Jenny. That was at Sunday dinner. Then suddenly he was living out there again. He could not have told himself how it happened. But all at once he realised that he had returned, not to that which he had walked all the way from Kinston to Jefferson to find, but to a certain amocable arrangement of communal sleeping and eating in which all thse engaged were aware that where you ate and slept was not important. He thought his reason was to be near a telephone and have the use of a car. Miss Jenny thought it was because of the flood. "And I suppose he is," he said. "His business out yonder is finished, even if they hadn't found his kettle and des--------"

"Kettle?" Miss Jenny said.

"His still. They hunted around until they found it before they brought him in. Once he was down, you see, they all jumped on him. All his good customers that had been buying from him and drinking what he'd give them free and trying to make love to her behind his back. You should hear them down town.

Sunday the Baptist minister took him for a text, and her too. Good God, can a man seriously voice the statement that by bringing a child into the world a woman can have put a noose about the neck of the man who begot it?"

"They're just Baptists," Miss Jenny said. "What about the money?"

"He had a little, almost a hundred and sixty dollars. It was buried in a can in the barn. They let him dig that up. 'That'll keep her' he says 'until it's over. Then we'll clear out. We've been intending to for a good while. If I'd listened to her, we'd have been gone already. You've been a good girl' he says. She was sitting on the cot beside him, holding the baby, and he took her chin in his hand and shook her head a little."

"It's a good thing Narcissa aint going to be on that jury," Miss Jenny said.

"Yes. But the fool wont even let me mention that that gorilla was ever on the place. He said 'They cant prove anything on me. I've been in a jam before. Everybody that knows anything about me knows that I wouldn't hurt a ~~feeb~~ feeb.' But that wasn't the reason he doesn't want it told about that thug. And ~~I/know/~~ he knew I knew it wasn't, because he kept on talking, sitting there in his overalls, rolling his cigarettes with the sack hanging in his teeth. 'I'll just stay here until it blows over. I'll be better off here; cant do anything outside, anyway. And this will keep her, with maybe something over for you until you're better paid.'

"But I knew what he was thinking. 'I didn't know you were a coward' I said.

" 'You do like I say' he said 'I'll be all right here'. But he doesn't........" He sat forward, rubbing his hands slowly. "He doesn't realise........Dammit, say what you want to, but there's a corruption about even looking upon evil, even by accident; you cannot haggle, traffic, with ~~putrifaction~~ putrifaction-------You've seen how Narcissa, just hearing about it, how it's made her restless and suspicious. I thought I had come back here of my own accord, but now I see that------Do you suppose she thought I was bringing that woman into the house at night, or something like that?"

"I did too, at first," Miss Jenny said. "But I reckon now she's learned that you'll work harder for whatever reason you think you have, than for anything anybody could offer you or give you."

"You mean, she'd let me think they never had any money, when she-------"

"Why not? Aint you doing all right without it?"

Narcissa entered.

"We were just talking about murder and crime," Miss Jenny said.

"I hope you're through, then," Narcissa said.

"Narcissa has her sorrows too," Miss Jenny said. "Dont you, Narcissa?"

"What now?" Horace said. "She hasn't caught Bory with alcohol on his breath, has she?"

"She's been jilted. Her beau's gone and left her."

"You're such a fool," Narcissa said.

"Yes, sir," Miss Jenny said, "Gowan Stevens has thrown her down. He didn't even come back from that Oxford dance to say goodbye. He just wrote her a letter." She began to search about her in the chair. "And now I flinch everytime the door-bell rings, thinking that his mother----------"

"Miss Jenny," Narcissa said, "you give me my letter."

"Wait," Miss Jenny said, "here it is. Now, what do you think of that for a delicate operation on the human heart without anaesthetic? I'm beginning to believe all this I hear, about how young folks learn all the things in order to get married, that we had to get married in order to learn."

Horace took the single sheet.

<u>Narcissa my dear</u>

<u>This has no heading. I wish it could have no date. But if my heart were as blank as this page, this would not be necessary at all. I will not see you again. I cannot write it, for I have gone through with an experience which I cannot face. I have but one rift in the darkness, that is that I have injured no one save myself by my folly, and that the extent of that folly you will never learn. I need not say</u>

that the hope that you never learn it is the sole ~~reason for my actions from now on that I have done.~~ reason why I will not see you again. Thank as well of me as you can. I wish I had the right to say, if you learn of my folly think not the less of me.

G.

"Good Lord," Horace said. "Someone mistook him for a Mississippi man on the dance floor."

"I think, if I were you-----" Narcissa said. After a moment she said: "How much longer is this going to last, Horace?"

"Not any longer than I can help. If you know of any way in which I can get him out of that jail by tomorrow......"

"There's only one way," she said. She looked at him a moment. Then she turned toward the door. "Which way did Bory go? Dinner'll be ready soon." She went out.

"And you know what that way is," Miss Jenny said. "If you aint got any backbone."

"She's jealous," Horace said. Miss Jenny looked at him, her gray eyes cold and keen. During the year before his sister's marriage she had received a series of anonymous ~~letters~~ love-letters written by a scarce literate man. Inarticulate, obscene and sincere, she read them with detached equanimity, seeming to have no curiosity whatever regarding the author,

that the hope that you never learn it is the sole
~~reason for my actions from now on what I have done~~
reason why I will not see you again. Think as well
of me as you can. I wish I had the right to say, if
you learn of my folly think not the less of me.

6.

"Good Lord," Horace said. "Someone mistook him for a Mississippi man on the dance floor."

"I think, if I were you-----" Narcissa said. After a moment she said: "How much longer is this going to last, Horace?"

"Not any longer than I can help. If you know of any way in which I can get him out of that jail by tomorrow......"

"There's only one way," she said. She looked at him a moment. Then she turned toward the door. "Which way did Bory go? Dinner'll be ready soon." She went out.

"And you know what that way is," Miss Jenny said. "If you aint got any backbone."

"She's jealous," Horace said. Miss Jenny looked at him, her gray eyes cold and keen. During the year before his sister's marriage she had received a series of anonymous ~~lett~~ ~~lets~~ love-letters written by a scarce literate man. Inarticulate, obscene and sincere, she read them with detached equanimity, seeming to have no curiosity whatever regarding the author,

that the hope that you never learn it

not even bothering to destroy them. One night they were stolen: that was the only time Horace ever saw her lose her poise. He saw her then in the throes of a passion nearer maternal than actual motherhood ever roused; not with ~~rage or fear~~ outrage or fear, but at the idea of having letters addressed to her read by someone she did not know. ~~Miss Jenny was watching~~

Miss Jenny was watching him. "She's jealous," he said.

"And you're saying to yourself, That's something. Aint you?" She said.

But still Goodwin would not permit him to divulge Popeye's presence on the place that day.

"I tell you, they've got nothing on me," he said.

"How do you know?" Horace said.

"Well, no matter what they've got, I stand a chance in court. But just let it get out that I said he was ~~there~~ anywher around there, what chance do you think I'd have?"

"You've got the law, justice, civilization."

"Sure, if I spend the rest of my life squatting in that corner yonder. Come here." He led Horace to the window. "There are five windows in that hotel yonder that look into this one. And I've seen him light matches with a pistol at twenty feet. Why, damn it all, I'd never get back her from the courtroom the day I testified that."

"But there's such a thing as obstruct---------"

"Obstructing damnation. Let them prove I did it. He was found in the barn, shot from behind. Let them find the pistol. I was there, waiting. I didn't try to run. I could have, but I didn't. It was me notified the sheriff. Of course my being there alone except for her and Pap looked bad. If it was a stall, dont common sense tell you I'd have invented a better one?"

"You're not being tried by common sense," Horace said. "You're being tried by a jury."

"Then let them make the best of it. That's all they'll get. The dead man is in the barn, hadn't been touched; me and my wife and child and Pap in the house; nothing in the house touched; me the one that sent for the sheriff. No, no; I know I run a chance this way, but let me just open my head about that fellow, and there's no chance to it. I know what I'll get."

"But you heard the shot," Horace said. "You have already told that.

"No," he said, "I didn't. I didn't hear anything. I dont know anything about it........Do you mind waiting outside a minute while I talk to Ruby?"

It was five minutes before she joined him. He said:

"There's something about this that I dont know yet; that you and Lee haven't told me. Something he just warned you not to tell me. Isn't there?" She walked beside him, carrying the child. It was still whimpering now and then, tossing its thin body in sudden jerks. She tried to soothe it, crooning to it, rocking it in her arms. "Maybe you carry it too much," Horace said; "maybe if you could leave it at the hotel......"

"I guess Lee knows what to do," she said.

"But the lawyer should know all the facts, everything. He is the one to decide what to tell and what not to tell. Else, why have one? That's like paying a dentist to fix your teeth and then refusing to let him look into your mouth, dont you see? You wouldn't treat a dentist or a doctor this way." She said nothing, her head bent over the child. It wailed.

"Hush," she said, "hush, now."

"And worse than that, there's such a thing called obstructing justice. Suppose he swears there was nobody else there, suppose he is about to be cleared---which is not likely ---and somebody turns up who saw Popeye about the place, or saw his car leaving. Then they'll say, if Lee didn't tell the truth about an unimportant thing, why should we believe him when his neck's in danger?"

They reached the hotel. He opened the door for her. She did not look at him. "I guess Lee knows best," she said, going in. The child wailed, a thin, whimpering, distressful cry. "Hush," she said. "Shhhhhhhhhhhh."

Isom had been to fetch Narcissa from a party; it was late when the car stopped at the corner and picked him up. A few of the lights were beginning to come on, and men were already drifting back toward the square after supper, but it was still too early for the negro murderer to begin to sing. "And he'd better sing fast, too," Horace said. "He's only got two days more." But he was not there yet. The jail faced west; a last faint copper-colored light lay upon the dingy grating and upon the small, pale blob of a hand, and in scarce any wind a blue wisp of tobacco floated out and dissolved raggedly away. "If it wasn't bad enough to have her husband there, without that poor brute counting his remaining breaths at the top of his voice........."

"Maybe they'll wait and hang them both together," Narcissa said. "They do that sometimes, dont they?"

After supper he went to Miss Jenny's room. He drew a chair up and sat down and began to fill his pipe. He filled it slowly, as though he were not conscious of his hands.

"Well," Miss Jenny said, "how's it going?"

"What?" he said. "Oh. All right. All right."

"That woman, I mean. A hotel's no place for a young baby. That bottle of milk you carry in, that's not enough. I'd like to see her."

"I wish you could. But Narcissa----------"

"I thought you might bring her out to supper some night."

"Yes. Some night." He lit the pipe, then he let it go out again, staring at the fire.

"You might get your spunk up and try it, anyway."

"Yes," he said. He moved suddenly. "When this is over, I think I'll go to Europe. I need a change. Either I or

Mississippi does, one."

At his window, undressed, the light off, he could smell the garden, the myriad earth, the myriad darkness. By God I will go, he said; I'll write Belle in the morning. They would be gathered along the fence, now, and the thick, small-headed shape of the negro clinging to the bars, gorilla-like, beneath the ragged grieving of the heaven-tree between the light, the last bloom fallen now in viscid smears. "They ought to clean that mess off the walk," he said. Damn, damn, damn.

The next morning Saddie knocked on his door before he was up. "Miss Jenny say fer you to come to her room."

He slipped on his robe and found Miss Jenny propped in bed, a woollen shawl about her shoulders. Beside the bed a desk telephone sat on the table. After her stroke the extension had been made from the instrument downstairs.

"You're in trouble," she said. "Your family."

"Was it Belle? What-------"

"Your pistol widow. I couldn't get her to wait. She wants you in a hurry. She didn't say so, but she wants you to come right away. You might try to call her back. Saddie, bring a chair for Mr Horace."

"No," Horace said, "I'll go on in. I'll get some breakfast in town. Saddie, will you run and ask Isom to get the car out?"

"Why not call her and find out what it is?" Miss Jenny

said. "I liked her voice."

"I'll have to go in, anyway."

"Then I'll have to wait until tonight to find out what it is, wont I?" Miss Jenny said.

"I'm afraid so," he said.

He dressed rapidly, without stopping to shave.

As he entered the hotel he passed a young man with a small black bag, such as doctors carry. Horace went on up. The woman was standing in the half-open door, looking down the hall.

"I finally got the doctor," she said. "But I wanted anyway........." The child lay on the bed, its eyes shut, flushed and sweating, its curled hands above its head in the attitude of one crucified, breathing in short, whistling gasps. "He was sick all last night. I went and got some medicine and I tried to keep him quiet until daylight. At last I got the doctor." She stood beside the bed, looking down at the child. "There was a woman there," she said. "A young girl."

"A------------" Horace said. "Oh," he said. "Yes. You'd better tell me about it."

VII.

Townspeople taking after-supper drives through the college grounds or an oblivious and bemused faculty-member or a candidate for a master's degree on his way to the library, would see her, a snatched coat under her ~~arm~~ arm and her long ~~blonde~~ legs blonde with running, in speeding silhouette against the lighted windows of the Coop, as the women's dormitory was known, vanishing into the shadow beside the library wall, and perhspa final squatting swirl of knickers or whatnot as she sprang into the car waiting there with engine running on that particular night. The cars belonged to twon boys. Students in the University were not permitted to keep cars, and the men---hatless, in knickers and bright pull-overs---looked down upon the town boys who wore hats cupped rigidly upon pomaded heads, and coats a little too tight and trousers a little too full, with superiority and rage.

This was on week nights. On alternate Saturday evenings, at the Letter Club dances, or on the occasion of the three formal yearly balls, the town boys, lounging in attitudes of belligerent casualness, with their identical hats and upturned collars, watched her enter the gymnasium upon black collegiate arms and vanish in a swirling glitter upon a glittering swirl of music, with her high deliwate head and her bold painted mouth and soft chin, her eyes blankly right and left looking, cool, predatory and discreet.

Later, the music wailing beyond the glass, they would watch her through the windows as she passed in swift rotation from one pair of black sleeves to the next, her waist shaped slender and urgent in the interval, her feet filling the rythmic gap with music. Stooping they would drink from flasks and light cigarettes, then erect again, motionless againt the light, the upturned collars, the hatted heads, would be like a row of hatted and muffled busts cut from black tin and nailed to the window-sills.

There would always be three or four of them there when the band played Home, Sweet Home, lounging near the exit, their faces cold, bellicose, a little drawn with sleeplessness, watching the couples emerge in a wan aftermath of motion and noise. Three of them watched Temple and Gowan Stevens come out, into the chill presage of spring dawn. Her face was quite pale, dusted over with recent powder, her hair in spent red curls. Her eyes, all pupil now, rested upon them for a blank moment. Then she lifted her hand in a wan gesture, whether at them or not, none could have said. They did not respond, no flicker in their cold eyes. They watched Gowan slip his arm into hers, and the fleet revelation of flank and thigh as she got into his car. It was a long, low roadster, with a jacklight.

"Who's that son bitch?" one said.

"My father's a judge," the second said in a bitter, lilting falsetto.

"Hell. Let's go to town."

They went on. Once they yelled at a car, but it did not stop. On the bridge across the railroad cutting they stopped and drank from a bottle. The last made to fling it over the railing. The second caught his arm.

"Let me have it," he said. He broke the bottle carefully and spread the fragments across the road. They watched him.

"You're not good enough to go to a college dance," the first said. "You poor bastard."

"My father's a judge," the other said, propping the jagged shards upright in the road.

"Here comes a car," the third said.

It had three headlights. They leaned against the railing, slanting their hats against the light, and watched Temple and Gowan pass. Temple's head was low and close. The car moved slowly. ~~They watched the fan of light, the receding tail lamp, come to a stop at the door. The lights went off~~

"You poor bastard," the ~~second said,~~ first said.

"Am I?" the ~~first said~~ second said. He took something ~~from~~ from his pocket and flipped it out, whipping the sheer, faintly scented web across their faces. "Am I?"

"That's what you say."

"Doc got that step-in in Memphis," the third said. "Off a damn whore."

"You're a lying bastard," Doc said.

They watched the fan of light, the diminishing ruby taillamp, come to a stop at the Coop. The lights went off. After a while the car door slammed. The lights came on; the car moved away. It approached again. They leaned against the rail in a row, their hats slanted against the glare. The broken glass glinted in random sparks. The car drew up and stopped opposite them.

"You gentlemen going to town?" Gowan said, opening the door. They leaned against the rail, then the first said "Much obliged" gruffly and they got in, the two others in the rumble seat, the first beside Gowan.

"Pull over this way," he said. "Somebody broke a bottle there."

"Thanks," Gowan said. The car moved on. "You gentlemen going to Starkville tomorrow to the game?"

The ones in the rumble said nothing.

"I dont know," the first said. "I dont reckon so."

"I'm a stranger here," Gowan said. "I ran out of liquor tonight, and I've got a date early in the morning. Can you gentlemen tell me where I could get a quart?"

"It's mighty late," the first said. He turned to the others. "You know anybody he can find this time of night, Doc?"

"Luke might," the third said.

"Where does he live?" Gowan said.

"Go on," the first said. "I'll show you." They crossed the square and drove out of town about a half mile.

"This is the road to Taylor, isn't it?" Gowan said.

"Yes," the first said.

"I've got to drive down there early in the morning," Gowan said. "Got to get there before the special does. You gentlemen not going to the game, you say."

"I reckon not," the first said. "Stop here." A steep slope rose, crested by stunted blackjacks. "You wait here," the first said. "Gowan switched off the lights. They could hear the other scrambling up the slope.

"Does Luke have good liquor?" Gowan said.

"Pretty good. Good as any, I reckon," the third said.

"If you dont like it, you dont have to drink it," Doc said. Gowan turned fatly and looked at him.

"It's as good as that you had tonight," the third said.

"You didn't have to drink that, neither," Doc said.

"They cant seem to make good liquor down here like they do up at school," Gowan said.

"Where you from?" the third said.

"Virgin------oh, Jefferson. I went to school at Virginia. Teach you how to drink, there."

The other two said nothing. The first returned, preceeded by a minute shaling of earth down the slope. He had a fruit jar. Gowan lifted it against the sky. It was pale, innocent looking. He removed the cap and extended it.

"Drink."

The first took it and extended it to them in the rumble.

"Drink."

The third drank, but Doc refused. Gowan drank.

"Good God," he said, "how do you fellows drink this stuff?"

"We dont drink rotgut at Virginia," Doc said. Gowan turned in the seat and looked at him.

"Shut up, Doc," the third said. "Dont mind him," he said. "He's had a bellyache all night."

"Son bitch," Doc said.

"Did you call me that?" Gowan said.

" 'Course he didn't," the third said. "Doc's all right. Come on, Doc. Take a drink."

"I dont give a damn," Doc said. "Hand it here."

They returned to town. "The shack'll be open," the first said. "At the depot."

It was a confectionery-lunchroom. It was empty save for a man in a soiled apron. They went to the rear and entered an alcove with a table and four chairs. The man brought four glasses and coca-colas. "Can I have some sugar and water and a lemon, Cap?" Gowan said. The man brought them. The others watched Gowan make a whisky sour. "They taught me to drink it this way," he said. They watched him drink. "Hasn't got much kick, to me," he said, filling his glass from the jar. He drank that.

"You sure do drink it," the third said.

"I learned in a good school." There was a high window. Beyond it the sky was paler, fresher. "Have another, gentlemen," he said, filling his glass again. The others helped themselves moderately. "Up at school they consider it better to go down t than to hedge," he said. They watched him drink that one. They saw his nostrils bead suddenly with sweat.

"That's all for him, too," Doc said.

"Who says so?" Gowan said. He poured an inch into the glass. "If we just had some decent liquor. I know a man in my county named Goodwin that makes---------"

"That's what they call a drink up at school," Doc said.

Gowan looked at him. "Do you think so? Watch this." He poured into the glass. They watched the liquor rise.

"Look out, fellow," the third said. Gowan filled the glass level full and lifted it and emptied it steadily/. He remembered setting the glass down carefully, then he became aware simultaneously of open air, of a chill gray freshness and an engine panting on a siding at the head of a dark string of cars, and that he was trying to tell someone that he had learned to drink like a gentleman. He was still trying to tell them, in a cramped dark place smelling of ammonia and creesote, vomiting into a receptacle, trying to tell them that he must be at Taylor at six-thirty, when the special arrived. The paroxysm passed; he felt extreme lassitude, weakness, a desire to lie down which was forcibly restrained, and in the flare of a match he leaned against the wall, his eyes focussing slowly upon a name written there in pencil. He shut one eye, propped against the wall, swaying and drooling, and read the name. Then he looked at them, wagging his head.

"Girl name.........Name girl I know. Good girl. Good sport. Got date take her to Stark........Starkville. No chap' rone, see?" Leaning there, drooling, mumbling, he went to sleep.

At once he began to fight himself out of sleep. It seemed to him that it was immediately, yet he was aware of time passing all the while, and that time was a factor in his need to wake; that otherwise he would be sorry. For a long while he knew that his eyes were open, waiting for vision to return. Then he was seeing again, without knowing at once that he was awake.

He lay quite still. It seemed to him that, by breaking out of sleep, he had accomplished the purpose that he had ~~needed/to/do~~ waked himself for. He was lying in a cramped position under a low canopy, looking at the front of an unfamiliar building above which small clouds rosy with sunlight drove, quite empty of any sense. Then his abdominal muscles completed the retch upon which he had lost consciousness and he heaved himself up and sprawled into the foot of the car, banging his head on the door. The blow fetched him completely to and he opened the door and half fell to the ground and dragged himself up and turned toward the station at a stumbling run. He fell. On hands and knees he looked at the empty siding and up at the sunfilled sky with unbelief and despair. He rose and ran on, in his stained dinner jacket, his burst collar and broken hair. I passed out, he thought in a kind of rage, I passed out. I passed out.

The platform was deserted save for a negro with a broom. "Gret Gawd, white folks," he said.

"The train," Gowan said, "the special. The one that was on that track."

"Hit done lef. But five minutes ago." With the broom still in the arrested gesture of sweeping he watched Gowan turn and run back to the car and tumble into it.

The jar lay on the floor. He kicked it aside and started the engine. He knew that he needed something on his stomach, but there wasn't time. He looked down at the jar. His inside coiled coldly, but he raised the jar and drank, guzzling, choking the stuff down, clapping a cigarette into his mouth to restrain the paroxysm. Almost at once he felt better.

He crossed the square at forty miles an hour. It was six-fifteen. He took the Taylor road, increasing speed. He drank again from the jar without slowing down. When he reached Taylor the train was just pulling out of the station. He slammed in between two wagons as the last car passed. The vestibule o-pened; Temple sprang down and ran for a few steps beside the car while an official leaned down and shook his fist at her.

Gowan had got out. She turned and came toward him, walk-ing swiftly. Then she paused, stopped, came on again, staring at his wild face and hair, at his ruined collar and shirt.

"You're drunk," she said. "You pig. You filthy pig."

"Had a big night. You dont know the half of it."

She looked about, at the bleak yellow station, the overalled men chewing slowly and watching her, down the track at the diminishing train, at the four puffs of vapor that had almost died away when the sound of the whistle came back. "You filthy pig," she said. "You cant go anywhere like this. You haven't even changed clothes." At the car she stopped again. "What's that behind you?"

"My canteen," Gowan said. "Get in."

She looked at him, her mouth boldly scarlet, her eyes watchful and cold beneath her brimless hat, a curled spill of red hair. She looked back at the station again stark and ugly in the fresh morning. She sprang in, tucking her legs under her. "Let's get away from here." He started the car and turned it. "You'd better take me back to Oxford," she said. She looked back at the station. It now lay in shadow, in the shadow of a high scudding cloud. "You'd better," she said.

At two oclock that afternoon, running at good speed through a high murmurous desolation of pines, Gowan swung the car from the gravel into a narrow road between eroded banks, descending toward a bottom of cypress and gum. He wore a cheap blue workshirt beneath his dinner jacket. His eyes were bloodshot, puffed, his jowls covered by blue stubble, and looking at him, braced and clinging at the car leaped and bounced in the worn ruts, Temple thought His whiskers have grown since we left Dumfries. It was hair-oil he drank. He bought a bottle of hair-oil at Dumfries and drank it.

He looked at her, feeling her eyes. "Dont get your back up, now. It wont take a minute to run up to Goodwin's and get a bottle. It wont take ten minutes. I said I'd get you to Starkville before the train does, and I will. Dont you believe me?"

She said nothing, thinking of the pennant-draped train already in Starkville; of the colorful stands; the band, the yawning glitter of the bass horn; the green diamond dotted with players, crouching, uttering short, yelping cries like marsh-fowl disturbed by an alligator, not certain of where the danger is, motionless, poised, encouraging one another with short meaningless cries, plaintive, wary and forlorn.

"Trying to come over me with your innocent ways. Dont think I spent last night with a couple of your barber-shop jellies for nothing. Dont think I fed them my liquor just because I'm bighearted. You're pretty good, aren't you? Think you can play around all week with any badger-trimmed hink that owns a ford, and fool me on Saturday, dont you? ~~Dont think he never showed me that step-in~~. Dont ~~you~~ think I didn't see your name where it's written on that lavatory wall. Dont you believe me?"

She said nothing, bracing herself as the car lurched from one bank to the other of the cut, going too fast. He was still watching her, making no effort to steer it.

"By God, I want to see the woman that can-------" The road flattened into sand, arched completely over, walled completely by a jungle of cane and brier. The car lurched from side to side in the loose ruts.

She saw the tree blocking the road, but she only braced herself anew. It seemed to her to be the logical and disastrous end to the train of circumstance in which she had become involved. She sat and watched rigidly and quietly as Gowan, apparently looking straight ahead, drove into the tree at twenty miles an hour. The car struck, bounded back, then drove into the tree again and turned onto its side.

She felt herself flying through the air, carrying a numbing shock upon her shoulder and a picture of two men peering from the fringe of cane at the roadside. She scrambled to her feet, her head reverted, and saw them step into the road, the one in a suit of tight black and a straw hat, smoking a cigarette, the other bareheaded, in overalls, carrying a shotgun, his bearded face gaped in slow astonishment. Still running her bones turned to water and she fell flat on her face, still running.

Without stopping she whirled and sat up, her mouth open upon a soundless wail behind her lost breath. The man in overalls was still looking at her, his mouth open in innocent astonishment within a short soft beard. The other man was leaning over the upturned car, his tight coat ridged across his shoulders. Then the engine ceased, though the lifted front wheel continued to spin idly, slowing.

Without stopping she whirled and sat up, her mouth open upon a soundless wail behind her lost breath. The man in overalls was still looking at her, his mouth open in innocent astonishment within a short soft beard. The other man was leaning over the upturned ear, his tight coat ridged across his shoulders. Then the engine ceased, though the lifted front wheel continued to spin idly, slowing.

109.

chils bowed with flattened noses against the glass, but the younger men of the town entered in 2s and 3s and looked at the dead man. He lay on a wooden table, in his overalls, barefoot, the sun-bleached curls on the back of his head matted with dried blood and singed with powder, while the coroner sat over him, trying to ascertain his last name. ~~But none knew it, not even neighbors who ... remembered him for 15 years~~

Several men and women living in that part of the county remembered him ~~as a~~ for 15 years, ~~and the merchants had seen him on infrequent Saturdays in town, barefoot, hatless, with his rapt, round and gaze, his cheek bulged innocently upon a peppermint jawbreaker~~ A few of them had known him as Tommy; to others about that sparse countryside he was merely an anonymous and familiar figure without age or origin, living in abandoned barns or cabins, ~~or now and then with a farmer~~ work about sawmills or now and then on a farm

VIII.

The man in overalls was barefoot also. He walked ahead of Temple and Gowan, the shotgun swinging in his hand, his splay feet apparently effortless in the sand into which Temple sand almost to the ankle at each step. From time to time he looked over his shoulder at them, at Gowan's bloody face and splotched clothes, at Temple struggling and lurching on her high heels.

"Putty hard walkin, aint it?" he said. "Ef she'll take off them high heel shoes, she'll git along better."

"Will I?" Temple said. She stopped and stood on alternate legs, holding to Gowan, and removed her slippers. The man watched her, looking at the slippers.

"Durn ef I could git air two of my fingers into one of them things," he said. "Kin I look at em?" She gave him one. He turned it slowly in his hand. "Durn my hide," he said. He looked at Temple again with his pale, empty gaze. His hair grew innocent and straw-like, bleached on the crown, darkening about his ears and neck in untidy curls. "She's a right tall gal, too," he said. "With them skinny legs of hern. How much she weigh?" Temple extended her hand. He returned the slipper slowly, looking at her, at her belly and loins. "He aint laid no crop by yit, has he?"

"Come on," Gowan said, "let's get going. We've got to get a car and get back to Jefferson by night."

When the sand ceased Temple sat down and put her slippers on. She found the man watching her lifted thigh and she jerked her skirt down and sprang up. "Well," she said, "go on. Dont you know the way?"

The house came into sight, above the cedar grove beyond whose black interstices an apple orchard flaunted in the sunny afternoon. It was set in a ruined lawn, surrounded by abandoned grounds and fallen outbuildings. But nowhere was any sign of husbandry---plow or tool; in no direction was a planted field in sight---only a gaunt weather-stained ruin in a sombre grove through which the breeze drew with a sad, murmurous sound. Temple stopped.

"I dont want to go there," she said. "You go on and get the car," she told the man. "We'll wait here."

"He said fer y'all to come on to the house," the man said.

"Who did?" Temple said. "Does that black man think he can tell me what to do?"

"Ah, come on," Gowan said. "Let's see Goodwin and get a car. It's getting late. Mrs Goodwin's here, isn't she?"

"Hit's likely," the man said.

"Come on," Gowan said. They went on to the house. The man mounted to the porch and set the shotgun just inside the door.

"She's around somewher," he said. He looked at Temple

again. "Hit aint no cause fer yo wife to fret," he said. "Lee'll git you to town, I reckon."

Temple looked at him. They looked at one another soberly, like two children or two dogs. "What's your name?"

"My name's Tawmmy," he said. "Hit aint no need to fret."

The hall was open through the house. She entered.

"Where you going?" Gowan said. "Why dont you wait out here?" She didn't answer. She went on down the hall. Behind her she could hear Gowan's and the man's voices. The back porch lay in sunlight, a sedgment of sunlight framed by the door. Beyond she could see a weed-choked slope and a huge barn, broken-backed, tranquil in sunny desolation. To the right of the door she could see the corner either of a detached building or of a wing of the house. But she could hear no sound save the voices from the front.

She went on, slowly. Then she stopped. On the square of sunlight framed by the door lay the shadow of a man's head, and she half spun, poised with running. But the shadow wore no hat, so she turned and on tiptoe she went to the door and peered around it. A man sat in a splint-bottom chair, in the sunlight, the back of his bald, white-fringed head toward her, his hands crossed on the head of a rough stick. She emerged onto the back porch.

"Good afternoon," she said. The man did not move. She advanced again, then she glanced quickly over her shoulder. With the tail of her eye she thought she had seen a thread of smoke drift out the door in the detached room where the porch made an L, but it was gone. From a line bwtween two posts in front of this door three square cloths hung damp and limp, as though recently washed, and a woman's undergarment of faded pink silk. It had been washed until the lace resembled a ragged, fibre-like fraying of the cloth itself. It bore a patch of pale calico, neatly sewn. Temple looked at the old man again.

For an instant she thought that his eyes were closed, then she believed that he had no eyes at all, for ~~bwtee~~ between the lids two objects like dirty yellowish clay marbles were fixed. "Gowan," she whispered, then she wailed "Gowan!" and turned running, her head reverted, just as a voice spoke beyond the door where she had thought to have seen smoke:

"He cant hear you. What do you want?"

She whirled again and without a break in her~~/~~ stride and still watching the old man, she ran right off the porch and fetched up on hands and knees in a litter of ashes and tin cans and bleached bones, and saw Popeye watching her from the corner of the house, his hands in his pockets and a slanted cigarette curling across his face. Still without stopping she scrambled onto the porch and sprang into the kitchen, where a woman sat at a table, a burning cigarette in her hand, watching the door.

Popeye went on around the house. Gowan was leaning over the edge of the porch, dabb~~l~~ing gingerly at his bloody nose. The barefooted man squatted on his heels against the wall.

"For Christ's sake," Popeye said, "why cant you take him out back and wash him off? Do you want him sitting around here all day looking like a damn hog with its throat cut?" He snapped the cigarette into the weeds and sat on the top step and began to scrape his muddy shoes with a platinum penknife on the end of his watch chain.

~~Tommy rose.~~ The barefoot man rose.

"You said something about-------" Gowan said.

"Pssst!" the other said. He began to wink and frown at Gowan, jerking his head at Popeye's back.

"And then you get on back down that road," Popeye said. "You hear?"

"I thought you was fixin to watch down ther," the man said.

"Dont think," Popeye said, scraping at his trouser-cuffs. "You've got along forty years without it. You do what I told you."

When they reached the back porch the barefoot man said: "He jest caint stand fer nobody-------Aint he a cur'us feller, now? I be dawg ef he aint better'n a circus to-------He wont stand fer nobody drinkin hyer cep Lee. Wont drink none hisself, and jest let me take one sup and I be dawg ef hit dont look ~~like a~~ like he'll have a catfit."

"He said you were forty years old," Gowan said.

" 'Taint that much," the other said.

"How old are you?/ Thirty?"

"I dont know. 'Taint as much as he said, though." The old man sat in the chair, in the sun. "Hit's jest Pap," the man said. The azure shadow of the cedars had reached the old man's feet. It was almost up to his knees. His hand came out and fumbled about his knees, dabbling into the shadow, and became still, wrist-deep in shadow. Then he rose and grasped the chair and, tapping ahead with the stick, he bore directly down upon them in a shuffling rush, so that they had to step quickly aside. He dragged the chair into the full sunlight and sat down again, his face lifted into the sun, his hands crossed on the head of the stick. "That's Pap," the man said. "Blind and deef both. I be dawg ef I wouldn't hate to be in a fix wher I couldn't tell and wouldn't even keer whut I was eatin."

On a plank fixed between two posts sat a galvanised pail, a tin basin, a cracked dish containing a lump of yellow soap. "To hell with water," Gowan said. "How about that drink?"

"Seems to me like you done already had too much. I be dawg ef you didn't drive that ere car straight into that tree."

"Come on. Haven't you got some hid out somewhere?"

"Mought be a little in the barn. But dont let him hyear us, er he'll find hit and po hit out." He went back to the door and peered up the hall. Then they left the porch and went toward the barn, crossing what had once been a kitchen garden choked now with cedar and blackjack saplings. Twice the man looked back over his shoulder. The second time he said:

"Yon's yo wife wantin somethin."

Temple stood in the kitchen door. "Gowan," she called.

"Wave yo hand er somethin," the man said. "Ef she dont hush, he's goin to hyear us." Gowan flapped his hand. They went on and entered the barn. Beside the entrance a crude ladder mounted. "Better wait twell I git up," the man said. "Hit's putty rotten; mought not hold us both."

"Why dont you fix it, then?/ Dont you use it everyday?"

"Hit's helt all right, so fur," the other said. He mounted. Then Gowan followed, through the trap, into yellow-barred gloom where the level sun fell through the broken walls and roof. "Walk wher I do," the man said. "You'll tromp on a loose boa'd and find yoself downstairs befo you know hit." He picked his way across the floor and dug an earthenware jug from a pile of rotting hay in the corner. "One place he wont look fer hit," he said. "Skeered of sp'ilin them gal's hands of hisn."

They drank. "I've seen you out hyer befo," the man said. "Caint call yo name, though."

"My name's Stevens. I've been buying liquor from Lee for three years. When'll he be back? We've got to get on to town."

"He'll be hyer soon. I've seen you befo. Nother feller fum Jefferson out hyer three-fo nights ago. I caint call his name neither. He sho was a talker, now. Kep on tellin how he up and ~~XX~~ quit his wife. Have some mo," he said; then he ceased and squatted slowly, the jug in his lifted hands, his head bent with listening. After a moment the voice spoke again, from the hallway beneath.

"Jack."

The man looked at Gowan. His jaw dropped into an expression of imbecile glee. What teeth he had were stained and ragged within his soft, tawny beard.

"You, Jack, up there," the voice said.

"Hyear him?" the man whispered, shaking with silent glee. "Callin me Jack. My name's Tawmmy."

"Come on," the voice said. "I know you're there."

"I reckon we better," Tommy said. "He jest lief take a shot up through the flo as not."

"For Christ's sake," Gowan said, "Why didn't you-----Here," he shouted, "here we come!"

Popeye stood in the door, his forefingers in his vest. The sun had set. When they descended and appeared in the door Temple stepped from the back porch. She paused, watching them, then she came down the hill. She began to run.

"Didn't I tell you to get on down that road?" Popeye said.

"Me an him jest stepped down hyer a minute," Tommy said.

"Did I tell you to get on down that road, or didn't I?"

"Yeuh," Tommy said. "You told me." Popeye turned without so much as ~~looking~~ a glance at Gowan. Tommy followed. His back still shook with secret glee. Temple met Popeye halfway to the house. Without ceasing to run she appeared to pause. Even her flapping coat did not overtake her, yet for an appreciable instant she faced Popeye with a grimace of taut, toothed coquetry. He did not stop; the finicking swagger of his narrow back did not falter. Temple ran again. She passed Tommy and clutched Gowan's arm.

"Gowan, I'm scared. She said for me not to------You've been drinking again; you haven't even washed the blood-----She says for us to go away from here......." Her eyes were quite black, her face small and wan in the dusk. She looked toward the house. Popeye was just turning the corner. "She has to walk all the way to a spring for water; she-------They've got the cutest little baby in a box behind the stove. Gowan, she said for me not to be here after dark. She said to ask him. He's got a car. She said she didn't think he----------"

"Ask who?" Gowan said. Tommy was looking back at them. Then he went on.

"That black man. She said she didn't think he would, but he might. Come on." They went toward the house. A path led around it to the front. The car was parked ~~behind~~ between the path and the house, in the tall weeds. Temple faced Gowan again, her hand lying upon the door of the car. "It wont take him any time, in this. I know a boy at home has one. It will run eighty.

All he would have to do is just drive us to a town, because she said if we were married and I had to say we were. Just to a railroad. Maybe there's one closer than Jefferson," she whispered, staring at him, stroking her hand along the edge of the door.

"Oh," Gowan said, "I'm to do the asking. Is that it? You're all nuts. Do you think that ape will? I'd rather stay here a week than go anywhere with him."

"She said to. She said for me not to stay here."

"You're crazy as a loon. Come on here."

"You wont ask him? You wont do it?"

"No. Wait till ~~he/comes~~ Lee comes, I tell you. He'll get us a car."

They went on in the path. Popeye was leaning against a post, lighting a cigarette. Temple ran on up the broken steps. "Say," she said, " dont you want to drive us to town?"

He turned his head, the cigarette in his mouth, the match cupped between his hands. Temple's mouth was fixed in that cringing grimace. Popeye leaned the cigarette to the match. "No," he said.

"Come on," Temple said. "Be a sport. It wont take you any time in that Packard. How about it? We'll pay you."

Popeye inhaled. He snapped the match into the weeds. He said, in his soft, cold voice: "Make your whore lay off of me, Jack."

Gowan moved thickly, like a clumsy, good-tempered horse goaded suddenly. "Look here, now," he said. Popeye exhaled, the smoke jetting downward in two thin spurts. "I dont like that," Gowan said. "Do you know who you're talking to?" He continued that thick movement, like he could neither stop it nor complete it. "I dont like that." Popeye turned his head and looked at Gowan. Then he quit looking at him and Temple said suddenly:

"What river did you fall in with that suit on? Do you have to shave it off at night?" Then she was moving toward the door with Gowan's hand in the small of her back, her head reverted, her heels clattering. Popeye leaned motionless against the post, his head turned over his shoulder in profile.

"Do you want------" Gowan hissed.

"You mean old thing!" Temple cried. "You mean old thing!"

Gowan shoved her into the house. "Do you want him to slam your damn head off?" he said.

"You're scared of him!" Temple said. "You're scared!"

"Shut your mouth!" Gowan said. He began to shake her. Their feet scraped on the bare floor as ~~they~~ though they were performing a clumsy dance, and clinging together they lurched into the wall. "Look out," he said, "you're getting all that stuff stirred up in me again." She broke free, running. He leaned against the wall and watched her in silhouette run out the back door.

She ran into the kitchen. It was dark save for a crack of light about the fire-door of the stove. She whirled and ran out the door and saw Gowan going down the hill toward the barn. He's going to drink some more, she thought; he's getting drunk again. That makes three times today. Still more dusk had grown in the hall. She stood on tiptoe, listening, thinking I'm hungry. I haven't eaten all day; thinking of the school, the lighted windows, the slow couples strolling toward the sound of the supper bell, and of her father sitting on the porch at home, his feet on the rail, watching a negro mow the lawn. She moved quietly on tiptoe. In the corner beside the door the shotgun leaned and she crowded into the corner beside it and began to cry.

Immediately she stopped and ceased breathing. Something was moving beyond the wall against which she leaned. It crossed the room with minute, blundering sounds, preceeded by a dry tapping. It emerged into the hall and she screamed, feeling her lungs emptying long after all the air was expelled, and her diaphragm laboring long after her chest was empty, and watched the old man go down the hall at a wide-legged shuffling trot, the stick in one hand and the other elbow cocked at an acute angle from his middle. Running, she passed him---a dim, spraddled figure standing at the edge of the porch---and ran on into the kitchen and darted into the corner behind the stove. Crouching she drew the box out and drew it before her. Her hand touched the child'd face, then she flung her arms around the box, clutching it, staring across it at the pale door and trying to pray. But she could not think of a single designation for the heavenly father, so she began to say "My father's a judge; my father's a judge" over and over until Goodwin ran lightly into the room. He struck a match and held it overhead and looked down at her until the flame reached his fingers.

"Hah," he said. She heard his light, swift feet twice, then his hand touched her cheek and he lifted her from behind the box by the scruff of the neck, like a kitten. "What are you doing in my house?" he said.

ing to pray. But she could not think of a single designation for the heavenly father, so she began to say "My father's a judge; my father's a judge" over and over until Goodwin ran lightly into the room. He struck a match and held it overhead and looked down at her until the flame reached his fingers.

"Hah," he said. She heard his light, swift feet twice, then his hand touched her cheek and he lifted her from behind the box by the scruff of the neck, like a kitten. "What are you doing in my house?" he said.

gardens in the profound and undisturbed foundations of the sea, seen as through green glass, poised for less than a breath, but no breath. Often in the green twilight of late spring, like that windless twilight of sea grottoes, lichened and fronded where were snared amid the seething bubbles of the waving shape, had he tried to learn that hand, small, clutching flush of heart-shaped hooves where the ravished vine, back-springing, revealed clustered head, [illegible] hand, scuttling flank and the cold pale chalk of sparks between spinning hoof and flag.

IX.

From somewhere beyond the lamplit hall she could hear the voices---a word; now and then a laugh: the harsh, derisive laugh of a man easily brought to mirth by youth or by age, cutting across the spluttering of frying meat on the stove where the woman stood. Once she heard two of them come down the hall in their heavy shoes, and a moment later the clatter of the dipper in the galvanised pail and the voice that had laughed, cursing. Holding her coat close she peered around the door with the wide, abashed curiosity of a child, and saw Gowan and a second man in khaki breeches. He's getting drunk again, she thought. He's got drunk four times since we left Taylor.

"Is he your brother?" she said.

"Who?" the woman said. "My what?" she turned the meat on the hissing skillet.

"I thought maybe your young brother was here."

"God," the woman said. She turned the meat with a wire fork. "I hope not."

"Where is your brother?" Temple said, peering around the door. "I've got four brothers. Two are lawyers and one's a newspaper man. The other's still in school. At Yale. My father's a judge. Judge Drake of Jackson." She thought of her father sitting on the veranda, in a linen suit, a palm leaf fan in his hand, watching the negro mow the lawn.

The woman opened the oven and looked in. "Nobody asked you to come out here. I didn't ask you to stay. I told you to go while it was daylight."

"How could I? I asked him. Gowan wouldn't, so I had to ask him."

The woman closed the oven and turned and looked at Temple, her back to the light. "How could you? Do you know how I get my water? I walk after it. A mile. Six times a day. Add that up. Not because I am somewhere I am afraid to stay." She went to the table and took up a pack of cogarettes and shook one out.

"May I have one?" Temple said. The woman flipped the pack along the table. She removed the chimney from the lamp and lit hers at the wick. Temple took up the pack and stood listening to Gowan and the other man go back into the house. "There are so many of them," she said in a wailing tone, watching the cigarette crush slowly in her fingers. "But maybe, with so many of them.........." The woman had gone back to the stove. She turned the meat. "Gowan kept on getting drunk again. He got drunk three times today. He was drunk when I got off the train at Taylor and I am on probation and I told him what would happen and I tried to get him to throw the jar away and when we stopped at that little country store to buy a shirt he got drunk again. And so we hadn't eaten and we stopped at Dumfries and he went into the restaurant but I was too worried to eat and I couldn't find him and then he came up another street and I felt the bottle in his pocket before he knocked my hand away. He kept on saying I had his lighter and then when he lost it and I told him he had, he swore he never owned one ih his life."

The meat hissed and spluttered in the skillet. "He got drunk three serarate times," Temple said. "Three separate times in one day. Buddy---that's Hubert, my youngest brother---said that if he ever caught me with a drunk man, he'd beat hell out of me. And now I'm with one that gets drunk three times in one day." Leaning her hip against the table, her hand crushing the cigarette, she began to laugh. "Dont you think that's funny?" she said. Then she quit laughing by holding her breath, and she could hear the faint guttering the lamp made, and the meat in the skillet and the hissing of the kettle on the stove, and the voices, the harsh, abrupt, meaningless masculine sounds from the house. "And you have to cook for all of them every night. All those men eating here, the house full of them at night, in the dark........" She dropped the crushed cigarette. "May I hold the baby? I know how; I'll hold him good." She ran to the box, stooping, and lifted the sleeping child. It opened its eyes, whimpering. "Now, now; Temple's got it." She rocked it, held high and awkward in her thin arms. "Listen," she said, looking at the woman's back, "will you ask him? your husband, I mean. He can get a car and take me somewhere. Will you? Will ask him?" The child had stopped whimpering. Its lead-colored eyelids showed a thin line of ~~white~~ eyeball. "I'm not afraid," Temple said. "Things like that dont happen. Do they? They're just like other people. You're just like other people. With a little baby. And besides, my father's a ju-judge. The gu-governor comes to our house to e-eat---------What a cute little bu-ba-a-by," she wailed, lifting the child to her face; "if bad mans hurts Temple, us'll tell the governor's soldiers, wont us?"

"Like what people?" the woman said, turning the meat. "Do you think Lee hasn't anything better to do than chase after every one of you cheap little----------" She opened the fire door and threw her cigarette in and slammed the door. In nuzzling at the child Temple had pushed her hat onto the back of her head at a precarious dissolute angle above her clotted curls. "Why did you come here?"

"It was Gowan. I begged him. We had already missed the ball game, but I begged him if he'd just get me to Starkville before the special started back, they wouldn't know I wasn't on it, because the ones that saw me get off wouldn't tell. But he wouldn't. He said we'd stop here just a minute and get some more whisky and he was already drunk then. He had gotten drunk again since we left Taylor and I'm on probation and Daddy would just die, But he wouldn't do it. He got drunk again while I was begging him to take me to a town anywhere and let

let me out."

"On probation?" the woman said.

"For slipping out at night. Because ~~they~~ only town boys can have cars, and when you had a date with a town boy on Friday or Saturday or Sunday, the boys in school wouldn't have a date with you, because they cant have cars. So I had to slip out. And a girl that didn't like me told the Dean, because I had a date with a boy she liked and he never asked her for another date. So I had to."

"If you didn't slip out, you wouldn't get to go riding," the woman said. "Is that it? And now when you slipped out once too often, you're squealing."

"Gowan's not a town boy. He's from Jefferson. He went to Virginia. He kept on saying how they had taught him to drink like a gentleman, and I begged him just to let me out anywhere and lend me enough money for a ticket because I only had two dollars, but he---------"

"Oh, I know your sort," the woman said. "Honest women. Too good to have anything to do with common people. You'll slip out at night with the kids, but just let a man come along." She turned the meat. "Take all you can get, and give nothing. 'I'm a pure girl; I dont do that'. You'll slip out with the kids and burn their gasoline and eat their food, but just let a man so much as look at you and you faint away because your father the judge and your four brothers might not like it. But just ~~let~~ let you get into a jam, then who do you come crying to?

to us, the ones that are not good enough to lace the judge's almighty shoes." Across the child Temple gazed at the woman's back, her face like a small pale mask beneath the precarious hat.

"My brother said he would kill Frank. He didn't say he would give me a whipping if he caught me with him; he said he would kill the goddam son of a bitch in his yellow buggy and my father cursed him and said he could run his family a while longer and he drove me into the house and locked me in and went down to the bridge to wait for Frank. But I wasn't a coward. I climbed down the gutter and headed Frank off and told him. I begged him to go away, but he said we'd both go. When we got back in the buggy I knew it had been the last time. I knew it, and I negged him again to go away, but he said he'd drive me home to get my suitcase and we'd tell father. He wasn't a coward either. My father was sitting on the porch. He said 'Get out of that buggy' and I got out and I begged Frank to go on, but he got out too and we came up the path and father reached around inside the door and got the shotgun. I got in front of Frank and father said 'Do you want it too?' and I tried to stay in front but he shoved me behind him and held me and father shot him and said 'Get down there and sup your dirt, you whore'."

"I have been called that," Temple whispered, holding the sleeping child in her high thin arms, ~~looking~~ gazing at the woman's back.

"But you good women. Cheap sports. Giving nothing, then when you're caught.......Do you know what you've got into now?" she looked across her shoulder, the fork in her hand. "Do you think you're meeting kids now? kids that give a damn whether you like it or not? Let me tell you whose house you've come into without being asked or wanted; who you're expecting to drop everything and carry you back where you had no business ever leaving. When he was a soldier in the Philippines he killed another soldier over one of those nigger women and they sent him to Leavenworth. Then the war came and they let him out to go to it. He got two medals, and when it was over they put him back in Leavenworth until the lawyer gat a congressman to get him out. Then I could quit jazzing again--------"

"Jazzing?" Temple whispered, holding the child, looking herself no more than an elongated and leggy infant in her scant dress and uptilted hat.

"Yes, putty-face!" the woman said. "How do you suppose I paid that lawyer? And that's the sort of man you think will care that much-----" with the fork in her hand she came and snapped her fingers softly and viciously in Temple's face "----what happens to you. And you, you little doll-faced slut, that think you cant come into a room where a man is without him.........." Beneath the ~~gray garment~~ faded garment her breast moved deep and full. With her hands on her hips she looked at Temple with cold, blazing eyes. "Man? You've never seen a real man. You dont know what it is to be wanted by a real man. And thank your stars you haven't and never will, for then you'd find just what that little putty face is worth, and all the rest of it you think you are jealous of when you're just scared of it. And if he is just man enough to call you whore, you'll say Yes Yes and you'll crawl naked in the dirt and the mire for him to call you that........Give me that baby." Temple held the child, gazing at the woman, her mouth moving as if she were saying Yes Yes Yes. The woman threw the fork onto the table. "Turn loose," she said, lifting the child. It opened its eyes and wailed. The woman drew a chair out and sat down, the child upon her lap. "Will you hand me one of those diapers on the line yonder?" she said. Temple stood in the floor, her lips still moving. "You're scared to go out there, aren't you?" the woman said. She rose.

"No," Temple said; "I'll get------"

"I'll get it." The unlaced brogans scuffed across the kitchen. She returned and drew another chair up to the stove and spread the two remaining cloths and the undergarment on it, and sat again and laid the child across her lap. It wailed. "Hush," she said, "hush, now," he face in the lamplight taking a serene, brooding quality. She changed the child and laid it in the box. Then she took a platter down from a cupboard curtained by a split towsack and took up the fork and came and looked into Temple's face again.

"Listen. If I get a car for you, will you get out of here?" she said. Staring at her Temple moved her mouth as though she were experimenting with words, tasting them. "Will you go ~~back~~ out the back and get into it and go away and never come back here?"

"Yes," Temple whispered, "anywhere. Anything."

Without seeming to move her cold eyes at all the woman looked Temple up and down. Temple could feel all her muscles shrinking like severed vines in the noon sun. "You poor little gutless fool," the woman said in her cold undertone. "Playing at it."

"I didn't. I didn't."

"You'll have something to tell them now, when you get back. Wont you?" Face to face, their voices were like shadows upon two close ~~walls~~ blank walls. "Playing at it."

"Anything. Just so I get away. Anywhere."

"It's not Lee I'm afriad of. Do you think he plays the dog after every ~~little~~ hot little bitch that comes ~~on~~ a-long? It's you."

"Yes. I'll go anywhere."

"I know your sort. I've seen them. All running, but not too fast. Not so fast you cant tell a real man when you see him. Do you think you've got the only one in the world?"

"Gowan," Temple whispered, "Gowan."

"I have slaved for that man," the woman whispered,

her lips scarce moving, in her still, dispassionate voice. It was as though she were reciting a formula for bread. "I worked night shift as a waitress so I could see him Sundays at the prison. I lived two years in a single room, cooking over a gas-jet, because I promised him. I lied to him and made money to get him out of prison, and when I told him, he beat me. And now you must come here where you're not wanted. Nobody asked you to come here. Nobody cares whether you are afraid or not. A-fraid? You haven't the guts to be really afraid, anymore than you have to be in love."

"I'll pay you," Temple whispered. "Anything you say. My father will give it to me." The woman watched her, her face motionless, as rigid as when she had been speaking. "I'll send you clothes. I have a new fur coat. I just wore it since Christmas. It's as good as new."

The woman laughed. Her mouth laughed, with no sound, no movement of her face. "Clothes? I had three fur coats once. I gave one of them to a woman in an alley by a saloon. Clothes? God." She turned suddenly. "I'll get a car. You get away from here and dont you ever come back. Do you hear?"

"Yes," Temple whispered. Motionless, pale, like a sleepwalker she watched the woman transfer the meat to the platter and pour the gravy over it. From the oven she took a pan of biscuits and put them on a plate. "Can I help you? Temple whispered. The woman said nothing. She took up the two plates and went out. Temple went to the table and took a cigarette from the pack and stood staring stupidly at the lamp. One side of the chimney was blackened. Across it a crack ran in a thin silver curve. The lamp was of tin, coated about the neck with dirty grease. She lit hers at the lamp, someway, Temple thought, holding the cigarette in her hand, staring at the uneven flame. The woman returned. She caught up the corner of her skirt and lifted the smutty coffee-pot from the stove.

"Can I take that?" Temple said.

"No. Come on and get your supper." She went out.

Temple stood at the table, the cigarette in her hand. The shadow of the stove feel upon the box where the child lay. Upon the lumpy wad of bedding it could be distinguished only by a series of pale shadows in soft small curves, and she went and stood over the box and looked down at its putty-colored face and bluish eyelids. A thin whisper of shadow cupped its head and lay moist upon its brow; one thin arm, upflung, lay curl-palmed beside its cheek.

"He's going to die," Temple whispered. Bending, her shadow loomed high upon the wall, her coat shapeless, her hat tilted monstrously above a monstrous escaping of hair. "Poor little baby," she whispered, "poor little baby." The men's voices grew louder. She heard a trampling of feet in the hall, a rasping of chairs, the voice of the man who had laughed above them,laughing again. She turned, motionless again, watching the door. The woman entered.

"Go and eat your supper," she said.

"The car," Temple said. "I could go now, while they're eating."

"What car?" the woman said. "Go on and eat. Nobody's going to hurt you."

"I'm not hungry. I haven't eaten today. I'm not hungry at all."

"Go on," the woman said.

"I'll wait and eat when you do."

"Go on and eat your supper. I've got to get done here some time tonight."

bright flowers, dusty-colored flowers of late summer blooms.

"Will you look at that back, now?" Miss Jenny said.

"Thanks," Horace said. "I thought it was her back, but I hated to .... and he'll doubtlss look the same from either side. Which is an advantage, I think ...... hope." They watched the 3 people — a broad, fattish man in brown and a straight-backed little boy flanking a woman in a white dress with a black ribbon at the waist.

X.

The woman leaned above the child, her face bent toward it in a musing attitude, as though she were not seeing it. It lay on the bed, beneath the blanket, its hands upflung beside its head, as though it had died in the presence of an unbearable agony which had not had time to touch it. Its eyes were half open, the balls rolled back into the skull so that only the white showed, in color like weak milk. Its face was still damp with perspiration, but its breathing was easier. It no longer breathed in those weak, whistling gasps as it had when Horace entered the room. On a chair beside the bed sat a tumbler half full of faintly discolored water, with a spoon in it. Through the open window came the myriad noises of the square---cars, wagons, footsteps on the pavement beneath---and through it Horace could see the courthouse, with men pitching dollars back and forth between holes in the bare earth beneath the locusts and water oaks.

The woman brooded above the child. "Nobody wanted her out there. Lee has told them and told them they must not bring women out there, and I told her before it got dark they were not her kind of people and to get away from there. It was that fellow that brought her. He was out there on the porch with them, still drinking, because when he came in to supper he couldn't hardly walk, even. He hadn't even tried to wash the blood off of his face. Little shirt-tail boys that think because Lee bseaks the law, they can come out there and treat our house like a..........Grown people are bad, but at least they take buying whisky ~~as a matter of course~~ like buying anything else; it's the ones like him, the ones that are too young to realise that people dont break the law just for a holiday." Horace could see her clenched hands writhing in her lap. "God, if I had my way, I'd hang every man that makes it or buys it or drinks it, every one of them./

"But why must it have been me, us? What had I ever done to her, to her kind? I told her to get away from there. I told her not to stay there until dark. But that fellow that brought her was getting drunk again, and him and Van picking at each other. If she'd just stopped running around where they had to look at her. She wouldn't stay anywhere. She'd just dash out one door, and in a minute she'd come running in from the other direction. And if he'd just let Van alone, because Van had to go back on the truck at midnight, and so Popeye would have made him behave. And Saturday night too, and them sitting up all night drinking anyway, and I had gone through it and gone through it and I'd tell Lee to let's get away, that he was getting nowhere, and he would have these spells like last night, and no doctor, no telephone. And then she had to come out there, after I had slaved for him, slaved for him." Deep full her bosom moved under the gray crepe. Horace watched her, the down-turned cheek, the hair bobbed once but drawn now to a knot at the back, at one rigid arm and the slow clenching of her hands in her lap.

"Standing there in the corner behind the bed, with that raincoat on. She was that scared, when they brought the fellow in, all bloody again. They laid him on the bed and Van hit him again and Lee caught Van's arm, and her standing there with her eyes like the holes in one of these masks. The raincoat was hanging on the wall, and she had it on, over her coat. Her dress was all folded up on the bed. They threw the fellow right on top of it, blood and all, and I said 'God, are you drunk too?' But Lee just looked at me and I saw that his nose was white already, like it gets when he's drunk.

"There wasn't any lock on the door, but I thought that pretty soon they'd have to go and see about the truck and then I could do something. Then Lee made me go out too, and he took the lamp out, so I had to wait until they went back to the porch before I could go back. I stood just inside the door. The fellow was snoring, in the bed there, breathing ~~xxx~~ hard, with his nose and mouth all battered up again, and I could hear them on the porch. Then they would be outdoors, around the house and at the back too I could hear them. Then they got quiet.

"I stood there, against the wall. He would snore and

choke and catch his breath and moan, sort of, and I would think about that girl lying there in the dark, with her eyes open, listening to them, and me having to stand there, waiting for them to go away so I could do something. I told her to go away. I said 'What fault is it of mine if you're not married? I dont want you here a bit more than you do'. I said 'I've lived my life without any help from ~~/ø~~ people of your sort; what right have you got to look to me for help?' Because I've done everything for him. I've been in the dirt for him. I've put everything behind me and all I ask was to be let alone.

"Then I heard the door open. I could tell Lee by the way he breathes. He went to the bed and said 'I want the raincoat. Sit up and take it off' and I could hear the shucks rattling while he took it off of her, then he went out. He just got the raincoat and went out. It was Van's coat.

"And I have walked around that house so much at night, with those men there, men living off of Lee's risk, men that wouldn't lift a finger for him if he got caught, until I could tell any of them by the way they breathed, and I could tell Popeye by the smell of that stuff on his hair. Tommy was following him. He came in the door behind Popeye and looked at me and I could see his eyes, like a cat. Then his eyes went away and I could feel him sort of squatting against me, and we could hear Popeye over where the bed was and that fellow snoring and snoring.

"I could just hear little faint sounds, from the

shucks, so I knew it was all right yet, and in a minute Popeye came on back, and Tommy followed him out, creeping along behind him, and I stood there until I heard them go down to the truck. Then I went to the bed. When I touched her she began to fight. I was trying to put my hand over her mouth so she couldn't make a noise, but she didn't anyway. She just lay there, thrashing about, rolling her head from one side to the other, holding to the coat.

" 'You fool!' I says 'It's me---the woman.'

"Then she begun to say 'I'll tell my father! I'll tell my father! until I had to hold her.

" 'Get up' I says 'Will you get up and walk quiet?'

" 'Will you get me out of here?' she says 'Will you? Will you?'

"When she got up she couldn't stand up, for shaking and trembling. I had to hold her up, telling her to be quiet. She got quiet. She wanted to stop and get her clothes, but I wouldn't let her. 'Do you want your clothes' I says 'or do you want to get out of here?'

" 'Yes' she says 'Anything, if you'll just get me out of here.' "

On their shoeless feet they moved like ghosts. They crossed the porch and went on toward the barn. When they were about fifty yards from the house the woman stopped and turned and jerked Temple up to her, and gripping her by the shoulders, their faces close together, she cursed Temple in a whisper, a sound no louder than a sigh and filled with fury. Then she flung her away and they went on. They entered the hallway. It was pitch dark. Temple heard the woman fumbling at the wall. A door creaked open; the woman took her arm and guided her up a single step into a floored room where she could feel walls and smell a faint, dusty odor of grain, and closed the door behind them. As she did so something rushed invisibly nearby in a scurrying scrabble, a dying whisper of fairy feet. Temple whirled, treading on something that rolled under her foot, and sprang toward the woman.

"It's just a rat," the woman said, but Temple hurled herself upon the other, flinging her arms about her, trying to snatch both feet from the floor.

"A rat?" she wailed, " a rat? Open the door! Quick!"

"Stop it! Stop it!" the woman hissed. She held Temple until she ceased. Then they knelt side by side against the wall. After a while the woman whispered: "There's some cotton-seed-hulls over there. You can lie down." Temple didn't answer. She crouched against the woman, shaking slowly, and they squatted there in the black darkness, against the wall.

She waked lying in a tight ball, with narrow bars of sunlight falling across her face like the tines of a gokden fork, and while the stiffened blood trickled and tingled through her cramped muscles she lay gazing quietly up at the ceiling.

Like the walls, it was of rough planks crudely laid, each plank separated from the next by a thin line of blackness; in the corner a square opening above a ladded gave into a gloomy loft shot with thin pencils of sun also. From nails in the walls broken bits of dessiccated harness hung, and she lay plucking tenatively at the subatance in which she lay. She gathered a handful of it and lifted her head, and saw within her fallen coat naked flesh between brassiere and knickers and knickers and stockings. Then she remembered the rat and scrambled up and sprang to the door, clawing at it, still clutching the fist full of cottonseed-hulls, her face puffed with the hard slumber of seventeen.

She had expected the door to be locked and for a time she could not pull it open, her numb hands scoring at the undressed planks until she could hear her finger nails. It swung back and she sprang out. At once she sprang back into the crib and banged the door to. The blind man was coming down the slope at a scuffling trot, tapping ahead with the stick, the other hand at his waist, clutching a wad of his trousers. He passed the crib with his braces dangling about his hips, his gymnasium shoes scuffing in the dry chaff of the hallway, and passed from view, the stick rattling lightly along the rank of emoty stalls.

Temple crouched against the door, clutching her coat about her. She could hear him back there in one of the stalls. She opened the door and peered out, at the house in the bright May sunshine, the sabbath peace, and she thought about the girls and men leaving the dormitories in their new Spring clothes, strolling along the shaded streets toward the cool, unhurried sound of bells. She lifted her foot and examined the soiled sole of her stocking, brushing at it with her palm, then at the other one.

The blind man's stick clattered again. She jerked her head back and closed the door to a crack and watched him pass, slower now, hunching his braces onto his shoulders. He mounted the slope and entered the house. Then she opened the door and stepped gingerly down.

She walked swiftly to the house, her stockinged feet flinching and cringing from the rough earth, watching the house. She mounted to the porch and entered the kitchen and stopped, listening into the silence. The stove was cold. Upon it the blackened coffee-pot sat, and a soiled skillet; upon the table soiled dishes were piled at random. I haven't eaten since...... since ......Yesterday was one day, she thought, but I didn't eat then. I haven't eaten since.......and that night was the dance, and I didn't eat any supper. I haven't eaten since dinner Friday, she thought. And now it's Sunday, thinking about the bells in cool steeples against the blue, and pigeons crooning about the belfries like echoes of the organ's bass. She returned to the door and peered out. Then she emerged, clutching the coat about her.

She entered the house and sped up the hall. The sun lay now on the front porch and she ran with a craning motion of her head, watching the patch of sun framed in the door. It was empty. She reached the door to the right of the entrance ahd opened it and sprang into the room and shut the door and leaned her back against it. The bed was empty. A faded patchwork quilt was wadded across it. A khaki-covered canteen and one slipper lay on the bed. On the floor her dress and hat lay.

She picked up the dress and hat and tried to brush them with her hand and with the corner of her coat. Then she sought the other slipper, moving the quilt, stooping to look under the bed. At last she found it in the fireplace, in a litter of wood ashes between an iron fire-dog and an overturned stack of bricks, lying on its side, half full of ashes, as though it had been flung of kicked there. She emptied it and wiped it on her coat and laid it on the bed and took the canteen and hung it on a nail in the wall. It bore the letters U S and a blurred number in black stencil. Then she removed the coat and dressed.

Long legged, thin armed, with high small buttocks ---a small childish figure no longer quite a child, not yet quite a woman---she moved swiftly, smoothing her stockings and writhing into her scant, narrow dress. Now I can stand anything, she thought quietly, with a kind of dull, ~~ddd~~ spent astonishment; I can stand just anything. From the top of one stocking she removed a watch on a broken black ribbon. Nine oclock. With her fingers she combed her matted curls, combing out trhee or four cottonseed-hulls. She took up the coat and hat and listened again at the door.

She returned to the back porch. In the basin was a residue of dirty water. She rinsed it and filled it and bathed her face. A soiled towel hung from a nail. She used it gingerly, then she took a compact from her coat and was using it when she found the woman watching her in the kitchen door.

"Goodmorning," Temple said. The woman held the child on her hip. It was asleep. "Hello, baby," Temple said, stooping; "you wan s'eep all day? Look at Temple." They entered the kitchen. The woman poured coffee into a cup.

"It's cold, I expect," she said. "Unless you want to make up the fire." From the oven she took a pan of bread.

"No," Temple said, sipping the lukewarm coffee, feeling her insides move in small, trickling clots, like loose shot. "I'm not hungry. I haven't eaten in two days, but I'm not hungry. Isn't that funny?/ I haven't eaten in........." She looked at the woman's back with a fixed placative grimace. "You haven't got a bathroom, have you?"

"What?" the woman said. She looked at Temple across her shoulder while Temple stared at her with that grimace of cringing and placative assurance. From a shelf the woman took a mail-order catalogue and tore out a few leaves and handed them to Temple. "You'll have to go to the barn, like we do/"

"Will I?" Temple said, holding the paper. "The barn."

"They're all gone," the woman said. "They wont be back this morning."

"Yes," Temple said. "The barn."

"Yes; the barn," the woman said. "Unless you're too pure to have to."

"Yes," Temple said. She looked out the door, across the weed-choked clearing. Between the sombre spacing of the cedars the orchard lay bright in the sunlight. She donned the coat and hat and went toward the barn, the torn leaves in her hand, splotched over with small cuts of clothes-pins and patent wringers and washing-powder, and entered the hallway. She stopped, folding and folding the sheets, then she went on, with swift, cringing glances at the empty stalls. She walked right through the barn. It was open at the back, upon a mass of jimson weed in savage white-and-lavender bloom. She walked on into the sunlight again, into the weeds. Then she began to run, snatching her feet up almost before they touched the earth, the weeds slashing at her with huge, moist, malodorous blossoms. She stooped and twisted through a fence of sagging rusty wire and ran downhill among trees.

At the bottom a narrow scar of sand divided the two slopes of a small valley, winding in a series of dazzling splotches where thesun found it. Temple stood in the sand, listening to the birds among the sunshot leaves, listening, looking about. She followed the dry runlet to where a jutting shoulder formed a nook matted with briers. Among the new green last year's dead leaves from the branches overhead clung, not yet fallen to earth. She stood here for a while, folding and folding the sheets in her fingers, in a kind of despair. When she rose she saw, upon the glittering mass of leaves along the crest of the ditch, the squatting outline of a man.

For an instant she stood and watched herself run out of her body, out of one slipper. She watched her legs twinkle against the sand, through the flecks of sunlight, for several yards, then whirl and run back and snatch up the slipper and whirl and run again.

When she caught a glimpse of the house she was opposite the front porch. The blind man sat in a chair, his face lifted into the sun. At the edge of the woods she stopped and put on the slipper. She crossed the ruined lawn and sprang onto the porch and ran down the hall. When she reached the back porch she saw a man in the door of the barn, looking toward the house. She crossed the porch in two strides and entered the kitchen, where the woman sat at the table, smoking, the child on her lap.

"He was watching me!" Temple said. "He was watching me all the time!" She leaned beside the door, peering out, then she came to the woman, her face small and pale, her eyes like holes burned with a cigar, and laid her hand on the cold stove.

"Who was?" the woman said.

"Yes," Temple said. "He was there in the bushes, watching me all the time." She looked toward the door, then back at the woman, and saw her hand lying on the stove. She snatched it up with a wailing shriek, clapping it against her mouth, and turned and ran toward the door. The woman caught her arm, still carrying the child on the other, and Temple sprang back into the kitchen. Goodwin was coming toward the house. He looked once at them and went on into the hall.

Temple began to struggle. "Let go," she whispered, "let go! Let go!" She surged and plunged, grinding the woman's hand against the door jamb until she was free. She sprang from the porch and ran toward the barn and into the hallway and climbed the ladder and scrambled through the trap and to her feet again, running toward the pile of rotting hay.

Then suddenly she ran upside down in a rushing interval; she could see her legs still running in space, and she struck lightly and solidly on her back and lay still, staring up at an oblong yawn that closed with a clattering vibration of loose planks. Faint dust sifted down across the bars of sunlight.

Her hand moved in the substance in which she lay, then she remembered the rat asecond time. Her whole body ~~made~~ surged in an involuted spurning movement that brought her to her feet in the loose hulls, so that she flung her hands out and caught herself upright, a hand on either ~~side~~ angle of the corner, her face not twelve inches from the cross beam on which the rat crouched. For an instant they stared eye to eye, then its eyes glowed suddenly like two tiny electric bulbs and it leaped at her head just as she sprang backward, treading again on something that rolled under her foot.

She fell ~~forward~~ toward the opposite corner, on her face in the hulls and a few scattered corn-cobs gnawed bone-clean. Something thudded against the wall and struck her head in rocochet. The rat was in that corner now, on the floor. Again their faces were not twelve inches apart, the rat's eyes glowing and fading as though worked by lungs. Then it stood erect, its back to the corner, its forepaws ~~crossed~~ curled against its chest, and began to squeak at her in tiny plaintive gasps. She backed away on hands and knees, watching it. Then she got to her feet and sprang at the door, hammering at it, watching the rat over her shoulder, her body arched against the door, rasping at the planks with her bare hands.

The woman stood in the kitchen door, holding the child, until Goodwin emerged from the house. The lobes of his nostrils were quite white against his brown face, and she said: "God, are you drunk too?" He came along the porch. "She's not here," the woman said. "You cant find her." He brushed past her, trailing a reek of whisky. She turned, watching him. He looked swiftly about the kitchen, then he turned and looked at her standing in the door, blocking it. "You wont find her," she said. "She's gone." He came toward her, lifting his hand. "Dont put your hand on me," she said. He gripped her arm, slowly. His eyes were a little bloodshot. The lobes of his nostrils looked like wax.

"Take your hand off me," she said. "Take it off." Slowly he drew her out of the door. She began to ~~xxxxxx~~ curse him. "Do you think ~~I'll let you~~ you cane? Do you think I'll let you? Or any other little slut?" Motionless, facing one another like the first position of a dance, they stood in a mounting terrific muscular hiatus.

With scarce any movement at all he flung her aside in a complete revolution that fetched her up against the table, her arm flung back for balance, her body bent and her hand fumbling behind her among the soiled dishes, watching him across the inert body of the child. He wakked toward her. "Stand back," she said, lifting her hand slightly, bringing the butcher knife into view. "Stand back." He came steadily toward her, then she struck at him with the knife.

He caught her wrist. She began to struggle. He plucked the child from her and laid it on the table and caught her other hand as it flicked at his face, and holding both wrists in one hand, he slapped her. It made a dry, flat sound. He slapped her again, first on one cheek, then the other, rocking her head from side to side. "That's what I do to them," he said, slapping her. "See?" He released her. She stumbled backward against the table and caught up the child and half crouched between the table and the wall, watching him as he turned and left the room.

She knelt in the corner, holding the child. It had not stirred. She laid her palm first on one cheek, then on the other. She rose and laid the child in the box and took a sunbonnet from a nail and put it on. From another nail she took a coat trimmed with what had once been white fur, and took up the child and left the room.

Tommy was standing in the barn, beside the crib, looking toward the house. The old man sat on the front porch, in the sun. She went dwon the steps and followed the path to the road and went on without looking back. When she came to the tree and the wrecked car she turned from the road, into a path. After a hundred yards or so she reached the spring and sat down beside it, the child on her lap and the hem of her skirt turned back over its sleeping face.

Popeye came out of the bushes, walking gingerly in his muddy shoes, and stood looking down at her across the spring. His hand flicked to his coat and he fretted and twisted a cigarette and put it into his mouth and snapped a match with his thumb. "Jesus Christ," he said, "I told him about letting them sit around all night, swilling that goddam stuff. There ought to be a law." He looked away in the direction in which the house lay. Then he looked at the woman, at the top of her sunbonnet. "Goofy house," he said. "That's what it is. It's not four days ~~since~~ ago I find a bastard squatting here, asking me if I read books. Like he would jump me with a book or something. Take me for a ride with the telephone directory." Again he looked off toward the house, jerking his neck forth as if his collar were too tight. He looked down at the top of the sunbonnet. "I'm going to town, see?" he said. "I'm clearing out. I've got enough of this." She did not look up. She adjusted the hem of the skirt above the child's face. Popeye went on, with light, finicking sounds in the underbrush. Then they ceased. Somewhere in the swamp a bird sang.

Before he reached the house Popeye left the road and followed a wooded slope. When he emerged he saw Goodwin standing behind a tree in the orchard, looking toward the barn. Popeye stopped at the edge of the wood and looked at Goodwin's back. He put another cigarette into his mouth and thrust his fingers into his vest. He went on across the orchard, walking gingerly. Goodwin heard him and looked over his shoulder. Popeye took a match from his vest, flicked it into flame and lit the cigarette. Goodwin looked toward the barn again and Popeye stood at his shoulder, looking toward the barn.

"Who's down there?" he said. Goodwin said nothing. Popeye jetted smoke from his nostrils. "I'm clearing out," he said. Goodwin said nothing, watching the barn. "I said, I'm getting out of here," Popeye said. Without turning his head Goodwin cursed him. Popeye smoked quietly, the cigarette wreathing across his still, soft, black gaze. Then he turned and went toward the house. The old man sat in the sun. Popeye did not enter the house. Instead he went on ~~through the garden and the weed-choked lot and entered the barn from the rear~~ across the lawn and into the cedars until he was hidden from the house. Then he turned and crossed the garden and the weed-choked lot and entered the barn from the rear.

Tommy squatted on his heels beside the crib door, looking toward the house. Popeye looked at him a while, smoking. Then he snapped the cigarette away and entered a stall quietly. Above the manger was a wooden rack for hay, just under an opening in the loft floor. Popeye climbed into the rack and drew himself silently into the loft, his tight coat strained into thin ridges across his narrow shoulders and back.

XI.

Temple heard Popeye curse Tommy and order him back down the road, and when she stood in the corner beside the shotgun, crying quietly in the dusk, she was thinking of him squatting there in the bushes beside the car; thinking of herself running down the road in the twilight, her coat streaming behind her, her ankles wrenching and lurching in the sand, until she overtook him and squatted beside him; of the two of them squatting there in the bushes until daylight. She had completely eliminated Gowan from her mind.

She did not even look for him when she entered the diningroom, her face fixed in a cringing, placative expression. She was looking for Tommy. She went swiftly toward him, across the turned faces. Someone intervened: a hard hand and arm; she attempted to evade him, looking at Tommy.

"Here," Gowan said across the table, his chair rasping back, "you come around here."

"Outside, brother," the one who had stopped her said, whom she recognised then as the one who had laughed so ~~muc~~/ often; "you're drunk. Come here, kid." His hard forearm came across her middle. She thrust against it, grinning rigidly at Tommy. "Move down, Tommy," the man said. "Aint you got no manners, you mat-faced bastard?" Tommy guffawed, scraping his chair along the floor. The man drew her toward him by the wrist. Across the table Gowan stood up, propping himself on the table. She began to resist, grinning at Tommy, picking at the man's fingers.

"Quit that, Van," Goodwin said.

"Right on my lap here," Van said.

"Let her go," Goodwin said.

"Who'll make me?" Van said. "Who's big enough?"

"Let her go," Goodwin said. Then she was free. She began to back slowly away. Behind her the woman, entering with a dish, stepped aside. Still smiling her aching, rigid grimace Temple backed from the room. In the hall she whirled and ran. She ran right off the porch, into the weeds, and sped on. She ran to the road and down it for fifty yards in the darkness, then without a break she whirled and ran back to the house and sprang onto the porch and crouched against the door just as someone came up the hall. It was Tommy.

"Oh, hyer you are," he said. He thrust something awkwardly at her. "Hyer," he said.

"What is it?" she whispered.

"Little bite of victuals. I bet you aint et since mawnin."

"No. Not then, even," she whispered.

"You eat a little mite and you'll feel better," he said, poking the plate at her. "You set down hyer and eat a little bite wher wont nobody bother you. Durn them fellers."

Temple leaned around the door, past his dim shape, her face wan as a small ghost in the refracted light from the diningroom. "Mrs--------Mrs........." she whispered.

"She's in the kitchen. Want me to go back there with you?" In the diningroom a chair scraped. Between blinks Tommy saw Temple in the path, her body slender and motionless for a moment as though waiting for some laggard part to catch up. Then she was gone like a shadow around the corner of the house. He stood in the door, the plate of food in his hand. Then he turned his head and looked into the hall just in time to see her flit across the darkness toward the kitchen."Durn them fellers."

He was standing there when the others returned to the porch.

"He's got a plate of grub," Van said. "He's trying to get his with a plate full of ham."

"Git my whut?" Tommy said.

"Look here," Gowan said.

Van struck the plate from Tommy's hand. He turned to Gowan. "Dont you like it?"

"No," Gowan said, "I dont."

"What are you going to do about it?" Van said.

"Van," Goodwin said.

"Do you think you're big enough to not like it?" Van said.

"I am," Goodwin said.

When Van went back to the kitchen Tommy followed him. He stopped at the door and heard Van in the kitchen.

"Come for a walk, little bit," Van said.

"Get out of here, Van," the woman said.

"Come for a little walk," Van said. "I'm a good guy. Ruby'll tell you."

"Get out of here, now," the woman said. "Do you want me to call Lee?" Van stood against the light, in a khaki shirt and breeches, a cigarette behind his ear against the smooth sweep of his blond hair. Beyond him Temple stood behind the chair in which the woman sat at the table, her mouth open a little, her eyes quite black.

When he went back to the porch with the jug he said to Goodwin: "Why dont them fellers quit pesterin that gal?"

"Who's pestering her?"

"Van is. She's skeered. Whyn't they leave her be?"

"It's none of your business. You keep out of it. You hear?"

"Them fellers ought to quit pesterin her," Tommy said. He squatted against the wall. They were drinking, passing the jug back and forth, talking. With the top of his mind he listened to them, to Van's gross and stupid tales of city life with rapt interest, guffawing now and then, drinking in his turn. Van and Gowan were doing the talking, and Tommy listened to them. "Them two's fixin to have hit out with one another," he whispered to Goodwin in a chair beside him. "Hyear em?" They were talking quite loud; Goodwin moved swiftly and lightly from his chair, his feet striking the floor with light thuds; Tommy saw Van standing and Gowan holding himself erect by the back of his chair.

"I never meant-------" Van said.

"Dont say it, then," Goodwin said.

Gowan said something. That durn feller, Tommy thought. Cant even talk no more.

"Shut up, you," Goodwin said.

"Think talk bout my-------" Gowan said. He moved, swayed against the chair. It fell over.

"By God, I'll-----" Van said.

"------ginia gentleman; I dont give a--------"Gowan said. Goodwin flung him aside with a backhanded blow of his arm, and grasped Van. Gowan fell against the wall.

"When I say sit down, I mean it," Goodwin said.

After that they were quiet for a while. Goodwin returned to his chair. They began to talk again, passing the jug, and Tommy listened. But soon he began to think about Temple again. He would feel his feet scouring on the floor and his whole body writhing in an acute discomfort. "They ought to let that gal alone," he whispered to Goodwin. "They ought to quit pesterin her."

"It's none of your business," Goodwin said. "Let every damned one of them.........."

"They ought to quit pesterin her."

Popeye came out the door. He lit a cigarette. Tommy

watched his face flare out between his hands, his cheeks sucking; he followed with his eyes the small comet of the match into the weeds. Him too, he said. Two of em; his body writhing slowly. Pore little crittur. I be dawg ef I aint a mind to go down to the barn and stay there, I be dawg ef I aint. He rose, his feet making no sound on the porch. He stepped down into the path and went around the house. There was a light in the window there. Dont nobody never use in there, he said, stopping, then he said, That's where she'll be stayin, and he went to the window and looked in. The sash was down. Across a missing pane a sheet of rusted tin was nailed.

Temple was sitting on the bed, her legs tucked under her, erect, her hands lying in her lap, her hat tilted on the back of her head. She looked quite small, her very attitude an outrage to muscle and tissue of more than seventeen and more compatible with eight or ten, her elbows close to her sides, her face turned toward the door against which a chair was wedged. There was nothing in the room save the bed, with its faded patchwork quilt, and the chair. The walls had been plastered once, but the plaster had cracked and fallen in places, exposing the lathing and molded shreds of cloth. On the wall hung a raincoat and a khaki-covered canteen.

Temple's head began to move. It turned slowly, as if she were following the passage of someone beyond the wall. It turned on to an excrutiating degree, though no other muscle moved, like one of those papier-mache Easter toys filled with candy, and became motionless in that reverted position. Then it turned back, slowly, as though pacing invisible feet beyond the wall, back to the chair against the door and became motionless there for a moment. Then she faced forward and Tommy watched her take a tiny watch from the top of her stocking and look at it. With the watch in her hand she lifted her head and looked directly at him, her eyes calm and empty as two holes. After a while she looked down at the watch again and returned it to her stocking.

She rose from the bed and removed her coat and stood motionless, arrowlike in her scant dress, her head bent, her hands clasped before her. She sat on the bed again. She sat with her legs close together, her head bent. She raised her head and looked about the room. Tommy could hear the voices from the dark porch. They rose again, then sank to the steady murmur.

Temple sprang to her feet. She ~~stepped out of her slippers~~ unfastened her dress, her arms arched thin and high, her shad-ow anticking her movements. In a single motion she was out of it, crouching a little, match-thin in her scant undergarments. Her head emerged facing the chair against the door. She hurled the dress away, her hand reaching for the coat. She scrabbled it up and swept it about her, pawing at the sleeves. Then, the coat clutched to her breast, she whirled and looked straight into Tommy's eyes and whirled and ran and flung herself upon ~~t~~ the chair. "Durn them fellers," Tommy whispered, "durn them fellers." He could hear them on the front porch and his body began again to writhe slowly in an acute unhappiness. "Durn them fellers."

When he looked into the room again Temple was moving toward him, holding the coat about her. She took the raincoat from the nail and put it on over her own coat and fastened it. She lifted the canteen down and returned to the bed. She laid the canteen on the bed and picked her dress up from the floor and brushed it with her hand and folded it carefully and laid it on the bed. Then she turned back the quilt, exposing the mattress. There was no linen, no pillow, and when she touched the mattress it gave forth a faint dry whisper of shucks.

She removed her slippers and set them on the bed and got in beneath the quilt. Tommy could hear the mattress crackle. She didn't lie down at once. She at upright, quite still, the hat tilted rakishly upon the back of her head. Then she moved the canteen, the dress and the slippers beside her head and drew the raincoat about her legs and lay down, drawing the quilt up, then she sat up and removed the hat and shook her hair out and laid the hat with the other garments and prepared to lie down again. Again she paused. She opened the raincoat and produced a compact from somewhere and, watching her motions in the tiny mirror, she spread and fluffed her hair with her fingers and powdered her face and replaced the compact and looked at the watch again and fastened the raincoat. She moved the garments one by one under the quilt and lay down and drew the quilt to her chin. The voices had got quiet for a moment and in the silence Tommy could hear a faint, steady chatter of the shucks inside the mattress where Temple lay, her hands crossed on her breast and her legs straight and close and decorous, like an effigy on an ancient tomb.

The voices were still; he had completely forgot them until he heard Goodwin say "Stop it. Stop that!" A chair crashed over; he heard Goodwin's light thudding feet; the chair clattered along the porch as though it had been kicked aside, and crouching, his ~~arms~~ elbows out a little in squat, bear-like alertness, Tommy heard dry, light sounds like billiard balls. "Tommy," Goodwin said.

When necessar he could move with that thick, lightning-like celerity of badgers or coons. He was around the house and on the porch in time to see Gowan slam into the wall and slump along it and plunge full length off the porch into the weeds, and Popeye in the door, his head thrust forward. "Grab him there!" Goodwin said. Tommy sprang upon Popeye in a sidling rush.

"I got----hah!" he said as Popeye slashed savagely at his face; "you would, would you? Hole up hyer."

Popeye ceased. "Jesus Christ. You let them sit around here all night, swilling that goddam stuff; I told you. Jesus

Christ."

Goodwin and Van were a single shadow, locked and hushed and furious. "Let go!" Van shouted. "I'll kill-------"Tommy sprang to them. They jammed Van against the wall and held him motionless.

"Got him?" Goodwin said.

"Yeuh. I got him. Hole up hyer. You done whupped him."

"By God, I'll---------"

"Now, now; whut you want to kill him fer? You caint eat him, kin you? You want Mr Popeye to start guttin us all with that ere artermatic?"

Then it was over, gone like a furious gust of black wind, leaving a peaceful vacuum in which they moved quietly about, lifting Gowan out of the weeds with low-spoken, amicable directions to one another. They carried him into the hall, where the woman stood, and to the door of the room where Temple was.

"She's locked it," Van said. He struck the door, high. "Open the door," he shouted. "We're bringing you a customer."

"Hush," Goodwin said. "There's no lock on it. Push it."

"Sure," Van said,; "I'll push it." He kicked it. The chair buckled and sprang into the room. Van banged the door open and they entered, carrying Gowan's legs. Van kicked the chair across the room. Then he saw Temple standing in the corner behind the bed. His hair was broken about his face, long as a girl's. He flung it back with a toss of his head. His chin was bloody and he deliberately spat blood onto the floor.

"Go on," Goodwin said, carrying Gowan's shoulders, "put him on the bed." They swung Gowan onto the bed. His bloody head lolled over the edge. Van jerked him aver and slammed him into the mattress. He groaned, lifting his hand. Van struck him across the face with his palm.

"Lie still, you------"

"Let be," Goodwin said. He caught Van's hand. For an instant they glared at one another.

"I said, Let be," Goodwin said. "Get out of here."

"Got proteck........" Gowan muttered "......girl. 'Ginia gem........ gemman got proteck........"

"Get out of here, now," Goodwin said.

The woman stood in the door beside Tommy, her back a-gainst the door frame. Beneath a cheap coat her nightdress dropped to her feet.

Van lifted Temple's dress from the bed. "Van," Goodwin said. "I said get out."

"I heard you," Van said. He shook the dress out. Then he looked at Temple in the corner, her arms crossed, her hands clutching her shoulders. Goodwin moved toward Van. He dropped the dress and went around the bed. Popeye came in the door, a cigarette in his fingers. Beside the woman Tommy drew his breath hissing through his ragged teeth.

He saw Van take hold of the raincoat upon Temple's breast and rip it open. Then Goodwin sprang between them; he saw Van duck, whirling, and Temple fumbling at the torn raincoat.

Van and Goodwin were now in the middle of the floor, swinging at one another, then he was watching Popeye walking toward Temple. With the corner of his eye he saw Van lying on the floor and Goodwin standing over him, stooped a little, watching Popeye's back.

"Popeye," Goodwin said. Popeye went on, the cigarette trailing back over his shoulder, his head turned a little as though he were not looking where he was going, the cigarette slanted as though his mouth were somewhere under the turn of his jaw. "Dont touch her," Goodwin said.

Popeye stopped before Temple, his face turned a little aside. His right hand lay in his coat pocket. Beneath the raincoat on Temple's breast Tommy could see the movement of the other hand, communicating a shadow of movement to the coat.

"Take your hand away," Goodwin said. "Move it."

Popeye moved his hand. He turned, his hands in his coat pockets, looking at Goodwin. He crossed the room, watching Goodwin. Then he turned his back on him and went out the door.

"Here, Tommy," Goodwin said quietly, "grab hold of this." They lifted Van and carried him out. The woman stepped aside. She leaned against the wall, holding her coat together. Across the room Temple stood crouched into the corner, fumbling at the torn raincoat. Gowan began to snore.

Goodwin returned. "You'd better go back to bed," he said. The woman didn't move. He put his hand on her shoulder. "Ruby."

"While you finish the trick Van started and you wouldn't let him finish? You poor fool. You poor fool."

"Come on, now," he said, his hand on her shoulder. "Go back to bed."

"But dont ~~bother to~~ come back. Dont bother to come back. I wont be there. You owe me nothing. Dont think you do."

Goodwin took her wrists and drew them steadily apart. Slowly and steadily he carried her hands around behind her and held them in one of his. With the other hand he opened the coat. The nightdress was of faded pink crepe, lace-trimmed, laundered and laundered until, like the garment on the wire, the lace was a fibrous mass.

"Hah," he said. "Dressed for company."

"Whose fault is it if this is the only one I have? Whose fault is it? Not mine. I've given them away to nigger maids after one night. But do you think any nigger would take this and not laugh in my face?"

He let the coat fall to. He released her hands and she drew the coat together. With his hand on her shoulder he began to push her toward the door. "Go on," he said. Her shoulder gave. It alone moved, her body turning on her hips, her face reverted, watching him. "Go on," he said. But her torso alone turned, her hips and head still touching the wall. He turned and crossed the room and went swiftly around the bed and caught Temple by the front of the raincoat with one hand.

He began to shake her. Holding her up by the gathered wad of coat he shook her, her small body clattering soundlessly inside the loose garment, her shoulders and thighs thumping against the wall. "You little fool!" he said. "You little fool!" Her eyes were quite wide, almost black, the lamplight on her face and two tiny reflections of his face in her pupils like peas in two inkwells.

He released her. She began to sink to the floor, the raincoat rustling about her. He caught her up and began to shake her again, looking over his shoulder at the woman. "Get the lamp," he said. The woman did not move. Her head was bent a little; she appeared to muse upon them. Gowan swept his other arm under Temple's knees. She felt herself swooping, then she was lying on the bed beside Gowan, on her back, jouncing to the dying chatter of the shucks. She watched him cross the room and lift the lamp from the mantel. The woman had turned her head, following him also, her face sharpening out of the approaching lamp in profile. "Go on," he said. She turned, her face turning into shadow, the lamp now on her back and on his hand on her shoulder. His shadow blotted the room completely; his arm in silhouette backreaching, drew to the door. Gowan snored, each respiration choking to a huddle fall, as though he would never breathe again.

Tommy was outside the door, in the hall.

"They gone down to the truck yet?" Goodwin said.

"Not yit," Tommy said.

"Better go and see about it," Goodwin said. They went on. Tommy watched them enter another door/. Then he went to the kitchen, silent on his bare feet, his neck craned a little with lis$tening. In the kitchen Popeye sat, straddling a chair, smoking. Van stood at the table, before a fragment of mirror, combing his hair with a pocket comb. Upon the table lay a damp, blood-stained cloth and a burning cigarette. Tommy squatted outs/ide the door, in the darkness.

He was there when Goodwin came out with the raincoat. He entered the kitchen without seeing him. "Where's Tommy?" he said. Tommy heard Popeye say something, then Goodwin emerged with Van following him, the raincoat on his arm now. "Come on, now," Goodwin said. "Let's get that stuff out of here."

Tommy's pale eye began to glow faintly, like those of a cat. The woman could see them in the darkness when he crept into the room after Popeye, and while Popeye stood over the bed where Temple lay. They glowed suddenly out of the darkness at her, then they went away and she could hear him breathing beside her; again they glowed up at her with a quality furious and qusetioning and sad and went away again and he crept behind Popeye from the room.

He saw that Popeye returned to the kitchen, but he did not follow at once. He stopped at the hall door and squatted there. His body began to writhe again in shocked indecision, his bare feet whispering on the floor with a faint, rocking movement as he swayed from side to side, his hands wringing slowly against his flanks. And Lee too, he said, And Lee too. Durn them fellers. Durn them fellers. Twice he stole along the porch until he could see the shadow of Popeye's hat on the kitchen floor, then returned to the hall and the door where Temple lay and where Gowan snored. The third time he smelled Popeye's cigarette. Ef he'll jest keep that up, he said. And Lee too, he said, rocking from side to side in a dull, excrutiating agony, And Lee too.

When Goodwin came up the slope and onto the back porch Tommy was squatting just outside the door again. "What in hell-----" Goodwin said. "Why didn't you come on? I've been looking for you for ten minutes." He glared at Tommy, then he looked into the kitchen. "You ready?" he said. Popeye came to the door. Goodwin looked at Tommy again. "What have you been doing?"

Popeye looked at Tommy. Tommy stood now, rubbing his instep with the other foot, looking at Popeye.

"What're you doing here?" Popeye said.

"Aint doin nothin," Tommy said.

"Are you following me around?"

"I aint trailin nobody," Tommy said sullenly.

"Well, dont, then," Popeye said.

"Come on," Goodwin said. "Van's waiting." They went on. Tommy followed them. Once he looked back at the house, then he shambled on behind them. From time to time he would feel that acute surge go over him, like his blood was too hot all of a sudden, dying away into that warm unhappy feeling that fiddle music gave him. Durn them fellers, he whispered, Durn them fellers.

He was standing in the hallway of the barn when Temple at last got the door of the crib open. When she recognised him she was half spun, leaping back, then she whirled and ran toward him and sprang down, clutching his arm. Then she saw Goodwin standing in the back door of the house and she whirled and leaped back into the crib and turned and leaned her head around the door, her voice making a thin eeeeeeeeeeeee sound like bubbles in a bottle. She leaned there, scrabbling her hands on the door, trying to pull it to, ~~Ke/ffint/Tok/listening/to/~~ hearing Tommy's voice.

".......Lee says hit wont hurt you none. All you got to do is lay down........" It was a dry sort of sound, not in her consciousness at all, nor his pale eyes beneath the shaggy thatch. She leaned in the door, wailing, trying to shut it. Then she felt his hand clumsily on her thigh. ".......says hit wont hurt you none. All you got to do is........."

She looked at him, his diffident, hard hand on her hip. "Yes," she said, "all right. Dont you let him in here."

"You mean fer me not to let none of them in hyer?"

"All right. I'm not scared of rats. You stay there and dont let him in."

"All right. I'll fix hit so caint nobody git to you. I'll be right hyer."

"All right. Shut the door. Dont let him in here."

"All right." He shut the door. She leaned in it, looking toward the house. He pushed her back so he could close the door. "Hit aint goin to hurt you none, Lee says. All you got to do is lay down."

"All right. I will. Dont you let him in here." The door closed. She heard him drive the hasp to. Then he shook the door.

"Hit's fastened," he said. "Caint nobody git to you now. I'll be right hyer."

He squatted on his heels in the chaff, looking at the house. After a while he saw Goodwin come to the back door and look toward ~~the barn~~ him, and squatting, clasping his knees, Tommy's eyes glowed again, the pale irises appearing for an instant to spin on the pupils like tiny wheels. He squatted there, his lip lifted a little, until Goodwin went back into the house. Then he sighed, expelling his breath, and he looked at the blank door of the crib and again his eyes glowed with a diffident, groping, hungry fire and he began to rub his hands slowly on his shanks, rocking a little from side to side. Then he ceased, became rigid, and watched Goodwin move swiftly across the corner of the house and into the cedars. He squatted rigid, his lip lifted a little upon his ragged teeth.

Sitting in the cottonseed-hulls, in the litter of gnawed corn-cobs, Temple lifted her head suddenly toward the trap at the top of the ladder. She heard Popeye cross the floor, then his foot ap eared, groping gingerly for the step. He descended, watching her over his shoulder.

She sat quite motionless, her mouth open a little. He stood looking at her. He gegan to thrust his chin out in a series of jerks, as though his collar were too tight. ~~Then~~. He lifted his elbows and brushed them with his palm, and the skirt of his coat, then he crossed her field of vision, moving without a sound, his hand in his coat pocket. He tried the door. Then he shook it.

"Open the door," he said.

There was no sound. Then Tommy whispered: "Who's that?"

"Open the door," Popeye said. The door opened. Tommy looked at Popeye. He blinked.

"I didn't know you was in hyer," he said. He made to look past Popeye, into the crib. Popeye laid his hand flat on Tommy's face and thrust him back and leaned past him and looked up at the house. Then he looked at Tommy.

"Didn't I tell you about following me?"

"I wasn't following you," Tommy said. "I was watching him," jerking his head toward the house.

"Watch him, then," Popeye said. Tommy turned his head and looked toward the house and Popeye drew his hand from his coat pocket.

To Temple, sitting in the cottonseed-hulls and the corn-cobs, the sound was no louder than the striking of a match:

a short, minor sound shutting down upon the scene, the instant, with a profound finality, completely isolating it, and she sat ~~t/~~ there, her legs straight before her, her hands ~~~~ limp and palm-up on her lap, looking at Popeye's tight back and the ridges across the shoulders as he leaned out the door, the pistol behind him, against his flank, wisping thinly along his leg.

He turned and looked at her. He waggled the pistol slightly and put it back in his coat, then he walked toward her. Moving, he made no sound at all; the released door yawned and clapped against the jamb, but it made no sound either; it was as though sound and silence had become inverted. She could hear silence in a thick rustling as he moved toward her through it, thrusting it aside, and she began to say Something is going to happen to me. She was saying it to the old man with the yellow clots for eyes. "Something is happening to me!" she screamed at him, sitting in his chair in the sunlight, his hands crossed on the top of the stick. "I toRd you it was!" she screamed, voiding the words like hot silent bubbles into the bright silence about them until he turned his head and the two phlegm-clots above her where she lay tossing and thrashing on the rough, sunny boards. "I told you! I told you all the time!"

XII.

"But that girl," Horace said. "You know she was all right. You know that."

The woman sat on the edge of the bed, looking down at the child. Motionless, her hands quiet now in her lap, she had that spent immobility of a chimney rising above the ruin of a house in the aftermath of a cyclone. "The car passed me about halfway back to the hose," she said in a flat, toneless voice. "She was in it. I dont know what time it was. It was about half way back to the house."

"You had turned around and were going back?"

"I forgot to bring his bottle," she said. Her hand went out and hovered about the child's face. For a time it performed those needless, brooding, maternal actions with the covers as though it responded instinctively to old compulsions of habit and care while the discretion of the mind slept. Then she sat again, her hands quiet in her lap, her face bent above the child. "So I had to go back. Lee was in our room. He came to the door and looked at me and I said 'Yes. What. What is it.' About noon the car came and he sent word for the sheriff."

Each time he passed the jail he would find himself looking up at the window, to see the hand or the wisp of tobacco smoke blowing along the sunshine. The wall was now in sunlight, the hand lying there in sunlight too, looking dingier, smaller,

smaller, more tragic than ever, yet he turned his head quickly away. It was as though from that tiny clot of knuckles he was about to reconstruct an edifice upon which he would not dare to look, like an archaeologist who, from a meagre sifting of vertebrae, reconstructs a shape out of the nightmares of his own childhood, and he looked quickly away as the car went smoothly on and the jail, the shabby purlieus of the square gave way to shady lawns and houses---all the stability which he had known always---a stage upon which tragedy kept to a certain predictableness, decorum.

Of course she's all right, he said. She's down there at school now. Probably just getten over being thoroughly scared, damn her. Damn her. They passed the final fringe of cabins and small houses like the fraying hem of a garment, and the final filling-station---that fatuous and optimistic dream of man in which the apotheosis of his indolence sits at the roadside, grinding coins out of a spigot furnished him gratis and with the very upkeep of which he need not concern himself. "Of course ~~she's~~ she's all right," he said. "Things like that dont happen."

"Sir?" Isom said.

"What? Oh, nothing. Nothing." The fields were stoutly green with young cotton and corn. Now and then men and animals, tiny with distance, moved among the rows in the level afternoon. Against patches of woods already darkening into the virile green of full summer the dogwwod was almost gone, less than a stain. Only the locust was still in bloom, in ragged foam above the green tunnel of the drive. When they turned in at the gate the scent of it was heavy on the air and at every breath it snowed down the sunny vista and lay in diffident snow upon the packed cinders.

"Things like that dont happen," he said. "This is a civilised age, say what you want to."

"Yes," Miss Jenny said. "I've heard that."

"It's when I think of little Belle; think that at any moment........." Against the book on the table the photograph sat under the lamp. Along the four edges of it was the narrow imprint of the missing frame. The face wore an expression of sweet and bemused self-consciousness. The short hair was straight and smooth, neither light nor dark; they eyes darker than light and with a shining quality beneath soft and secret lids; a prim smooth mouth innocently travestied by the painted bow of the period. He began to whisper Damn him, damn him, tramping back and forth before the photograph.

In the window the faint curtains moved in shadowy peristalsis upon the smooth belly of the dark. The darkness was shrill with the drowsy dissonance of early summer cicadas, and with darkness the scents of the garden seemed to have increased tenfold, permeant, corruptive, and he thought of that afternoon last fall when he had first watched Gowan walking there in the garden, impeccable, decorous, plumply cavalier.

"He came out to the kitchen while I was getting breakfast," the woman said. "Wild looking, with his face all bloody and swollen. I tried to get him to wash it off, but he kept on jabbering about her until I made him understand she was down there in the crib asleep, then he calmed down some and said he was going to get a car. I told him where the nearest one was, and he wouldn't even wait for breakfast."

When he left the house he was still groggy and he thought that he was still drunk. He could remember only vaguely what had happened. He had got Van and the wreck confused and he did not know that he had been knocked out twice. He only remembered that he had passed out some time early in the night, and he thought that he was still drunk. But when he reached the wrecked car and saw the path and followed it to the spring and drank of the cold water, he found that it was a drink he wanted, and he knelt there, bathing his face in the cold water and trying to examine his reflection in the broken surface, whispering Jesus Christ to himself in a kind of despair. He thought about returning to the house for a drink, then he thought of having to face Temple, the men; of Temple there among them.

When he reached the highroad the sun was well up, warm. I'll get cleaned up some, he said. And coming back with a car. I'll decide what to say to her on the way to town; thinking of Temple returning among people who knew him, who might know

~~swept,/reeled/against/~~ him. I passed out twiśe, he said. <u>I passed out twice.</u> Jesus Christ, Jesus Christ he whispered, his body writhing inside his disreputable and bloody clothes in an agony of rage and shame.

His head began to clear with air and motion, but as he began to feel better physically the blackness of the future increased. Town, the world, began to appear as a black cul-de-sac; a place in which he must walk forever more, his whole body cringing and flinching from whispering eyes when he had passed, and when in midmorning he reached the house he sought, the prospect of facing Temple again was more than he could bear. So he engaged the car and directed the man and paid him and went on. A little later a car going in the opposite direction stopped and picked him up.

Damn it, it is a civilised age, Horace thought, tramping back and forth while the sweet, soft, secret face came and went beneath the cylindrical blur of highlight which the lamp cast upon the glossy surface of the portrait, We are civilised, no matter how hard we try not to be. The stupfdity of it, of believing that evil is merely an empty sound called daring; merely a closet of shiny costumes from which you can dress yourself for an evening. It's because they are fools enough to believe that older people, grown people, are wiser than they; because they believe that they must do all the things the magazines and movies tell them are expected of young people. Teaching them that the courageous thing is to live your own life, when nobody has an own life at sixty, let alone sixteen. "Damn him, damn him," he whispered, tramping back and forth before the photograph.

If we'd just let them alone, he thought, thinking of the potential evil in everyone, even children; thinking of Temple back at school, spending perhaps one sleepless night in which for a little while and for the first time since she was born, she had completely forgot herself. Not over one night, he said. Then she'll realise that she has escaped and then it'll be a whispered tale over a box of candy, probably clumped pinpoints of cigarettes in the secure dark and soft gasps and crowding surges under fleeting silk, like puppies in a basket, five or six in the bed. But to think that by merely existing, drawing breath, they should be at the mercy of such......"Damn him," he whispered,"damn him," tramping back and forth while the soft, bemused face blurred and faded in and out of the photograph.

The curtains billowed steadily and faintly, as though to the shrill pulsing of the cicadas, and he thought how darkness is that agent which destroys the edifice with which light shapes people to a certain predictable behavior, as though by the impact of eyes; thinking of the grape arbor, of the murmur of young voices darkening into silence and into the pale whisper of Little Belle's small white dress, of the delicate and urgent mammalian whisper of that curious small flesh in which was vatted delicately a seething sympathy of the blossoming grape. He drew a chair to the table and moved the photograph until the face was clear of the highlight, gazing at the sweet, veiled enigma. As though there were in events a fatality which takes its color from the minds privy to the events, he thought. As though a disaster not a part of the plan could be engendered by his lack of concern and my fundamental pessimism and her furious woman's desire for retributive justice.........He rose quickly, the chair scraping on the floor. Again the face blurred into the highlight, yet the familiarity of the face's planes enabled him still to see it, as though beneath disturbed water or through steam, and he looked down at the face with a sort of still horror and despair, at a face more blurred than sweet, at eyes more secret than soft. He reached for it so quickly that he knocked it flat, whereupon once more the face mused tenderly behind the rigid travesty of the painted mouth.

The hall was dark. In moccasins his feet made no noise. Though slowing, the initial impulse carried him halfway down the stairs before he stopped, one hand on the balustrade, his head and shoulders still in that faint diffusion of light from the transom above Miss Jenny's door, remembering the extension of the telephone in Miss Jenny's room, telling himself that the reason was that he did not want to disturb her, knowing that the ~~real~~ reason was that he did not want even Miss Jenny to know what an old woman he was. But the real reason was that he was afraid to face in darkness what he might find at the other end of the wire.

He turned abd mounted the stairs and tapped at Miss and tapped at Miss Jenny's door. She bade him enter and he found her reading in bed. In the shadow beside the bed the cot ~~on/which~~ presented an unbroken surface, ridged in a faint curve.

"Dont get tangled in the cord," Miss Jenny said. One end of it was tied to the bedpost beside her head, the other end ~~disapp~~ disappeard at the top of the ridge of bedclothing on the cot. "Did you dream who committed the murder?"

"Your nice, wellbred young man," Horace said. "I know why he wont come back."

"Who? Gowan?"

"Yes. Gowan. And, by the Lord, he'd better not come back. By God, when I think that I had the opportunity-------"

"What? What did he do?"

"He carried a little fool girl out there with him that day and got drunk and ran off and left her. That's what he did. If it hadn't been for/ that woman--------And when I think of people like that walking the earth with impunity just because he has a balloon-tailed suit and went through the astonishing experience of having attended Virginia........ On any train or in any hotel, on the street; anywhere, mind you--------"

"Oh," Miss Jenny said. "I didn't understand at first who you meant. Well," she said. "You remember that last time he was here, just after you came? the day he ~~left~~ wouldn't stay for supper and went to Oxford?"

"Yes. And when I think how I could have------"

"He asked Narcissa to marry him. She said that one child was enough for her."

"I said she has no heart. She cannot be satisfied with less than insult."

"So he got mad and said he would go to Oxford, where there was a woman he was reasonably confident he would not appear ridiculous to: somthing like that. Well." She looked at him, her neck bowed to see across her spectacles. "I'll declare, a male parent is a funny thing, but just let a man have a hand in one that's no kin to him....... What is it that makes a man think that the female flesh he marries or begets might misbehave, but all he didn't marry or get is bound to?"

"Yes," Horace said, "and thank God she isn't my flesh and blood. I can reconcile myself to her having to be exposed to a scoundrel now and then, but to think that at any moment she may become involved with a fool."

"Well, what are you going to do about it? Start some kind of roach campaign?"

"I'm going to do what she said; I'm going to have a law passed making it obligatory upon everyone to shoot any man less than fifty years old that makes, buys, sells or thinks whiskey. ....scoundrel I can face, but to think of her being exposed to any fool.........."

In his room again he stood at the window, feeling the dark soft whisper of the curtains against his cheek. Invisible, stirred seemingly by the cicadas, since there was scarce any movement of the darkness itself; the cicadas become now a drowsy sound, numbing, almost pleasant, as prolonged dissonnance does. There was no movement, yet the body of night, darkness, was filled with that yawning sense of teeming and accomplished space. The window looked south. Four miles of peaceful night lay between, yet he believed that he could see the glow of town low in the sky; dark flat shapes of rooflines; a square building with a dim grated window, a pale blob of knuckles motionless in one of the interstices.

It was three oclock when he passed the jail on foot and looked up at the window. It was empty: an orderly checker-boarding of pale squares in a blank wall under the low morning star. The square was empty, the air chill with dawn. He moved in echoing isolation beneath the lighted face of the clock on the court-house and the sparse lights which filled the doorways nd/ and niches in the blank facades of stores with shadows in humped shapes like ranks of patient vultures.

The station was still three quarters of a mile away. The waiting-room, lit by a single dirt-crusted globe, was empty save for a man in overalls sprawled on his back, his head on a folded coat, snoring, and a woman in a calico dress, a dingy shawl and an awkward hat bright with rigid and moribund flowers, her head bent and her hands crossed on a paper-wrapped parcel on her lap, a straw suit-case at her feet. He discovered then that he had forgottan the book. The photograph was still propped against it---the very thing which had driven him from bed to walk four and three quarters miles in the darkness---and his inner eye~~s~~ showed it to him suddenly, blurred by the highlight, and beside it his freshly loaded pipe. He searched his coat again, finding only the pouch.

The train came, finding him tramping back and forth along the cider-packed right-of-way. The man and woman got on, the man carrying his rumpled coat, the woman the parcel and the suitcase. He followed them into the day coach filled with snoring, with bodies sprawled half into the aisle as though in the aftermath of a sudden and violent destruction, with dropped heads. open-mouthed, their throats turned profoundly upward as though waiting the stroke of knives.

He dozed. The train clicked on, stopped, jolted. He waked and dozed again. Someone shook him out of sleep into a primrose dawn, among unshaven puffy faces washed lightly over as though with the paling ultimate stain of a holocaust, blinking at one another with dead eyes into which personality returned in secret opaque waves. He got off, had breakfast, and ~~entered another~~ took another accomodation, entering a car where a child wailed hopelessly, crunching peanut-shells under his feet as he moved up the car in a stale ammoniac odor until he found a seat beside a man. A moment later the man leaned forward and spat tobacco juice between his knees. Horace rose quickly and went forward into the smoking car. It was full too, the door between it and the jim crow car swinging open. Standing in the aisle he could look forward into a diminishing corridor of green plush seat-backs topped by hatted cannonballs swaying in unison, while gusts of talk and laughter blew back and kept in steady motion the blue acrid air in which white men sat, spitting into the aisle.

He changed again. The waiting crowd was composed half of young men in collegiate clothes with small cryptic badges on their shirts and vests, and two girls with painted small faces and scant bright dresses like identical artificial flowers surrounded each by bright and restless bees. When the train came they pushed gaily forward, talking and laughing, shouldering aside older people with gay rudeness, clashing and slamming seats back and settling themselves, turning their faces up out of laughter, their cold faces still toothed with it, as three middle-aged women moved down the car, looking tenatively left and right at the filled seats.

The two girls sat together, removing a fawn and a blue hat, lifting slender hands and preening not-quite-formless fingers about their close heads seen between the sprawled elbows and the leaning heads of two youths hanging over the back of the seat and surrounded by colored hat bands at various heights where the owners sat on the seat arms or stood in the aisle; and presently the conductor's cap as he thrust among them with plaintive, fretful cries, like a bird.

"Tickets. Tickets, please," he chanted. For an instant they held him there, invisible save for his cap. Then two young men slipped swiftly back and into the seat behind Horace. He could hear them breathing. Forward the conductor's punch clicked twice. He came on back. "Tickets," he chanted. "Tickets." He took Horace's and stopped where the youths sat.

"You already got mine," one said. "Up there."

"Where's your check?" the conductor said.

"You never gave us any. You got our tickets, though. Mine was number--------" he repeated a number glibly, in a frank, pleasant tone. "Did you notice the number of yours, Shack?"

The second one repeated a number in a frank, pleasant tone. "Sure you got ours. Look and see." He began to whistle between his teeth, a broken dance rythm, unmusical.

"Do you eat at Gordon hall?" the other said.

"No. I have natural halitosis." The conductor went on. The whistle reached crescendo, clapped off by his hands on his knees, ejaculating ~~duh~~ duh-duh-duh. Then he just squalled, meaningless, vertiginous; to Horace it was like sitting before a series of printed pages turned in furious snatches, leaving a series of cryptic, headless and tailless evocations on the mind.

"She's travelled a thousand miles without a ticket."

"Marge too."

"Beth too."

"Duh-duh-duh."

"Marge too."

"I'm going to punch mine Friday night."

"Eeeeyow."

"Do you like liver?"

"I cant reach that far."

"Eeeeeyow."

They whistled, clapping their heels on the floor to furious crescendo, saying duh-duh-duh. The first jolted the seat back against Horace's head. He rose. "Come on," he said. "He's done gone." Again the seat jarred into Horace and he watched them return and join the group that blocked the aisle, saw one of them lay his bold, rough hand flat upon one of the bright, soft faces uptilted to them. Beyond the group a countrywoman with an infant in her arms stood braced against a seat. From time to time she looked back at the blocked aisle and the empty seats beyond.

At Oxford he descanded into a throng of them at the station, hatless, in bright dresses, now and then with books in their hands and surrounded still by swarms of colored shirts. Impassable, swinging hands with their escorts, objects of casual and puppyish pawings, they dawdled up the hill toward the college, swinging their little hips, looking at Horace with cold, blank eyes as he stepped off the walk in order to pass them.

At the top of the hill three paths diverged through

a broad grove beyond which, in green vistas, buildings in red brick or gray stone ~~gear~~ gleamed, and where a clear soprano bell began to ring. The procession became three streams, thinning rapidly upon the dawdling couples, swinging hands, strolling in erratic surges, lurching into one another with puppyish squeals, with the random intense purposelessness of children. Watching them Horace began to laugh, without mirth. And this is what I have been losing sleep over, he thought. What can a creature like that suffer, else where the dignity in tragedy---that one quality which we do not possess in common with the ~~beasts~~ beasts of the field, standing there in the bright dappling of noon, thinking that she might have been the very one who forced him to step off the walk in order to pass her: the supreme gesture of that irony which ordered his life.

The broader path led to the postoffice. He entered and waited until the window was clear.

"I'm trying to find a young lady, Miss Temple Drake. I probably just missed her, didn't I?"

"She's not here any longer," the clerk said. "She quit school about two weeks ago." He was young: a dull, smooth face behind horn glasses, the hair meticulous. After a time Horace heard himself asking quietly:

"You dont know where she went?"

The clerk looked at him. He leaned, lowering his

voice: "Are you another detective?"

"Yes," Horace said, "yes. No matter. It doesn't matter." Then he was walking quietly down the steps, into the sunlight again. He stood there while on both sides of him they passed in a steady stream of little colored dresses, bare-armed, with close bright heads, with that identical cool, innocent, unabashed expression which he knew well in their eyes, above the savage identical paint upon their mouths; like music moving, like honey poured in sunlight, pagan and evanescent and serene, thinly evocative of all lost days and outpaced delights, in the sun. Bright, trembling with heat, it lay in the open gladesof miragelike glimpses of stone or brick: columns without tops, towers apparently floating above a green cloud in slow ruin against the soithwest wind, sinister, imponderable, bland; and he standing there listening to the swwet cloistral bell, thinking Now what? What now? and answering himself: Why, nothing. Nothing. It's finished.

He returne to the station an hour before the train was due, a filled but unlighted cob pipe in his hand. In the lavatory he saw, scrawled on the foul, stained wall, ~~the pencilled name~~ her pencilled name. Temple Drake. He read it quietly, his head bent, slowly fingering the unlighted pipe.

A half hour before the train came they began to gather, strolling down the hill and gathering along the platform with thin, bright, raucous laughter, their blonde legs monotonous, their bodies moving continually inside their scant garments with that awkward and voluptuous purposelessness of the young.

The return train carried a pullman. He went on through the day coach and entered it. There was only one other occupant: a man in the center of the car, next the window, bareheaded, leaning back, his elbow on the window sill and an unlighted cigar in his ringed hand. When the train drew away, passing the sleek crowns in increasing reverse, he rose and went forward toward the day coach. He carried an overcoat on his arm, and a soiled, light-colored felt hat. With the corner of his eye Horace saw his hand fumbling at his breast pocket, and he remarked the severe trim of hair across the man's vast, soft, white neck. Like with a guillotine, Horace thought, watching the man sidle past the porter in the aisle and vanish, passing out of his sight and his mind in the act of flinging the hat onto his head. The train sped on, swaying on the curves, flashing past an occasional house, through cuts and across valleys where young cotton wheeled slowly in fanlike rows.

The train checked speed; a jerk came back, and four whistle-blasts. The man in the soiled hat entered, taking a cigar from his breast pocket. He came down the aisle swiftly, looking at Horace. He slowed, the cigar in his fingers. The train jolted again. The man flung his hand out and caught the back of the seat facing Horace.

"Aint this Judge Benbow?" he said. Horace looked up into a vast, puffy face without any mark of age or thought whatever---a majestic sweep of flesh on either side of a small blunt nose, like looking out over a mesa, yet withal some indefinable quality of delicate paradox, as though the Creator had completed his joke by lighting the munificent expenditure of putty with something originally intended for some weak, acquisitive creature like a squirrel or a rat. "Dont I address Judge Benbow?" he said, offering his hand. "I'm Senator Snopes, Cla'ence Snopes."

"Oh," Horace said, "yes. Thanks," he said, "but I'm afraid you anticipate a little. Hope, rather."

The other waved the cigar, the other hand, palm-up, the third finger discolored faintly at the base of a huge ring, in Horace's face. Horace shook it and freed his hand. "I thought I recognised you when you got on at Oxford," he said, "but I--------May I set down?" he said, already shoving at Horace's knee with his leg. He flung the overcoat---a shoddy blue garment with a greasy velvet collar---on the seat and sat down as the train stopped. "Yes, sir, I'm always glad to see any of the boys, any time......" He leaned across Horace and peered out the window at a small dingy station with its cryptic bulletin board ~~chalk~~ chalked over, an express truck bearing a wire chicken coop containing two forlorn fowls, at three or four men in overalls gone restfully against the wall, chewing. " 'Course you aint in my county no longer, but what I say a man's friends is his friends, whichever way they vote. Because a friend is a friend, and whether he can do anything for me or not........." He leaned back, the unlighted cigar in his fingers. "You aint come all the way up from the big town, then."

"No," Horace said.

"Anytime you're in Jackson, I'll be glad to accomodate you as if you was still in my county. Dont no man stay so busy he aint a time for his old friends, what I say. Let's see, you're in Kinston, now, aint you? I know your senators. Fine men, both of them, but I just caint call their names."

"I really couldn't say, myself," Horace said. The train started. Snopes leaned into the aisle. looking back. His light gray suit had been pressed but not cleaned. "Well," he said. He rose and took up the overcoat. "Any time you're in the city.......You going to Jefferson, I reckon?"

"Yes," Horace said.

"I'll see you again, then."

"Why not ride back here?" Horace said. "You'll find it more comfortable."

"I'm going up and have a smoke," Snopes said, waving the cigar. "I'll see you again."

"You can smoke here. There aren't any ladies."

"Sure," Snopes aid. "I'll see you ~~again~~ at Holly

Springs." He went on back toward the day coach and passed out of sight with the cigar in his mouth. By the Lord, Horace thought, he'll stay out now. He'll worry all the way home for fear I'll tell. Horace remembered him ten years ago as a hulking, dull youth, son of a restaurant-owner, member of a family which had been moving from the Frenchman's Bend neighborhood into Jefferson for the past twenty years, in sections; a family of enough ramifications to have elected him to the legislature without recourse to a public polling. But once more the man went out of his mind and he was thinking of the jail window, of the hand lying in it; of the woman. ~~Tell/Tell~~ Tell me again about that girl.

She was in the car. ~~He/was/going/fast/rough/road/and/all/and/I/thought/~~ It passed me about halfway back to the house. I dont know what time it was. He was going fast, rough road and all, and I thought then about how he was going to get around that tree. She looked at me when they passed. Just looked at me. She didn't wave or anything. She just looked at where I was standing when they passed. Her hat was on crooked, like it was last night, and I thought then that when she put it on that morning in the kitchen it was on straight, but I just thought that..........

He sat quite still, the cold pipe in his hand. He rose and went forward through the day coach, then into the smoker. Snopes was in the aisle, his thigh draped over the arm of a seat where four men sat, using the unlighted cigar to gesture with. Horace caught his eye and beckoned from the vestibule. A moment later Snopes joined him, the overcoat on his arm.

"How are things going at the capital?" Horace said.

Snopes began to speak in his harsh, assertive voice. there emerged gradually a picture of stupid chicanery and petty corruption for stupid and petty ends, conducted principally in hotel rooms into which bellboys whisked with bulging jackets upon discreet flicks of skirts in swift closet doors. "Anytime you're in town," he said. "I always like to show the boys around. Ask anybody in town; they'll tell you if it's there, Cla'ence Snopes'll know where it is. You got a pretty tough case up home there, what I hear."

"Cant tell yet," Horace said. He said: "I stopped off at Oxford today, at the university, speaking to some of my step-daughter's friends. One of her best friends is no longer in school there. A young lady from Jackson named Temple Drake."

Snopes was watching him with thick, small, opaque eyes. "Oh, yes; Judge Drake's gal," he said. "The one that ran away."

"Ran away?" Horace said. "Ran back home, did she? What was the trouble? Fail in her work?"

"I dont know. When it come out in the paper folks thought she'd run off with some fellow. One of them companionate marriages."

"But when she turned up at home, they knew it wasn't

that, I reckon. Well, well, Belle'll be surprised. What's she doing now? Running around Jackson, I suppose?"

"She aint there."

"Not?" Horace said. He could feel the other watching him. "Where is she?"

"Her paw sent her up north somewhere, with an aunt. Michigan. It was in the papers couple days later."

"Oh," Horace said. He still held the cold pipe, and he discovered his hand searching his pocket for a match. He drew a deep breath. "That Jackson paper's a pretty good paper. It's considered the most reliable paper in the state, isn't it?"

"Sure," Snopes said. "You was at Oxford trying to locate her?"

"No, no. I just happened to meet a friend of my daughter who told me she had left school. Well, I'll see you at Holly Springs."

"Sure," Snopes said. Horace returned to the pullman and sat down and lit the pipe, realising that he had not smoked all day.

When the train slowed for Holly Springs he went to the vestibule, then he stepped quickly back into the car. Snopes emerged from the day coach as the porter opened the door and swung down the step, stool in hand. Snopes descended. He took something from his breast pocket and gave it to the porter. "Here, George," he said, "have a cigar."

Horace descended. ~~He/watched~~ Snopes went on, the soiled hat towering half a head above any other. Horace looked at the porter.

"He gave it to you, did he~~/~~?"

The porter chucked the cigar on his palm. He put it in his pocket.

"What're you going to do with it?" Horace said.

"I wouldn't give it to nobody I know," the porter said.

"Does he do this very often?"

"Three-four times a year. Seems like I always git him, too......Thank' suh."

Horace saw Snopes enter the waiting-room; ~~he/watched~~ the soiled hat, the vast neck, passed again out of his mind. He filled the pipe again.

From a block away he heard the Memphis-bound train come in. It was at the platform when he reached the station. Beside the open vestibule Snopes stood, talking with two youths in new straw hats, with something vaguely mentorial about his thick shoulders and his gestures. The train whistled. The two youths got on. Horace stepped back around the corner of the station.

When his train came he saw Snopes get on ahead of him and enter the smoker. Horace knocked out his pipe and entered the day coach and found a seat at the rear, facing backward.

Isom was at the station, with the car. When they crossed the square the lighted clock-hands stood at half past eight. He looked up at the hotel wall and leaned forward suddenly. "I want to stop at the hotel a minute, Isom."

The drummers sat along the curb, with cigars and cigarettes; ~~but there was now no more singing at the jail~~ across the way and a little further down the street the barred window of the jail was empty beneath the ragged shadow of the tree, and there were no figures leaning along the fence any more.

The lobby was empty. After a moment the proprietor appeared: a tight, iron-gray man with a toothpick, his vest open upon a neat paunch. The woman was not there. "It's these church ladies," he said. He lowered his voice, the toothpick in his fingers. "They come in this morning. A committee of them. You know how it is, I reckon."

"You mean to say you let the Baptist church dictate who your guests shall be?"

"It's them ladies. You know how it is, once they get set on a thing. A man might just as well give up and do like they say. Of course, with me--------"

"By God, if there was a man-------"

"Shhhhhh," the proprietor said. "You know how it is when them-------"

"But of course there wasn't a man who would------And you call yourself one, that'll let-------"

"I got a certain position to keep of myself," the proprietor said in a placative tone. "If you come right down to it." He stepped back a little, against the desk. "I reckon I can say who'll stay in my house and who wont," he said. "~~I/aint/be/holden/to/no/man~~ "And I know some more folks around here that better do the same thing. Not no mile off, neither. I aint beholden to no man. Not to you, noways."

By God, by God, Horace whispered. He said: "Where is she now? or did they drive her out of town?"

"That aint my affair, where folks go after they check out," the proprietor said, turning his back. He said: "I reckon somebody took her~~t~~ in, though."

"Yes," Horace said. "Christians. Chriatians." He turned toward the door. The proprietor called him. He turned. the other was taking a paper down from a pigeon-hole. Horace returned to the desk. The paper lay on the desk. The proprietor leaned with his hands on the desk, the toothpick tilted in his mouth.

"She said you'd pay it," he said.

He paid the bill, counting the money down with shaking hands. Isom watched him emerge and cross the street swiftly. He called, but Horace went on and entered the jail yard and went to the door and knocked. After a while a lank, slattern woman came with a lamp, holding a man's coat across her breast. She peered at him and said before he could speak:

"You're lookin fer Miz Goodwin, I reckon."

"Yes. How did-----Did-----"

"You're the lawyer. I've seed you befo. She's hyer. Sleepin now."

"Thanks," Horace said, "Thanks. I knew that someone ----I didn't believe that------"

"I reckon I kin always find a bed fer a woman and child," the woman said. "I dont keer whut Ed says. Was you wantin her special? She's sleepin now."

"No, no; I just wanted to--------"

The woman watched him across the lamp. " 'Taint no need botherin her, then. You kin come around in the mawnin and git her a boa'din-place. 'Taint no hurry."

XIII.

Popeye drove swiftly but without any quality of haste or of flight, down the clay ~~M~~ road and into the sand. Temple was beside him. Her hat was jammed onto the back of her head, her hair escaping beneath the crumpled brim in matted clots. Her face looked like a sleep-walker's as she swayed limply to the lurching of the car. She lurched against Popeye, lifting her hand in limp reflex. Without releasing the wheel he thrust her back with his elbow. "Brace yourself," he said. "Come on, now."

Before they came to the tree they passed the woman. She stood beside the road, carrying the child, the hem of her dress folded back over its face, and she looked at them quietly from beneath the faded sunbonnet, flicking swiftly in and out of Temple's vision without any motion, any sign.

When they reached the tree Popeye swung the car out of the road and drove it crashing into the undergrowth and through the prone tree-top and back into the road again in a running popping of cane-stalks like musketry along a trench, without any diminution of speed. Beside the tree Gowan's car lay on its side. Temple looked vaguely and stupidly at it as it too shot behind.

Popeye swung back into the sandy ruts. Yet there was no flight in the action: he performed it with a certain vicious petulance, that was all. It was a powerful car. Even in the sand it held forty miles an hour, and up the narrow gulch to the highroad, where he turned north. Sitting beside him, braced against jolts that had already given way to a smooth increasing hiss of gravel, Temple gazed dully forward as the road she had traversed yesterday began to flee backward under the wheels as onto a spool, feeling her blood seeping slowly inside her loins. She sat limp in the corner of the seat, watching the steady backward rush of the land---pines in opening vistas splashed with fading dogwood; sedge; fields green with new cotton and empty of any movement, peaceful, as though Sunday were a quality of atmosphere, of light and shade---sitting with her legs close together, listening to the hot minute seeping of her blood, saying dully to herself, I'm still bleeding. I'm still bleeding.

It was a bright, soft day, a wanton morning filled with that unbelievable soft radiance of May, rife with a promise of noon and of heat, with high fat clouds like gobs of whipped cream floating lightly as reflections in a mirror, their shadows scudding sedately across the road. It had been a lavender spring. The fruit trees, the white ones, had been in small leaf when the blooms matured; they had never attained that brilliant whiteness of last spring, and the dogwood had come into full bloom after the leaf also, in green retrograde before crescendo. But lilac and wistaria and redbud, even the shabby heaven-trees, had never been finer, fulgeant, with a burning scent blowing for a hundred yards along the vagrant air of April and May. The bougainvillia against the veranda would be large as basketballs and lightly poised as balloons, and looking wacantly and stupidly at the rushing roadside Temple began to scream.

It started as a wail, rising, cut suddenly off by Popeye's hand. With her hands lying on her lap, sitting erect, she screamed, tasting the gritty acridity of his fingers while the car slewed squealing in the gravel, feeling her secret blood. Then he gripped her by the back of the neck and she sat motionless, her mouth round and open like a small empty cave. He shook her head.

"Shut it," he said, "shut it;" gripping her silent. "Look at yourself. Here." With the other hand he swung the mirror on the windshield around and she looked at her image, at the uptilted hat and her matted hair and her round mouth. She began to fumble at her coat pockets, looking at her reflection. He released her and she produced the compact and opened it and peered into the mirror, whimpering a little. She powdered her face and rouged her mouth and straightened her hat, whimpering into the tiny mirror on her lap while Popeye watched her. He lit a cigarette. "Aint you ashamed of yourself?" he said.

"It's still running," she whimpered. "I can feel it." With the lipstick poised she looked at him and opened her mouth again. He gripped her by the back of the neck.

"Stop it, now. You going to shut it?"

"Yes," she whimpered.

"See you do, then. Come on. Get yourself fixed."

She put the compact away. He started the car again.

The road began to thicken with pleasure cars Sunday-bent ---small, clay-crusted Fords and Chevrolets; an occasional larger car moving swiftly, with swathed women,and dust-covered hampers; trucks filled with wooden-faced country people in garments like colored wood meticulously carved; now and then a wagon or a buggy. Before a weathered frame church on a hill the grove was full of tethered teams and battered cars and trucks. The woods gave away to fields; houses became more frequent. Low above the skyline, above roofs and a spire or two, smoke hung. The gravel became asphalt and they entered Dumfries.

Temple began to look about, like one waking from sleep. "Not here!" she said. "I cant------"

"Hush it, now," Popeye said.

"I cant-----I might------" she whimpered. "I'm hungry," she said. "I haven't eaten since........."

"Ah, you aint hungry. Wait till we get to town."

She looked about with dazed, glassy eyes. "There might be people here........." He swung in toward a filling-station. "I cant get out," she whimpered. "It's still running, I tell you!"

"Who told you to get out?" He descended and looked at her across the wheel. "Dont you move." She watched him go up the street and enter a door. It was a dingy confectionery. He bought a pack of cigarettes and put one in his mouth. "Gimme a couple of bars of candy," he said.

"What kind?"

"Candy," he said. Under a glass bell on the counter a plate of sandwiches sat. He took one and flipped a dollar on the counter and turned toward the door.

"Here's your change," the clerk said.

"Keep it," he said. "You'll get rich faster."

When he ~~reached~~ saw the car it was empty. He stopped ten feet away and changed the sandwich to his left hand, the unlighted cigarette slanted beneath his chin. The mechanic, hanging the hose up, saw him and jerked his thumb toward the corner of the building.

Beyond the corner the wall made an offset. In the niche was a greasy barrel half full of scraps of metal and rubber. Between the barrel and the wall Temple crouched. "He nearly saw me!" she whispered. "He was almsot looking right at me!"

"Who?" Popeye said. He looked back up the street. "Who saw you?"

"He was coming right toward me! A boy. At school. He was looking right toward--------"

"Come on. Come out of it."

"He was look-------" Popeye took her by the arm. She

crouched in the corner, jerking at the arm he held, her wan face craned around the corner.

"Come on, now." Then he hsi hand was at the back of her neck, gripping it.

"Oh," she wailed in a choked voice. It was as theugh he were lifting her slowly erect by that one hand. Excepting that, there was no movement between them. Side by side, almost of a height, they appeared as decorous as two acquaintances stopped to pass the time of day before entering church.

"Are you coming?" he said. "Are you?"

"I cant. It's down to my stocking now. Look." She lifted her skirt away in a shrinking gesture, then she dropped the skirt and rose again, her torso arching backward, her soundless mouth open as he gripped her. He released her.

"Will you come now?"

She came out from behind the barrel. He took her arm.

"It's all over the back of my coat," she whimpered. "Look and see."

"You're all right. I'll get you another coat to-morrow. Come on."

They returned to the car. At the corner she hung back again. "You want some more of it, do you?" he whispered, not touching her. "Do you?" She went on and got into the car quiet-ly. He took the wheel. "Here, I got you a sandwich." He took it from his pocket and put it in her hand. "Come on, now. Eat it." She took a bite obediently. He started the car and took the Memphis road. Again, the bitten sandwich in her hand, she ceased chewing and opened her mouth in that round, hopeless expression of a child; again his hand let the wheel and gripped the back of her neck and she sat motionless, gazing straight at him, her mouth open and the half chewed mass of bread and meat lying upon her tongue.

They reached Memphis in midafternoon. At the foot of the bluff below Main Street Popeye turned into a narrow street of smoke-grimed frame houses with tiers of wooden galleries, set a little back in grassless plots, with now and then a forlorn and hardy tree of some shabby species---gaunt, lop-branched magnolias, a stunted elm or a locust in grayish, cadaverous bloom---interspersed by rear ends of garages; a scrap-heap in a vacant lot; a low-doored cavern of an equivocal appearan ance where an oilcloth-covered counter and a row of backless stools, a metal coffee-urn and a fat man in a dirt apron with a toothpick in his mouth, stood for an instant out of the gloom with an effect as of a sinister and meaningless photograph poorly made. From the bluff, beyond a line of office buildings terraced sharply against the sunfilled sky, came a sound of traffic---motor horns, trolleys---passing high overhead on the river breeze; at the end of the street a trolley materialised in the narrow gap with an effect as of magic and vanished with a stupendous clatter. On a second storey gallery a young negress in her underclothes smoked a cigarette sullenly, her arms on the balustrade.

Popeye drew up before one of the dingy three-storey houses, the entrance of which was hidden by a dingy lattice cubicle leaning a little awry. In the grimy grassplot before it two of those small, wooly, white, worm-like dogs, one with a pink, the other a blue, ribbon about its neck, moved about with an air of sluggish and obscene paradox. In the sunlight their coats looked as though they had been cleaned with gasoline.

Later Temple could hear them outside her door, whimpering and scuffing, or, rushing thickly in when the negro maid opened the door, climbing and sprawling onto the bed and into Miss Reba's lap with wheezy, flatulent sounds, billowing into the rich pneumasis of her breast and tonguing along the metal tankard which she waved in one ringed hand as she talked.

"Anybody in Memphis can tell you who Reba Rivers is. Ask any man on the street, cop or not. I've had some of the biggest men in Memphis right here in this house, bankers, lawyers, doctors---all of them. I've had two police captains drinking beer in my dining-room and the commisioner himself upstairs with one of my girls. They got drunk and crashed the door in on him and found him buck-nekkid, dancing the highland fling. A man fifty years old, seven foot tall, with a head like a peanut. He was a fine fellow. He knew me. They all know Reba Rivers. Spend their money here like water, they have. They know me. I aint never double-crossed nobody, honey." She drank beer, breathing thickly into the tankard, the other hand, ringed with yellow diamonds as large as gravel, lost among the lush billows of her breast.

Her slightest movement appeared to be accomplished by an expenditure of breath out of all proportion to any pleasure the movement could afford her. Almost as soon as they entered the house she began to ~~tee~~ tell Temple about her asthma, toiling up the stairs in front of them, planting her feet heavily in worsted bedroom slippers, a wooden rosary in one hand and the tankard in the other. She had just returned from church, in a black silk gown and a hat savagely flowered; the lower half of the tankard was still frosted with inner chill. She moved heavily from big thigh to thigh, the two dogs moiling underfoot, talking steadily back across her shoulder in a harsh, expiring, maternal voice.

"Popeye knew better than to bring you anywhere else but to my house. I been after him for, how many years I been after you to get you a girl, honey? What I say, a young fellow cant no more live without a girl than.........." Panting, she fell to cursing the dogs under her feet, stopping to shove them aside. "Get back down there," she said, shaking the rosary at them. They snarled at her in vicious falsetto, baring their teeth, and she leaned against the wall in a thin aroma of beer, her hand to her breast, her mouth open, her eyes fixed in a glare of sad terror of all breathing as she ~~beseeched breath,~~ besought breath the tankard a squat soft gleam like dull silver lifted in the gloom.

The narrow stairwell turned back upon itself in a succession of niggard reaches. The light, falling through a thickly-curtained door at the front and through a shuttered window at the rear of each stage, had a weary quality. A spent quality; defunctive, exhausted---a protracted weariness like a vitiated backwater beyond sunlight and the vivid noises of sunlight and day. There was a defunctive odor of irregular food, vaguely alcoholic, and Temple even in her ignorance seemed to be surrounded by a ghostly promiscuity of intimate garments, of discreet whispers of flesh stale and oft-assailed and impregnable beyond each silent door which they passed. Behind her, about hers and Miss Reba's feet the two dogs scrabbled in nappy gleams, their claws clicking on the metal strips which bound the carpet to the stairs.

Later, lying in bed, a towel wrapped about her naked loins, she could hear them sniffing and whining outside the door. Her coat and hat hung on nails in the door, her dress and stockings lay upon a chair, and it seemed to her that she could hear the rythmic splush-splush of the washing-board somewhere and she flung herself again in an agony for concealment as she had when they took her knickers off.

"Now, now," Miss Reba said. "I bled for four days, myself. It aint nothing. Doctor Quinn'll stop it in two minutes, and Minnie'll have them all washed and pressed and you wont never know it. That blood'll be worth a thousand dollars to you, honey." She lifted the tankard, the flowers on her hat rigidly moribund, nodding in macabre was hael. "Us poor girls," she said. The drawn shades, cracked ii̸nto a myriad pattern like old skin, blew faintly on the bright air, breathing into the room on waning surges o̸f̸ the sound of Sabbath traffic, festive, steady, evanescent. Temple lay motionless in the bed, her legs straight and close, to covers to her chin and her face small and wan, framed in the rich sprawl of her hair. Miss Reba lowered the tankard, gasping for breath. In her hoarse, fainting voice she began to tell Temple how lucksy she was.

"Every girl in the district has been trying to get him, honey. There's one, a little married woman slips d̸o̸w̸n̸/ down here sometimes, she offered Minnie twenty-five dollars just to get him into the room, that's all. But do you think he'd so much as look at one of them? Girls that have took in a hundred dollars a night. No, sir. Spend his money like water, but do you think he'd look at one of them except to dance with her? I always knowed it wasn't going to be none of these here common whores he'd take. I'd tell them, I'd say, the one of yez that gets him'll/ wear diamonds, I says, but it aint going to be none of you common whores, and now Minnie'll have them washed and pressed until you wont know it."

"I cant wear it again," Temple whispered. "I cant."

"No more you'll have to, if you dont want. You can

give them to Minnie, though I dont know what she'll do with them except maybe--------" At the door the dogs began to whimper louder. Feet approached. The door opened. A negro maid entered, carrying a tray bearing a quart bottle of beer and a glass of gin, the dogs surging in around her feet. "And tomorrow the stores'll be open and me and you'll go shopping, like he said for us to. Liks I said, you girl that gets him'll wear diamonds: you just see if I wasn't----------" she turned, mountainous, the tankard lifted, as the two dogs scrambled onto the bed and then onto her lap, snapping viciously at one another. From their curled shapeless faces bead-like eyes glared with choleric ~~savageness~~ ferocity, their mouths gaped pinkly upon needle-like teeth. "Reba!" Miss Reba said, "get down! You, Mr Binford!" flinging them down, their teeth clicking about her hands. "You just bite me, you--------Did you get Miss------What's your name, honey? I didn't quite catch it."

"Temple," Temple whispered.

"I mean, your first name, honey. We dont stand on no ceremony here."

"That's it. Temple. Temple Drake."

"You got a boy's name, aint you?-----Miss Temple's things washed, Minnie?"

"Yessum," the maid said. "Hit's dryin now hind the stove." She came with the tray, shoving the dogs gingerly aside while they clicked their teeth at her ankles.

"You wash it out good?"

"I had a time with it," Minnie said. "Seem like that the most hardest blood of all to get-------" With a convulsive momement Temple flopped over, ducking her head beneath the covers. She felt Miss Reba's hand.

"Now, now. Now, now. Here, take your drink. This one's on me. I aint going to let no girl of Popeye's-------"

"I dont want anymore," Temple said.

"Now, now," Miss Reba said. "Drink it and you'll feel better." She lifted Temple's head. Temple clutched the covers to her throat. Miss Reba held the glass to her lips. She gulped it, writhed down again, clutching the covers about her, her eyes wide and black above the covers. "I bet you got that towel disarranged," Miss Reba said, putting her hand on the covers.

"No," Temple whispered. "It's all right. It's still there." She shrank, cringing; they could see the cringing of her legs beneath the covers.

"Did you get Dr Quinn, Minnie?" Miss Reba said.

"Yessum." Minne was filling the tankard from the bottle, a dull frosting pacing the rise of liquor within the metal. "He say he dont make no Sunday afternoon calls."

"Did you tell him who wanted him? Did you tell him Miss Reba wanted him?"

"Yessum. He say he dont--------"

"You go back and tell that suh-------You tell him I'll------No; wait." She rose heavily. "Sending a message like that back to me, that can put him in jail three times over." She waddled toward the door, the dogs crowding about the felt slippers. The maid followed and closed the door. Temple could hear Miss Reba cursing the dogs as she descended the stairs with terrific slowness. The sounds died away.

The shades blew steadily in the windows, with faint rasping sounds. Temple began to hear a clock. It sat on the mantel above a grate filled with fluted green paper. The clock was of flowered china, supported by four china nymphs. It had only one hand, scrolled and gilded, halfway between ten and e-leven, lending to the otherwise blank face a quality of unequivocal assertion, as though it had nothing whatever to do with time.

Temple rose from the bed. Holding the towel about her she stole toward the door, her ears acute, her eyes a little blind with the strain of listening. It was twilight; in a dim mirror, a pellucid oblong of dusk set on end, she had a glimpse of herself like a thin ghost, a pale shadow moving in the ut-termost profundity of shadow. She reached the door. At once she began to hear a hundred conflicting sounds in a single converg-ing threat and she clawed furiously at the door until she found the bolt, dropping the towel to drive it home. Then she caught up the towel, her face averted, and ran back and sprang into the bed and clawed the covers to her chin and lay there, listening to the secret whisper of her blood.

They knocked at the door for some time before she made any sound. "It's the doctor, honey," Miss Reba panted harshly. "Come on, now. Be a good girl."

"I cant," Temple said, her voice faint and small. "I'm in bed."

"Come on, now. He wants to fix you up." She panted harshly. "My God, if I could just get one full breath again. I aint had a full breath since........." Low down beyond the door Temple could hear the dogs. "Honey."

She rose from the bed, holding the towel about her. She went to the door, silently.

"Honey," Miss Reba said.

"Wait," Temple said. "Let me get back to the bed before Let me get."

"There's a good girl," Miss Reba said. "I knowed she was going to be good."

"Count ten, now," Temple said. "Will you count ten, now?" she said against the wood. She slipped the bolt soundlessly, then she turned and sped back to the bed, her naked feet in pattering ~~diminuendo~~ diminuendo.

The doctor was a fattish man with thin, curly hair. He wore horn-rimmed glasses which lent to his eyes no distortion at all, as though they were of clear glass and worn for decorum's sake. Temple watched him across the covers, holding them to her throat. "Make them go out," she whispered; "if they'll just go out."

"Now, now," Miss Reba said, "he's going to fix you up."

Temple clung to the covers.

"If the little lady will just let. ..." the doctor said. His hair evaporated finely from his brow. His mouth nipped in at the corners, his lips full and wet and red. Behind the glasses his eyes loo ed like little bicycle wheels at dizzy speed; a metallic hazel. He put ~~a thick white hand~~ out a thick, white hand bearing a ~~signet ring~~ masonic ring, haired over with fine reddish fuzz to the second knuckle-joints. Cold air slipped down her body, below her thighs; her eyes were closed. Lying on her back, her legs close together, she began to cry, hopelessly and passively, like a child in a dentist's waiting-room.

"Now, now," Miss Reba said, "take another sup of gin, honey. It'll make you feel better."

XIV.

In the window the cracked shade, yawning now and then with a faint rasp against the frame, let twilight into the room in fainting surges. From beneath the shade the smoke-colored twilight emerged in slow puffs like signal smoke from a blanket, thickening in the room. The china figures which supported the clock gleamed in hushed smooth flexions: knee, elbow, flank, arm and breast in attitudes of voluptuous lassitude. The glass face, become mirror-like, appeared to hold all reluctant light, holding it its tranquil depths a quiet gesture of moribund time, one-armed like a veteran from the wars. Half past ten oclock. Temple lay in the bed, looking at the clock, thinking about half-past-ten-oclock.

She wore a too-large gown of cerise crepe, black against the linen. Her hair was a black sprawl, combed out now; her face, throat and arms outside the covers were gray. After the others left the room she lay for a time, head and all beneath the covers. She lay so until she heard the door shut and they descending feed, the doctor's light, unceasing voice and Miss Reba's labored breath grow twilight-colored in the dingy hall and die away. Then she sprang from the bed and ran to the door and shot the bolt and ran back and hurled the covers over her head again, lying in a tight knot until the air was exhausted.

A final saffron-colored light lay upon the ceiling and the upper walls, tinged already with purple by the serrated palisade of Main Street high against the western sky. She watched it fade as the successive yawns of the shade consumed it. She watched the final light condense into the clock face, and the dial change from a round orifice in the darkness to a disc suspended in nothingness, the original chaos, and change in turn to a crystal ball holding in its still and cryptic depths the ordered chaos of the intricate and shadowy world upon ~~which the ot scars of the ancient wounds whirl onward at dizzy speed into the darkness lurking with new disasters. She was thinking about half-past-ten-oclock~~ whose scarred flanks the old wounds whirl onward at dizzy speed into darkness lurking with new disasters.

She was thinking about half-past-ten-oclock. The hour for dressing for a dance, if you were popular enough not to have to be on time. The air would be steamy with recent baths, and perhaps powder in the light like chaff in barn-lofts, and they looking at one another, comparing, talking whether you could do more damage ~~if~~ if you could just walk out on the floor like you were now. Some wouldn't, mostly ones with short legs. Some of them were all right, but they just wouldn't. They wouldn't say why. The worst one of all said boys thought all girls were ugly except when they were dressed. She said the Snake had been seeing Eve for several days and never noticed her until Adam made her put on a fig leaf. How do you know? they said, and she said because the Snake was there before Adam, because he was the first one thrown out of heaven; he was there all the time. But that wasn't what they meant and they said, How do you know, and Temple thought of her kind of backed up against the dressing table and the rest of them in a circle around her with their combed hair and their shoulders smelling of scented soap and the light powder in the air and their eyes like knives until you could almost watch her flesh where the eyes were touching it, and her eyes in her ugly face courageous and frightened and daring, and they all saying, How do you know? until she told them and held up her hand and swore she had. That was when the youngest one turned and ran out of the room. She locked herself in the bath and they could hear her being sick.

She thought about half-past-ten-oclock in the morning. Sunday morning, and the couples strolling toward church. She remembered it was still Sunday, the same Sunday, looking at the fading peaceful gesture of the clock. Maybe it was half-past-ten this morning, that half-past-ten-oclock. Then I'm not here, she thought. This is not me. Then I'm at school. I have a date tonight with.......thinking of the student with whom she had the date. But she couldn't remember who it would be. She kept the dates written down in her Latin 'pony', so she didn't have to bother about who it was. She'd just dress, and after a while somebody would call for her. So I better get up and dress, she said, looking at the clock.

She rose and crossed the room quietly. She watched the clock face, but although she could see a warped turmoil of faint light and shadow in geometric miniature swinging across it, she could not see herself. It's this nightie, she thought, looking at her arms, her breast rising out of a dissolving pall beneath which her toes peeped in pale, fleet intervals as she walked. She drew the bolt quietly and returned to the bed and lay with her head cradled in her arms.

There was still a little light in the room. She found that she was hearing her watch; had been hearing it for some time. She discovered that the house was full of noises, seeping into the room muffled and indistinguishable, as though from a distance. A bell rang faintly and shrilly somewhere; someone mounted the stairs in a swishing garment. The feet went on past the door and mounted another stair and ceased. She listened to the watch. A car started beneath the window with a grind of gears; again the faint bell rang, shrill and prolonged. She found that the faint light yet in the room was from a street lamp. Then she realised that it was night and that the darkness beyond was full of the sound of the city.

She heard the two dogs come up the stairs in a furious scrabble. The noise passed the door and stopped, became utterly still; so still that she could almost see them crouching there in the dark against the wall, watching the stairs. One of them was named Mister something, Temple thought, waiting to hear Miss Reba's feet on the stairs. But it was not Miss Reba; they came too steadily and too lightly. The door opened; the dogs surged in in two shapeless blurs and scuttled under the bed and crouched, whimpering. ~~Minnie entered~~ "You, dawgs!" Minnie's voice said. "You make me spill this." The light came on. Minnie carried a tray. "I got you some supper," she said. "Where them dawgs gone to?"

"Under the bed," Temple said. "I dont want any."

Minnie came and set the tray on the bed and looked down at Temple, her ~~placid face~~ pleasant face knowing and placid. "You want me to------" she said, extending her hand. Temple turned her face quickly away. She heard Minnie kneel, cajoling the dogs, the dogs snarling back at her with whimpering, asthmatic snarls and clicking teeth. "Come outen there, now," Minnie said. "They know fo Miss Reba do when she fixing to get drunk. You, Mr Binford!"

Temple raised her head. "Mr Binford?"

"He the one with the blue ribbon," Minnie said. Stooping, she flapped her arm at the dogs. They were backed against the wall at the head of the bed, snapping and snarling at her in mad terror. "Mr Binford was Miss Reba's man. Was landlord here eleven years until he die bout two years ago. Next day Miss Reba get these dawgs, name one Mr Binford and other Miss Reba. Whenever she go to the cemetary she start drinking like this evening, then they both got to run. But Mr Binford ketch it sho nough. Last time she throw him outen upstair window and go down and empty Mr Binford's clothes closet and throw everything out in the street except what he buried in."

"Oh," Temple said. "No wonder they're scared. Let them stay under there. They wont bother me."

"Reckon I have to. Mr Binford aint going to leave this room, not if he know it." She stood again, looking down at Temple. "Eat that supper," she said. "You feel better. I done slip you a drink of gin, too."

"I dont want any," Temple said, turning her face away. She heard Minnie leave the room. The door closed quietly. Under the bed the dogs crouched against the wall in that rigid and furious terror.

The light hung from the center of the ceiling, beneath a fluted shade of rose-colored paper browned where the bulb bulged it. The floor was covered by a figured maroon-tinted carpet tacked down in strips; the olive-tinted walls bore two framed lithographs. From the two windows curtains of machine lace hung, dust-colored, like strips of lightly congealed dust set on end. The whole room had an air of musty stodginess, dee corum; in the wavy mirror of a cheap varhished dresser, as in a stagnant pool, there seemed to linger spent ghosts of voluptuous gestures and dead lusts. In the corner, upon a faded scarred strip of oilcloth tacked over the carpet, sat a washstand bearing a flowered bowl and pitcher and a row of towels; in the corner ~~[illegible]~~ behind it sat a slop jar dressed also in fluted rose-colored paper.

Beneath the bed the dogs made no sound. Temple moved slightly; the dry complaint of mattress and springs died into the terrific silence in which they crouched. She thought of them, woolly, shapeless; savage, petulant, spoiled, the flatulent monotony of their sheltered lives snatched up without warning by an incomprehensible moment of terror and fear of bodily annihilation at the ~~hands~~ very hands which symbolised by ordinary the licensed tranquillity of their lives.

The house was full of sounds. Indistinguishable, remote, they came in to her with a quality of awakening, resurgence, as though the house itself had been asleep, rousing itself with dark; she heard something which might have been a burst of laughter in a shrill woman voice. Steamy odors from the tray drifted across her face. She turned her head and looked at it, at the covered and uncovered dishes of thick china. In the midst of them sat the glass of pale gin, a pack of cigarettes and a box of matches. She rose on her elbow, catching up the slipping gown. She lifted the covers upon a thick steak, potatoes, green peas; rolls; an anonymous pinkish mass which some sense---elimination, perhaps---identified as a sweet. She drew the slipping gown up again, thinking about them eating down at school in a bright uproar of voices and clattering forks; of her father and brothers at the supper table at home; thinking about the borrowed gown and Miss Reba saying that they would go shopping tomorrow. And I've just got two dollars, she thought.

When she looked at the food she found that she was not hungry at all, sisn't even want to look at it. She lifted the glass and gulped it empty, her face wry, and set it down and turned her face hurriedly from the tray, fumbling for the cigarettes. Wheh she went to strike the match she looked at the tray again and took up a strip of potato gingerly in her fingers and ate it. She ate another, the unlighted cigarette in her other hand. Then she put the cigarette down and took up the knife and fork and began to eat, pausing from time to time to draw the gown up onto her shoulder.

When she finished eating she lit the cigarette. She heard the bell again, then anothet in a slightly different key. Across a shrill rush of a woman's voice a door ~~bang~~ banged. Two people mounted the stairs and passed the door; she heard Miss Reba's voice booming from somewhere and listened to her toiling slowly up the stairs. Temple watched the door until it opened and Miss Reba stood in it, the tankard in her hand. She now wore a bulging house dress and a widow's bonnet with a veil. She entered on the flowered felt slippers. Beneath the bed the two dogs made a stifled concerted sound of utter despair.

The dress, unfastened in the back, hung lumpily about Miss Reba's shoulders. One ringed hand lay on her breast, the other held the tankard high. Her open mouth, ~~fill~~ studded with gold-fillings, gaped upon the harsh labor of her breathing.

"Oh~~,~~ God oh God," she said. The dogs surged out from beneath the bed and hurled themselves toward the door in a mad scrabble. As they rushed~~p~~ past her she turned and flung the tankard at them. It struck the door jamb, splashing up the wall, and rebounded with a forlorn clatter. She drew her breath whistling, clutching her breast. She came to the bed and looked down at Temple through the veil. "We was happy as two doves," she wailed, choking, her ~~hand gleaming in hot glints~~ rings smoldering in hot glints within her billowing breast. "Then he had to go and die on me." She drew her breath whistling, her mouth gaped, shaping the hidden agony of her thwarted lungs, her eyes pale and round with striken bafflement, pro-~~truding~~ tuberant, "As two doves," she roared in a harsh, choking voice.

XV.

Again time had overtaken the dead gesture behind the clock crystal: Temple's watch on the table beside the bed said half-past-ten. For two hours she had lain undisturbed, listening. She could distinguish voices now from below stairs. She had been hearing them for some time, lying in the room's musty isolation. Later a mechanical piano began to play. Now and then she heard automobile brakes in the street beneath the window; once two voices quarrelling bitterly came up and beneath the shade.

She heard two people---a man and a woman---mount the stairs and enter~~d~~ the room next hers. Then she heard Miss Reba toil up the stairs and pass her door, and lying in the bed, her eyes wide and still, she heard Miss Reba hammering at the next door with the metal tankard and shouting into the wood. Beyond the door the man and woman were ~~[illegible]~~ utterly quiet, so quiet that Temple thought of the dogs again, thought of them crouching against the wall under the ~~bed~~ bed in that rigid fury of terror and despair. She listened to Miss Reba's voice shouting hoarsely into the blank wood. It died away into terrific gasping, then it rose again in the gross and virile cursing of a man. Beyond the wall the man and woman made no sound. Temple lay staring at the wall beyond which Miss Reba's voice rose again as she hammered at the door with the tankard.

Temple neither saw nor heard her door when it opened. She just happened to look toward it after how long she did not know, and saw Popeye standing there, his hat slanted across his face. Still without making any sound he entered and shut the door and shot the bolt and came toward the bed. As slowly she began to shrink into the bed, drawing the covers up to her chin, watching him across the covers. He came and looked down at her. She writhed slowly in a cringing movement, cringing upon herself in as complete an isolation as though she were bound to a church steeple. She grinned at him, her mouth warped over the rigid, placative porcelain of her grimace.

When he put his hand on her she began to whimper. "No,no," she whispered, "he said I cant now he said.........." He jerked the covers back and flung them aside. She lay motionless, her palms lifted, her flesh beneath the envelope of her loins cringing rearward in furious ~~separate~~/ disintegration like frightened people ~~on~~/~~a~~ in a crowd. When he advanced his hand again she thought he was going to strike her. Watching his face, she saw it beginning to twitch and jerk like that of a child about to cry, and she heard him begin to make a whimpering sound. He gripped the top of the gown. She caught his wrists and began to toss from side to side, opening her mouth to scream. His hand clapped over her mouth, and gripping his wrist, the saliva drooling between his fingers, her body thrashing furiously from thigh to thigh, she saw him crouching beside the bed, his face wrung above his absent chin, his bluish lips protruding as though he were blowing upon hot soup, making a high whinnying sound like a horse. Beyond the wall Miss Reba filled the hall, the house, with a harsh choking uproar of obscene cursing.

XVI.

As the train neared Memphis Virgil Snopes ceased talking and began to grow quieter and quieter, while on the contrary his companion, eating from a parrafin-paper package of popcorn and molasses, grew livelier and livelier with a quality something like intoxication, seeming not to notice the inverse state of his friend. He was still talking away when, carrying their new, imitation leather suitcases, their new hats slanted above their shaven necks, they descended at the station. In the waiting room Fonzo said:

"Well, what're we going to do first?" Virgil said nothing. Someone jostled them; Fonzo caught at his hat. "What we going to do?" he said. Then he looked at Virgil, at his face. "What's the matter?"

"Aint nothing the matter," Virgil said.

"Well, what're we going to do? You been here before. I aint."

"I reckon we better kind of look around," Virgil said.

Fonzo was watching him, his blue eyes like china. "What's the matter with you? All the time on the train you was talking about how many times you been to Memphis. I bet you aint never bu-------" Someone jostled them, thrust them apart; a stream of people began to flow between them. Clutching his suitcase and hat Fonzo fought his way back to his friend.

"I have, too," Virgil said, looking glassily about.

"Well, what we going to do, then? It wont be open till eight oclock in the morning."

"What you in such a rush for, then?"

"Well, I dont aim to stay here all night......What did you do when you was here before?"

"Went to the hotel," Virgil said.

"Which one? They got more than one here. You reckon all these folks could stay in one hotel? Which one was it?"

Virgil's eyes were also a pale, false blue. He looked glassily about. "The Gayoso hotel," he said.

"Well, let's go to it," Fonzo said. They moved toward the exit. A man shouted "taxi" at them; a redcap tried to take Fonzo's bag. "Look out," he said, drawing it back. On the street more cabmen barked at them.

"So this is Memphis," Fonzo said. "Which way is it, now?" He had no answer. He looked around and saw Virgil in the act of turning away from a cabman. "What you---------"

"Up this way," Virgil said. "It aint far."

It was a mile and a half. From time to time they swapped hands with the bags. "So this is Memphis," Fonzo said. "Where have I been all my life?" When they entered the Gayoso a porter offered to take the bags. They brushed past him and entered, walking gingerly on the tile floor. Virgil stopped.

"Come on," Fonzo said.

"Wait," Virgil said.

"Thought you was here before," Fonzo said.

"I was. This hyer place is too high. They'll want a dollar a day here."

"What we going to do, then?"

"Let's kind of look around."

They returned to the street. It was five oclock. They went on, looking about, carrying the suitcases. They came to another hotel. Looking in they saw marble, brass cuspidors, hurrying bellboys, people sitting among potted plants.

"That un'll be just as bad," Vbrgil said.

"What we going to do then? We caint walk around all night."

"Let's git off this hyer street," Virgil said. They left Main Street. At the next corner Virgil turned again. "Let's look down this-a-way. Git away from all that ere plate glass and monkey niggers. That's maht you have to pay for in them places."

"Why? It's already bought when we got there. How come we have to pay for it?"

"Suppose somebody broke it while we was there. Suppose they couldn't ketch who done it. Do you reckon they'd let us out withouten we paid our share?"

At five-thirty they entered a narrow dingy street of frame houses and junk yards. Presently they came to a three storey in a small grassless yard. Before the entrance a lattice-work false entry leaned. On the steps sat a big woman in a mother hubbard, watching two fluffy white dogs which moved about the yard.

"Let's try that un," Fonzo said.

"That aint no hotel. Where's air sign?"

"Why aint it?" Fonzo said. " 'Course it is. Who ever heard of anybody just living in a three storey house?"

"We cant go in this-a-way," Virgil said. "This hyer's the back. Dont you see that privy?" jerking his head toward the lattice.

"Well, let's go around to the front, then," Fonzo said. "Come on."

They went around the block. The opposite side was filled by a row of automobile sales-rooms. They stood in the middle of the block, their suitcases in their right hands.

"I dont believe you ever was here before, noways," Fonzo said.

"Let's go back. That must a been the front."

"With the privy built onto the front door?" Fonzo said.

"We can ask that lady."

"Who can? I aint."

"Let's go back and see, anyway."

They returned. The woman and the dogs were gone.

"Now you done it," Fonzo said. "Aint you?"

"Let's wait a while. Maybe she'll come back."

"It's almost seven oclock," Fonzo said.

They set the bags down beside the fence. The lights had come on, quivering high in the serried windows against the tall serene western sky.

"I can smell ham, too," Fonzo said.

A cab drew up. A plump blonde woman got out, followed by a man. They watched them go up the walk and enter/ the lat-tice. Fonzo sucked his breath across his teeth. "Durned if they didn't," he whispered.

"Maybe it's her husband," Virgil said.

Fonzo picked up his bag. "Come on."

"Wait," Virgil said. "Give them a little time."

They waited. The man came out and got in the cab and went away.

"Caint be her husband," Fonzo said. "I wouldn't a never left. Come on." He entered the gate.

"Wait," Virgil said.

"You can," Fonzo said. Virgil took his bag and fol-lowed. He stopped while Fonzo opened the lattice gingerly and peered in. "Aw, hell," he said. He entered. There was another door, with curtained glass. Fonzo knocked.

"Why didn't you push that ere button?" Virgil said. "Dont you know city folks dont answer no knock?"

"All right," Fonzo said. He rang the bell. The door opened. It was the woman in the mother hubbard; they could hear the dogs behind her.

"Got air extra room?" Fonzo said.

Miss Reba looked at them, at their new hats and the suitcases.

"Who sent you here?" she said.

"Didn't nobody. We just picked it out." Miss Reba looked at him. "Them hotels is too high."

Miss Reba breathed harshly. "What you boys doing?"

"We come hyer on business," Fonzo said. "We aim to stay a good spell."

"If it aint too high," Virgil said.

Miss Reba looked at him. "Where you from, honey?"

They told her, and their names. "We aim to be hyer a month or more, if it suits us."

"Why, I reckon so," she said after a while. She looked at them. "I can let you have a room, but I'll have to charge you extra whenever you do business in it. I got my living to make like everybody else."

"We aint," Fonzo said. "We'll do our business at the college."

"What college?" Miss Reba said.

"The barber's college," Fonzo said.

"Look here," Miss Reba said, "you little whipper-snapper." Then she began to laugh, her hand at her breast. They watched her soberly while she laughed in harsh gasps. "Lord, Lord," she said. "Come in here."

The room was at the top of the house, at the back. Miss Reba showed them the bath. When she put her hand on the door a woman's voice said: "Just a minute, dearie" and the door opened and she passed them, in a kimono. They watched her go up the hall, rocked a little to their young foundations by a trail of scent which she left. Fonzo nudged Virgil surreptitiously. In their room again he said:

"That was another one. She's got two daughters. Hold me, big boy; I'm heading for the hen-house."

They didn't go to sleep for some time that first night, what with the strange bed and room and the voices. They could hear the city, evocative and strange, imminent and remote; threat and promise both---a deep, steady sound upon which invisible lights glittered and wavered: colored coiling shapes of splendor in which already women were beginning to move in suave attitudes of new delights and strange nostalgic promises. Fonzo thought of himself surrounded by tier upon tier of drawn shades, rose-colored, beyond which, in a murmur of silk, in panting whispers, the apotheosis of his youth assumed a thousand avatars. Maybe it'll begin tomorrow, he thought; maybe by tomorrow night........ A crack of light came over the top of the shade and sprawled in a spreading fan upon the ceiling. Beneath the window he could hear a voice, a woman's, then a man's: they blended, murmured; a door closed. Someone came up the stairs in swishing garments, on the swift hard heels of a woman.

He began to hear sounds in the house: voices, laughter; a mechanical piano began to play. "Hear them?" he whispered.

"She's got a big family, I reckon," Virgil said, his voice already dull with sleep.

"Family, hell," Fonzo said. "It's a oarty. Wish I was at it."

On the third day as they were leaving the house in the morning, Miss Reba met them at the door. She wanted to use their room in the afternoons while they were absent. There was to be a detective's convention in town and business would look up some, she said. "Your things'll be all right. I'll have Minnie lock everything up before hand. Aint nobody going to steal nothing from you in my house."

"What business you reckon she's in?" Fonzo said when they reached the street.

"Dont know," Virgil said.

"Wish I worked for her, anyway," Fonzo said. "With all them women in kimonos and such running around."

"Wouldn't do you no good," Virgil said. "They're all married. Aint you heard them?"

The next afternoon when they returned from the school they found a woman's undergarment under the washstand..Fonzo picked it up. "She's a dress-maker," he said.

"Reckon so," Virgil said. "Look and see if they taken anything of yourn."

The house appeared to be filldd with peole who did not sleep at night at all. They could hear them at all hours, running up and down the stairs, and always Fonzo would be conscious of women, of female flesh. It got to where he seemed to lie in his celibate bed surrounded by women, and he would lie beside the steadily snoring Virgil, his ears strained for the murmurs, the whispers of silk that came through the walls and the floor, that seemed to be as much a part of both as the planks and the plaster, thinking that he had been in Memphis ten days, yet the extent of his acquaintance was a few of ~~the~~ his fellow pupils at the school. After Virgil was asleep he would rise and unlock the door and leave it ajar, but nothing happened.

On the twelfth day he told Virgil they were going visiting, with one of the barber-students.

"Where?" Virgil said.

"That's all right. You come on. I done found out something. And when I think I been here two weeks without knowing about it........"

"What's it going to cost?" Virgil said.

"When'd you ever have any fun for nothing?" Fonzo said. "Come on."

"I'll go," Virgil said. "BUt I aint going to promise to spend nothing."

"You wait and say that when we get there," Fonzo said.

The barber took them to a brothel. When they came out Fonzo said: "And to think I been here two weeks without never knowing about that house."

"I wisht you hadn't never learned," Virgil said. "It cost three dollars."

"Wasn't it worth it?" Fonzo said.

"Aint nothing worth ~~two~~ three dollars you caint tote off with you," Virgil said.

When they reached home Fonzo stopped. "We got to sneak in, now," he said. "If she was to find out where we been and what we been doing, she might not let us stay in the house with them ladies no more."

"That's so," Virgil said. "Durn you. Hyer you ~~made~~ done made me spend three dollars, and now you fixing to git us both throwed out."

"You do like I do," Fonzo said. "That's all you got to do. Dont say nothing."

Minnie let them in. The piano was going full blast. Miss Reba appeared in a door, with a tin cup in her hand. "Well, well," she said, "you boys been out mighty late tonight."

"Yessum," Fonzo said, prodding Virgil toward the stairs. "We been to prayer-meeting."

In bed, in the dark, they could still hear the piano.

"You made me spend three dollars," Virgil said.

"Aw, shut up," Fonzo said. "When I think I been here

for two whole weeks almost........."

The next afternoon they came home through the dusk, with the lights winking on, beginning to flare and gleam, and the women on their twinkling blonde legs meeting men and getting into automobiles and such.

"How about that three dollars now?" Fonzo said.

"I reckon we better not go ever night," Virgil said. "It'll cost too much."

"That's right," Fonzo said. "Somebody might see us and tell her."

They waited two nights. "Now it'll be six dollars," Virgil said.

"Dont come, then," Fonzo said.

When they returned home Fonzo said: "Try to act like something, this time. She near about caught us before on account of the way you acted."

"What if she does?" Virgil said in a sullen voice. "She caint eat us."

They stood outside the lattice, whispering.

"How you know she caint?" Fonzo said.

"She dont want to, then."

"How you know she dont want to?"

"Maybe she dont," Virgil said. Fonzo opened the lattice door. "I caint eat that six dollars, noways," Virgil said. "Wisht I could."

Minnie let them in. She said: "Somebody huntin you

all." They waited in the hall.

"We done caught now," Virgil said. "I told you about throwing that money away."

"Aw, shut up," Fonzo said.

A man emerged from a door, a big man with his hat cocked over one ear, his arm about a blonde woman in a read dress. "There's Cla'ence," Virgil said.

In their room Clarence said: "How'd you get into this place?"

"Just found it," Virgil said. They told him about it. He sat on the bed, in his soiled hat, a cigar in his fingers.

"Where you been tonight?" he said. They didn't answer. They looked at him with blank, watchful faces. "Come on. I know. Where was it?" They told him.

"Cost me three dollars, too," Virgil said.

"I'll be durned if you aint the biggest fool this side of Jackson," Clarence said. "Come on here." They followed sheepishly. He led them from the house and for three or four blocks. They crossed a street of negro stores and theatres and turned into a narrow, dark street and stopped at a house with red shades on the lighted windows. Clarence rang the bell. They could hear music inside, and shrill voices, and feet. They were admitted into a bare hallway where two shabby negro men argued with a drunk man in greasy overalls. Through an open door they saw a room filled with coffee-colored women in bright dresses, with ornate hair and golden smiles.

"Them's niggers," Virgil said.

" 'Course they're niggers," Clarence said. "But see this?" he waved a banknote in his cousin's face. "This stuff is color-blind."

XVII.

Horace met Snopes emerging from the barbershop, his jowls gray with powder, moving in an effluvium of pomade. In the bosom of his shirt, beneath his bow tie, he wore an imitation ruby stud which matched his ring. The tie was of blue polka-dots. the very white spots on it appeared dirty when seen close; the whole man with his shaved neck and pressed clothes and gleaming shoes emanated somehow the idea that he had been dry-cleaned rather than washed.

"Well, Judge," he said, "I hear you're having some trouble gittin a boarding-place for that client of yourn. Like I always say-----" he leaned, his voice lowered, his mud-colored eyes roving aside "-----the church aint got no place in politics, and women aint got no place in neither one, let alone the law. let them stay at home and they'll find plenty to do without upsetting a man's law-suit. And besides, a man aint no more than human, and what he does aint nobody's business but his. What you done with her?"

"She's at the jail," Horace said. He spoke shortly, making to pass on. The other blocked his way with an effect of clumsy accident.

"You got them all stirred up, anyhow. Folks is saying you wouldn't git Goodwin no bond, so he'd have to stay------" again Horace made to pass on. "Half the trouble in this world is caused by women, I always say. Like that girl gittin her paw all stirred up, running off like she done. I reckon he done the right thing sending her clean outen the state."

"Yes," Horace said in a dry, furious voice.

"I'm mighty glad to hear your case is going all right. Between you and me, I'd like to see a good lawyer make a monkey ~~of~~ outen that District Attorney. Give a fellow like that a little county office and he gits too big for his pants right away. Well, glad to've saw you. I got some business up town for a day or two. I dont reckon you'll be going up that-a-way?"

"What?" Horace said. "Up where?"

"Memphis. Anything I can do for you?"

"No," Horace said. He went on. For a short distance he could not see at all. He tramped steadily, the muscles beside his jaws beginning to ache, passing people who spoke to him, unawares.

When he reached home on his return from Oxford he said: "Well, I guess I'll have to take her to the house, now. By God, when I think of those------If there'd just been a man. But you cant hit a ~~doddering~~ damned doddering old he-goat. I swear, I believe it was that hotel man did it. I dont believe that even a Baptist woman would........." Then he became aware that his sister was speaking. She had not looked up from the magazine on her lap.

"Not in my house."

He looked at her. Then he began to fill his pipe

slowly and carefully. "It's not a matter of choice, my dear. You must see that."

"Not in my house," Narcissa said. "I thought we settled that."

He struck the match and lit the pipe and put the match carefully into the fireplace. "Do you realise that she has been practically turned into the streets? That-------"

"That shouldn't be a hardship. She ought to be used to that."

He looked at her. He put the pipe in his mouth and smoked it to a careful coal, watching his hand tremble upon the stem. "Listen. By tomorrow they will probably ask her to leave town. Just because she happens not to be married to the man whose child she carries about these sanctified streets. But who told them? That's what I want to know. I know that nobody in Jefferson knew it except---------"

"You were the first I heard tell it," Miss Jenny said. "But, Narcissa, why-------"

"Not in my house," Narcissa said, turning the magazine.

"Well," Horace said. He drew the pipe to an even coal. "That settles it, of course," he said, in a dry, light voice.

When he went to his room he packed the suitcase again. He went to bed. He lay tossing in the darkness, laughing now and then with savage mirthlessness. He thought of Temple. He thought of her floating in a canoe under the Michigan moon, with a ukelele perhaps, and an entranced and fatuous male leaning across the paddle toward the studiedly consonantless sound of her voice. Then he thought of the woman again, lying yonder at the jail, on the charity of the keeper of a house of public detention, where the authorities would doubtless not permit her to stay. He thought of himself before them, facing them across a smug table, saying Gentlemen, give me the key to that cell and I'll solve your problem in ten minutes, and unsully your fair city beyond fear of repetition and dread of recourse. Then he began to laugh again, writhing slowly, the sheets becoming unbearable with the temperature of his impotent rage.

The door opened. He lifted his head, looking across the black footboard into the black darkness where the door had yawned, felt rather than seen or heard. His sister spoke.

"Horace."

"Yes/?" He rose to his elbow. He could hear her garments, then she took shape, vaguely. "Look out for the bag," he said. "I dont remember where I left it. So it's probably where it can be stumbled over with the minimum of effort."

"I see it." She approached and stood beside the bed, looking down at him, solidifying into that immobility which was a part of all her movements, passing from attitude to attitude with that tranquillity of pagan statuary.

"How much longer are you going to keep this up?" she said.

"Just until morning," he said. "I'm going back to town. You need not see me again."

She sto d beside the bed, motionless. After a moment her cold unbending voice came down to him: "You know what I mean."

"I promise not to bring her into your house again. You can send Isom in to hide in the canna bed." She said nothing. "Surely you dont object to my living there, do you?"

"I domt care where you live. The question is, where I live. I live here, in this town. I'll have to stay here. But you're a man. It doesn't matter to you. You can go away."

"Oh," he said. He lay quite still. She stood above him, motionless. They spoke quietly, as though they were discussing wall-paper, food.

"Dont you see, this is my home, where I must spend the rest of my life. Where I was born. I dont care where else you go nor what you do. I dont care how many women you have nor who they are. But I cannot have my brother mixed up with a woman people are talking about. I dont expect you to have consideration for me; I ask you to have consideration for our father and mother. Take her to Memphis. They say you refused to let the man have bond to get out of jail; take her on to Memphis. You can think of a lie to tell him about that, too."

"Oh. So you think that, do you?"

"I dont think anything about it. I dont care. That's what people in town think. So it doesn't matter whether it's true or not. What I do mind is, everyday you force me to have to tell lies for you. Go away from here, Horace. Anybody but you would realise it's a case of cold-blooded murder."

"And over her, of course. I suppose they say that too, out of their odorous and omnipotent sanctity. Do they say yet that it was I killed him?"

"I dont see that it makes any difference who did it. The question is, are you going to stay mixed up with it? When people already believe you and she are slipping into my house at night." Her cold, unbending voice shaped the words in the darkness above him. Through the window, upon the blowing darkness, came the drowsy dissonnance of cicada and cricket.

"Do you believe that?" he said.

"I doesn't matter what I believe. Go on away, Horace. I ask it."

"And leave her--them, flat?"

"Hire a lawyer, if he wtill insists he's innocent. I'll pay for it. You can get a better criminal lawyer than you are. She wont know it. She wont even care. Cant you see that she is just leading you on to get him out of jail for nothing? Dont you know that woman has got money hidden away somewhere?" She had not moved, yet suddenly it was as though she had shrugged. Her voice, never less than cold, was quite empty now. "You're going back into town tomorrow, are you?" She turned, began to dissolve into the blackness. "You wont leave before breakfast, I suppose." He followed the sound of her garments with his eyes. The door yawned again.

The shrill darkness leaned steadily upon the curtains. I'm going to Europe, Horace said. Soon as this business is finished. This damned country. I'll write Belle for a divorce and-------he lay for a tense moment, then he started to swing his feet to the floor, but refrained. I'll write tomorrow. I couldn't even write a sane letter to anyone now.

When he went down to breakfast he carried the bag with him. She and the boy were at the table.

"Are you going in this morning?" she said.

"Yes. I'll be closer to my work. I hope to be too busy from now on to change my mind anymore."

She poured his coffee. "Who will be on the other side of the case?"

"District Attorney. Why?"

She rang the bell. The pantry door opened. "Bring Mr Horace some hot bread, Isom."

Horace was still watching her. "Why did you ask that? I never knew you to ask an idle question before......Damned little squirt," he said. "I swear, I believe he was at the bottom of that, last night. Getting her turned out of the hotel for public effect, political capital. By God, if I knew he did a thing like that just to get elected to Congress.......When there's not a member of the bar in the state can bawl louder about the sanctity of the home, motherhood..... ."

On the third day he found a domicile for the woman. It was in the ramshackle house of an old half-crazed white woman who was believed to manufacture spells for negroes. It was on the edge of town, set in a tiny plot of ground choked and massed with waist-high herbage in an unbroken jungle across the front. At the back a path had been trodden from the broken gate to the door. All night a dim light burned in the crazy depths of the house and at almost any hour of the twenty-four a wagon or a buggy might be seen tethered in the lane behind it and a negro entering or leaving the back door.

The house had been entered once by officers searching for whisky. They found nothing save a few dried bunches of weeds, and a collection of dirty bottles containing liquid of which they could say nothing surely save that it was not alcoholic, while the old woman, held by two men, her lank grayish hair shaken before the glittering collapse of her face, screamed invective at them in her cracked voice. In a lean-to shed room containing a bed and a barrel of anonymous refuse and trash in which mice rattled all night long, the woman found a home.

"You'll be all right here," Horace said. "You can always get me by ~~telephoning~~ telephone, at--------" giving her the name of a neighbor. "No: wait; tomorrow I'll have the telephone ~~put~~ put back in. Then you can--------"

"Yes," the woman said. "I reckon you better not be coming out here."

"Why? Do you think that would-----that I'd care a damn what-------"

"You have to live here."

"I'm damned if I do. I've already let too many women run my affairs for me as it is, and if these uxorious......." But he knew he was just talking. He knew that she knew it too, out of that ~~unflagging~~ feminine reserve of unflagging suspicion of all peoples' actions which seems at first to be mere affinity for evil but which is in reality practical wisdom.

"I guess I'll find you if there's any need," she said. "There's not anything else I could do."

"By God," Horace said, "dont you let them......Bitches," he said; "bitches."

The next day he had the telephone installed. He did not see his sister for a week; she had no way of learning that he had a phone, yet when, a week before the opening of Court, the telephone shrilled into the quiet where he ~~sa~~ sat reading one evening, he thought it was Narcissa until, across a remote blaring of victrola or radio music, a man's voice spoke in a guarded, tomblike tome.

"This is Snopes," it said. "How're you, Judge?"

"What?" Horace said. "Who is it?"

"Senator Snopes, Cla'ence Snopes." The victrola blared, faint, far away; he could see the man, the soiled hat, the thick shoukders, leaning above the instrument---in a drugstore or a restaurant---whispering into it behind a soft, huge, ringed hand, the telephone toylike in the other.

"Oh," Horace said. "Yes? What is it?"

"I got a little piece of information that might interest you."

"Information that would interest me?"

"I reckon so. That would interest a couple of parties." Against Horace's ear the radio or the victrola performed a reedy arpeggio of saxophones. Obscene, facile, they seemed to be quarreling with one another like two desterous monkeys in a cage. He could hear the gross breathing ~~of~~ of the man at the other end of the wire.

"All right," he said. "What do you know that would interest me?"

"I'll let you judge that."

"All right. I'll be down town in the morning. You can find me somewhere." Then he said immediately: "Hello!" The man sounded as though he were breathing in Horace's ear: a placid, gross sound, suddenly portentous somehow. "Hello!" Horace said.

"It evidently dont interest you, then. I reckon I'll dicker with the other party and not trouble you no more. Goodbye."

"No; wait," Horace said. "Hello! Hello!"

"Yeuh?"

"I'll come down tonight. I'll be there in about fifteen-------"

" 'Taint no need of that," Snopes said. "I got my car. I'll drive up there."

But not in this house, Horace said~~, wondering~~, wondering what the man could know, his mind flicking here and there while the voice still libgered in his ear with that nameless portent, thinking of the implements which evil employed and of the implements with which it had to be combatted.

~~There~~ He walked down to the gate. There was a moon tonight. Within the black-and-silver tunnel of cedars fireflies drifted in fatuous oinpricks. The cedars were black and pointed on the sky like a paper silhouette; the sloping lawn had a faint sheen, a patina like silver. Somewhere a whipporwill called, reiterant, tremulous, plaintful above the insects. Three cars passed. The fourth slowed and swung toward the gate. Horace stepped into the light. Behind the wheel Snopes loomed bulkily, giving the impression of having been inserted into the car before the top was put on. He extended his hand.

"How're you tonight, Judge?/ Didn't know you was living in town again until I tried to call you out to Mrs Sartorises."

"Well, thanks," Horace said. He freed his hand. "What's this you've got hold of?"

Snopes creased himself across the wheel and peered out beneath the top, toward the house.

"We'll talk here," Horace said. "Save you having to turn around."

"It aint very private here," Snopes ~~s~~ said. "But that's for you to say." Huge and thick he loomed, hunched, his featureless face moonlike itself in the refraction of the moon. Horace could feel Snopes watching him, with that sense of portent which had come over the wire; a quality calculating and cunning and pregnant. It seemed to him that he watched his mind flicking this way and that, striking always that vast, soft, inert bulk, as though it were caught in an avalanche of cottonseed-hulls.

"Let's go to the house," Horace said. Snopes opened the door. "Go on," Horace said. "I'll walk up." Snopes drove on. He was getting out of the car when Horace overtook him. "Well, what is it?" Horace said.

Again Snopes looked at the house. "Keeping batch, are you?" he said. Horace said nothing. "Like I always say, ever married man ought to have a little place of his own, where he can git off to himself without it being nobody's business what he does. 'Course a man owes something to his wife, but what they dont know caint hurt them, does it? Long's he does that, I caint see where she's got air kick coming. Aint that what you say?"

"She's not here," Horace said, "if that's what you're hinting at. What did you want to see me about?"

Again he felt Snopes watching him, the unabashed stare calculating and completely unbelieving. "Well, I always say, caint nobody tend to a man's private business but himself. I aint blaming you. But when you know me better, you'll know I aint loose-mouthed. I been around. I been there..... .Have a cigar?" His big hand flicked to his breast and offered two cigars.

"No, thanks."

Snopes lit a cigar, his face coming out of the match like a pie set on edge.

"What did you want to see me about?" Horace said.

Snopes puffed the cigar. "Couple days ago I come onto a piece of information which will be of value to you, if I aint mistook."

"Oh. Of value. What value?"

"I'll leave that to you. I got another party I could dicker with, but being as me and you was fellow-townsmen and all that."

Here and there Horace's mind flicked and darted. Snopes' family originated somewhere near Frenchman's Bend and still lived there. He knew ofthe devious means by which information passed from man to man of that illiterate race which populated that section of the county. But surely it cant be something he'd try to sell to the State, he thought. Even he is not that big a fool.

"You'd better tell me what it is, then," he said.

He could feel Snopes watching him. "You remember one day you got on the train at Oxford, where you'd been on some bus----"

"Yes," Horace said.

Snopes puffed the cigar to an even coal, carefully, at some length. ~~"You recall speaking to me about a girl."~~ ~~"Yes. Then what?"~~ ~~"That's for you to say."~~ He raised his hand and drew it across the back of his neck. "You recall speaking to me about a girl."

"Yes. Then what?"

"That's for you to say."

He could smell the honeysuckle as it bore up the silver slope, and he heard the whipporwill, liquid, plaintful, reiterant. "You mean, you know where she is?" Snopes said nothing. "And that for a price you'll tell?" Snopes said nothing. Horace shut his hands and put them in his pockets, shut against his flanks. "What makes you think that information will interest me?"

"That's for you to judge. I aint conducting no murder case. I wasn't down there at Oxford looking for her. Of course, if it dont, I'll dicker with the other party. I just give you the chance."

~~"If I dont, say tel, you'll go and sell it to her father"~~ Horace turned toward the steps. He moved gingerly, like an old man. "Let's sit down," he said. Snopes followed and sat on the step. They sat in the moonlight. "You know where she is?"

"I seen her." Again he drew his hand across the back of his neck. "Yes, sir. If she aint----hasn't been there, you can git your money back. I caint say no fairer, can I?"

"And what's your price?" Horace said. Snopes ~~[illegible]~~ puffed the cigar to a careful coal. "Go on," Horace said. I'm not going to haggle." Snopes told him. "All right," Horace said. "I'll pay it." He drew his knees up and set his elbows on them and laid his hands to his face. "Where is-----Wait. Are you a Baptist, by any chance?"

"My folks is. I'm putty liberal, myself. I aint hide-bound in no sense, as you'll find when you know me better."

"All right," Horace said from behind his hands. "Where is she?"

"I'll trust you," Snopes said. "She's in a Memphis 'ho'-house."

When he had gone Horace entered the house and turned on the light, blinking after the subtle treachery of the moon. Little Belle's photograph sat on the mantel. He took it down, looking at it. The light hung on a shadeless cord, low; the shadow of his body lay upon the photograph. He moved it so that the light fell upon it, then drew it back into the shadow again. The difference was too intangible to discern, even by its own immediate comparison; the white still white, the black still black, the secret, musing expression unaltered. Delicate, evocative, strange, looking up out of the shadow with a crass brazenness, a crass belief that the beholder were blind. He set it back on the mantel and sat down and wrote the letter to Belle in Kentucky, offering a divorce.

XVIII.

As Horace entered Miss Reba's gate and approached the lattice door, someone called his name from behind him. It was evening; the windows in the weathered, scaling wall were close pale squares. He ~~psued~~ paused and looked back. Around an adjacent corner Snopes' head peered, ~~turkey~~ turkey-like. He stepped into view. He looked up at the house, then both~~e~~ ways along the street. He came along the fence and entered the gate with a ~~at~~ wary air.

"Well, Judge," he said. "Boys will be boys, wont they?" He didn't offet to shake hands. Instead he bulked above Horace with that air somehow assured and alert at the ~~same~~ same time, glancing over his shoulder at the street. "Like I say, it never done no man no harm to git out now and then and-------"

"What is it now?" Horace said. "What do you want with me?"

"Now, now, Judge. I aint going to tell this at home. Git that idea clean out of your mind. If us boys started telling what we know, caint none of us git off a train at Jefferson again, hey?"

"You know as well as I do what I'm doing here. What do you want with me?"

"Sure; sure," Snopes said. "I know how a feller feels, married and all and not being sho~~e~~ where his wife is at." Between jerky glances over his shoulder he winked at Horace. "Make your mind easy. It's the same with me as if the grave knowed it. Only I hate to see a good-------" Horace had gone on toward the door. "Judge," Snopes said in a penetrant undertone. Horace turned. "Dont stay."

"Dont stay?"

"See/ her and then leave. It's a sucker place. Place for farm-boys. Higher'n Monte Carlo. I'll wait out hyer and I'll show you a place where---------" Horace went on and entered the lattice. Two hours later, as he sat talking to Miss Reba in her room while beyond the door feet and now and then voices came and went in the hall and on the stairs, Minnie entered with a torn scrap of paper and brought it to Horace.

"What's that?" Miss Reba said.

"That big pie-fasted man left it fer him," Minnie said. "He say fer you to come on down there."

"Did you let him in?" Miss Reba said.

"Nome. He never tried to git in."

"I guess not," Miss Reba said. She grunted. "Do you know him?" she said to Horace.

"Yes. I cant seem to help myself," Horace said. He opened the paper. Torn from a handbill, it bore an address in pencil in a neat, flowing hand.

"He turned up here about two weeks ago," Miss Reba said. "Come in looking for two boys and sat around the diningroom blowing his head off and feeling the girls' behinds, but if he ever spent a cent I dont know it. Did he ever give you an order, Minnie?"

"Nome," Minnie said.

"And couple of nights later he was here again. Didn't spend ~~noth~~ nuttin, didn't do nuttin but talk, and I says to him 'Look here, mister, folks what uses this waiting-room has got to get on the train now and then.' So next time he brought a half-pint of whisky with him. I dont mind that, from a good customer. But when a fellow like him comes here three times, pinching my girls and bringing one ~~half/~~ half-pint of whiskey and ordering four coca-colas.........Just a cheap, vulgar man, honey. So I told Minnie not to let him in anymore, and here one afternoon I aint no more than laid down for a nap when-------I never did find out what he done to Minnie to get in. I know he never give her nuttin. ~~What~~ How did he do it, Minnie? He must a showed you something you never seen before. Didn't he?"

Minnie tossed her head. "He aint got nothing I wantin to see. I done seed too many now fer my own good." Minnie's husband had quit her. He didn't approve of Minnie's business. He was a cook in a restaurant and he took all the clothes and jewelry the white ladies had given Minnie and went off with a waitress in the restaurant.

"He kept on asking ~~ab/about/her~~ and hinting around about that girl," Miss Reba said, "and me telling him to go ask

Popeye if he wanted to know right bad. Not telling him nuttin except to get out and stay out, see; so this day it's about two in the afternoon and I'm asleep and Minnie lets him in and he asks her who's here and she tells him aint nobody, and he goes on up stairs. And Minnie says about that time Popeye comes in. She says she dont know what to do. She's scared not to let him in, and she says she knows if she does and he spatters that big bastard all over the upstairs floor, she knows I'll fire her and her husband just quit her and all.

"So Popeye goes on upstairs on them cat feet of his and comes on your friend on his knees, peeping through the key-hole. Minnie says Popeye stood behind him for about a minute, with his hat cocked over one eye. She says he took out a cigar-ette and struck a match on his thumbnail without no noise and lit it and then she says he reached over and held the match to the back of your friend's neck, and Minnie says she stood there halfway up the stairs and watched them: that fellow kneeling there with his face like a pie took out of the oven too soon and Popeye squirting smoke through his nose and kind of jerking his head at him. Then she come on down and in about ten seconds here he comes down the stairs with both hands on top of his head, ~~sakin~~ going wump-wump-wump inside like one of these here big dray-horses, and he pawed at the door for about a minute, moaning to himself like the wind in a chimney Minnie says, un-til she opened the door and left him out. And that's the last time he's even rung this bell until tonight......Let me see that." Horace gave her the paper. "That's a nigger whore-house," she said. "The lous------Minnie, tell him his friend aint here. Tell him I dont know where he went."

Minnie went out. Miss Reba said.

"I've had all sorts of men in my house, but I ~~draw~~ got to draw the line somewhere. I had lawyers, too. I had the biggest lawyer in Memphis back there in my diningroom, treating my girls. A millionair. He weighed two hundred and eighty pounds and he had his own special bed made and sent down here. It's upstairs right this minute. But all in the way of my business, not theirs. I aint going to have none of my girls pestered by lawyers without good reason."

"And you dont consider this good reason? that a man is being tried for his life for something he didn't do? You may be guilty right now of harboring a fugitive from justice."

"Then let them come take him. I got nuttin to do with it. I had too many police in this house to be scared of them." She rasied the tankard and drank and drew the back of her hand across her mouth. "I aint going to have nuttin to do with nuttin I dont know about. What Popeye done outside is his business. When he starts killing folks in my house, then I'll take a hand."

"Have you any children?" She looked at him. "I dont mean to pry into your affairs," he said. "I was just thinking about that woman. She'll be on the streets again, and ~~I dont~~

God only knows what will become of that baby."

"Yes," Miss Reba said. "I'm supporting four, in a Arkansaw home now. Not mine, though." She lifted the tankard and looked into it, oscillating it gently. She set it down again. "It better not been born at all," she said. "None of them had." She rose and came toward him, moving heavily, and stood above him with her harsh breath. She put her hand on his head and tilted his face up. "You aint lying to me, are you?" she said, her eyes piercing and intent and sad. "No, you aint." She released him. "Wait here a minute. I'll see." She went out. He heard her speak to Minnie in the hall, then he heard her toil up the stairs.

He sat quietly as she had left him. The room contained a wooden bed, a painted screen, three over-stuffed chairs, a wall safe. The dressing-table was littered with toilet articles tied in pink satin bows. The mantel supported a wax lily beneath a glass bell; above it, draped in black, the photograph of a meek-looking man with an enormous moustache. On the walls hung a few lithographs of spurious Greek scenes, and one picture done in tatting. Horace rose and went to the door. Minnie sat in a chair in the dim hall.

"Minnie," he said, "I've got to have a drink. A big one."

He had just finished it when Minnie entered again. "She say fer you to come on up," she said.

He mounted the stairs. Miss Reba waited at the top. She led the way up the hall and opened a door into a dark room. "You'll have to talk to her in the dark," she said. "She wont have no light." Light from the hall fell through the door and across the bed. "This aint here," Miss Reba said. "Wouldn't even see you in her room at all. I reckon you better humor her until you find out what you want." They entered. The light fell across the bed, upon a motionless curving ridge of bedclothing, the general tone of the bed unbroken. She'll smother, Horace thought. "Honey," Miss Reba said. The ridge did not move. "Here he is, honey. Long as you're all covered up, let's have some light. Then we can close the door." She turned the light on.

"She'll smother," Horace said.

"She'll come out in a minute," Miss Reba said. "Go on. Tell her what you want. I better stay. But dont mind me. I couldn't a stayed in my business without learning to be deaf and dumb a long time before this. And if I'd ever a had any curiosity, I'd have worn it out long ago in this house. Here's a chair." She turned, but Horace anticipated her and drew up two chairs. He sat down beside the bed and, talking at the top of the unstirring ridge, he told her what he wanted.

"I just want to know what really happened. You wont commit yourself. I know that you didn't do it. I'll promise before you tell me a thing that you wont have to testify in Court unless they are going to hang him without it. I know how you feel. I wouldn't bother you if the man's life were not at stake."

The ridge did not move.

"They're going to hang him for something he never done," Miss Reba said. "And she wont have nuttin, nobody. And you with diamonds, and her with that poor little kid. You seen it, didn't you?"

The ridge did not move.

"I know how you feel," Horace said. "You can use a different name, wear clothes nobody will recognise you in, glasses."

"They aint going to catch Popeye, honey," Miss Reba said. "Smart as he is. You dont know his name, noway, and if you have to go and tell them in the court, I'll send him word after you leave and he'll go somewheres and send for you. You and him dont want to stay here in Memphis. The lawyer'll take care of you and you wont have to tell nuttin you---------" The ridge moved. Temple flung the covers back and sat up. Her head was touseled, her face puffed, two spots of rouge on her cheekbones and her mouth painted into a savage cupid's bow. She stared for an instant at Horace with black antagonism, then she looked away.

"I want a drink," she said, p lling up the shoulder of her gown.

"Lie down," Miss Reba said. "You'll catch cold."

"I want another drink," Temple said.

"Lie down and cover up your nekkidness, anyway," Miss

Reba said, rising. "You already had three since supper."

Temple dragged the gown up again. She looked at Horace. "You give me a drink, then."

"Come on, honey," Miss Reba said, trying to push her down. "Lie down and get covered up and tell him about that business. I'll get you a drink in a minute."

"Let me alone," Temple said, writhing free. Miss Reba drew the covers about her shoulders. "Give me a cigarette, then. Have you got one?" she asked Horace.

"I'll get you one in a minute," Miss Reba said. "Will you do what he wants you to?"

"What?" Temple said. She looked at Horace with her black, belligerent stare.

"You needn't tell me where your----he-----" Horace said.

"Dont think I'm afraid to tell," Temple said. "I'll tell it anywhere. Dont think I'm afraid. I want a drink."

"You tell him, and I'll get you one," Miss Reba said.

Sitting up in the bed, the covers about her shoulders, Temple told him of the night she had spent in the ruined house, from the time she entered the room and tried to wedge the door with the chair, until the woman came to the bed and led her out. That was the only part of the whole experience which appeared to have left any impression on her at all: the night which she had spent in comparative inviolation. Now and then Horace would attempt to get her on ahead to the crime itself, but she would elude him and return to herself sitting on the bed, listening to the men on the porch, or lying in the dark while they entered the room and came to the bed and stood there above her.

"Yes; that," she would say. "It just happened. I dont know. I had been scared so long that I guess I had just gotten used to being. So I just sat there in those cottonseeds and watched him. I thought it was the rat at first. There were two of them there. One was in one corner looking at me and the other was in the other corner. I dont know what they lived on, because there wasn't anything there but corn-cobs and cottonseeds. Maybe they went to the house to eat. But there wasn't any in the house. I never did hear one in the house. I thought it might have been a rat when I first heard them, but you can feel people in a dark room: did you know that? You dont have to see them. You can feel ~~them~~ them like you can in a car when they begin to look for a good place to stop----you know: park for a while." She went on like that, in one of those bright, chatty monologues which women can carry on when they realise that they have the center of the stage; suddenly Horace realised that she was recounting the experience with actual pride, a sort of naive and impersonal vanity, as though she were making it up, looking from him to Miss Reba with quick, darting glances like a dog driving two cattle along a lane.

"And so whenever I breathed I'd hear those shucks. I dont see how anybody ever sleeps on a bed like that. But maybe you get used to it. Or maybe they're tired at night. Because when I breathed I could hear them, even when I was just sitting on the bed. I didn't see how it could be just breathing, so I'd sit as still as I could, but I could still hear them. That's because breathing goes down. You think it goes up, but it doesn't. It goes down you, and I'd hear them getting drunk on the porch. I got to thinking I could see where their heads were leaning back against the wall and I'd say Now this one's drinking out of the jug. Now that one's drinking. Like the mashed-in place on the pillow after you got up, you know.

"That was when I got to thinking a funny thing. You know how you do when you're scared. I was looking at my legs and I'd try to make like I was a boy. I was thinking about ~~//~~ if I just was a boy and then I tried to make myself into one by thinking. You know how you do things like that. Like when you know one problem in class and when they come to that you look at him and think right hard, Call on me. Call on me. Call on me. I'd think about what they tell children, about kissing your elbow, and I tried to. I actually did. I was that scared, and I'd wonder if I could tell when it happened. I mean, before I looked, and I'd think I had and how I'd go out and show them ---you know. I'd ~~////~~ strike a match and say Look. See? Let me alone, now. And then I could go back to bed. I'd think how I could go to bed and go to sleep then, because I was sleepy. I was so sleepy I simply couldn't hardly hold my eyes open.

"So I'd hold my eyes tight shut and say Now I am. I

am now. I'd look at my legs and I'd think about how much I had done for them. I'd think about how many dances I had taken them to---crazy, like that. Because I thought how much I'd done for them, and now they'd gotten me into this. So I'd think about praying to be changed into a boy and I would pray and then I'd sit right still and wait. Then I'd think maybe I couldn't tell it and I'd get ready to look. Then I'd think maybe it was too soon to look; that if I looked too soon I'd spoil it and then it wouldn't, sure enough. So I'd count. I said to count fifty at first, then I thought it was still too soon, and I'd say to count fifty more. Then I'd think if I didn't look at the right time, it would be too late.

"Then I thought about fastening myself up some way. There was a girl went abroad one summer that told me about a kind of iron belt in a museum a king or something used to lock the queen up in when he had to go away, and I thought if I just had that. That was why I got the raincoat and put it on. The canteen was hanging by it and I got it too and put it in the-------"

"Canteen?" Horace said. "Why did you do that?"

"I dont know why I took it. I was just scared to leave it there, I guess. But I was thinking if I just had that French thing. I was thinking maybe it would have long sharp spikes on it and he wouldn't know it until too late and I'd jab it into him. I'd jab it all the way through him and I'd think about the blood running on me and how I'd say I guess that'll teach you! I guess you'll let me alone now! I'd say. I didn't know it was going to be just the other way.......I want a drink."

"I'll get you one in a minute," Miss Reba said. "Go on and tell him."

"Oh, yes; this was something else funny I did." She told about lying in the darkness with Gowan snoring beside her, listening to the shucks and hearing the darkness full of movement, feeling the man approaching. She could hear the blood in her veins, and the little muscles at the corners of her eyes cracking faintly wider and wider, and she could feel her nostrils going alternately cool and warm. Then he was standing over and she was saying Come on. Touch me. Touch me! You're a coward if you dont. Coward! Coward!

"I wanted to go to sleep, you see. And he just kept on standing there. I thought if he'd just go on and get it over with, I could go to sleep. So I'd say You're a coward if you dont! You're a coward if you dont! and I could feel my mouth getting fixed to scream, and that little hot ball inside you that screams. Then it touched me, that nasty little cold hand, fiddling around inside the coat where I was naked. It was like alive ice and my skin started jumping away from it/ like those little flying fish in front of a boat. It was like my skin knew which was it was going to go before it started moving, and my skin would keep on jerking just ahead of it like there wouldn't be anything there when the hand got there.

"Then it got down to where my insides begin, and I hadn't eaten ~~sinceyesterday~~ since yesterday at dinner and my insides started bubbling and going on and the shucks began to make so much noise it was like laughing. I'd think they were laughing at me because all the time his hand was going inside the top of my knickers and I hadn't changed into a boy yet.

"That was the funny thing, because I wasn't breathing then. I hadn't breathed in a long time. So I thought I was dead. Then I did a funny thing. I could see myself in the coffin. I looked sweet---you know: all in white. I had on a veil like a bride, and I was crying because I was dead or looked sweet or something. No: it was because they had put shucks in the coffin. I was crying because they had put shucks in the coffin where I was dead, but all the time I could feel my nose going cold and hot and cold and hot, and I could see all the people sitting around the coffin, saying Dont she look sweet. Dont she look sweet.

But I kept on saying Coward! Coward! Touch me, coward! I got mad, because he was so long doing it. I'd talk to him. I'd say Do you think I'm going to lie here all night, just waiting on you? I'd say. Let me tell you what I'll do, I'd say. And I'd lie there with the shucks laughing at me and me jerking away in front of his hand and I'd think what I'd say to him. I'd talk to him like the teacher does in school, and then I was a teacher in school and it was a little black thing like a nigger boy, kind of, and I was the teacher. Because I'd say How old am I? and I'd say I'm forty-five years old. I had iron-gray hair and spectacles and I was all big up here like women get. I had on a gray tailored suit, and I never could wear gray. And I was telling it what I'd do, and it kind of ~~getting/littler/and/littler/~~ drawing up and drawing up like it could already see the switch.

Then I said That wont do. I ought to be a man. So I was an old man, with a long white beard, and then the little black man got littler and littler and I was saying Now. You see now. I'm a man now. Then I thought about being a man, and as soon as I thought it, it happened. It made a kind of plopping sound, like blowing a little rubber tube wrong-side outward. It felt cold, like ~~when/you/hold~~ the inside of your mouth when you hold it open. I could feel it, and I lay right still to keep from laughing about how surprised he was going to be. I could feel the jerking going on inside my knickers ahead of his hand and me lying there trying not to laugh about how surprised and mad he was going to be in about a minute. Then all of a sudden I went to sleep. I couldn't even stay awake until his hand got there. I just went to sleep. I couldn't even feel myself jerking in front of his hand, but I could hear the shucks. I didn't wake up until that woman came and took me down to the crib."

As he was leaving the house Miss Reba said: "I wish you'd get her down there and not let her come back. I'd find her folks myself, if I knowed how to go about it. But you know how....... She'll be dead, or in the asylum in a year, wya him and her go on up there in that room. There's something funny about it that I aint found out about yet. Maybe it's her. She wasn't born for this kind of life. You have to be born for this like you have to be born a butcher or a barber, I guess. Wouldn't anybody so either of them just for money or fun."

Better for her if she were dead tonight, Horace thought, walking on. For me, too. He thought of her, Popeye, the woman, the child, Goodwin, all put into a single chamber, bare, lethal, immediate and profound: a single blotting instant between the indignation and the surprise. And I too; thinking how that were the only solution. Removed, cauterised out of the old and tragic flank of the world. And I, too, now that we're all isolated; thinking of a gentle dark wind blowing in the long corridors of sleep; of lying beneath a low cozy roof under the long sound of the rain: the evil, the injustice, the tears. In an alley-mouth two figures stood, face to face, not touching; the man speaking in a low tone unprintable epithet after epithet in a caressing whisper, the woman motionless before him as though in a musing swoon of voluptuous ecstasy. Perhaps it is upon the instant that we realise, admit, that there is a logical pattern to evil, that we die, he thought, thinking of the expression he had once seen in the eyes of a dead child, and of other dead: the cooling indignation, the shocked despair fading, leaving two empty globes in which the motionless world lurked profoundly in miniature.

He did not even return to his hotel. He went to the

station. He could get a train at midnight. He had a cup of coffee and wished immediately that he had not, for it lay in a hot ball on his stomach. Three hours later, when he got off at Jefferson, it was still there, unassimilated. He walked to town and crossed the deserted square. He thought of the other morning when he had crossed it. It was as though there had not been any elapsed time between: the same gesture of the lighted clock-face, the same vulture-like shadows in the doorways; it might be the same morning and he had merely crossed the square, about-faced and was returning; all between a dream filled with all the nightmare shapes it had taken him forty-three years to invent, concentrated in a hot, hard lump in his stomach. Suddenly he was walking fast, the coffee jolting like a hot, heavy rock inside him.

He walked quietly up the drive, beginning to smell the honeysuckle from the fence. The house was dark, still, as though it were marooned in space by the ebb of all time. The insects had fallen to a low monotonous pitch, everywhere, nowhere, spent, as though the sound were the chemical agony of a world left stark and dying above the tide-edge of the fluid in which it lived and breathed. The moon stood overhead, but without light; the earth lay beneath, without darkness. He opened the door and felt his way into the room and to the light. The voice of the night---insects, whatever it was---had followed him into the house; he knew suddenly that it was the friction of the earth on its axis, approaching that moment when it must decide to turn on or to remain forever still: a motionless ball in cooling space, across which a thick smell of honeysuckle writhed like cold smoke.

He found the light and turned it on. Belle's letter was propped on the mantel. He took it up and looked at the superscription, at the small disfigurations which held a name, a juxtaposition of letters which did not move him at all, scrawled there by a hand that had no actual relation to his life, feeling the hard ball of coffee inside him.

Then he was looking at the photograph, holding it in his hands. Enclosed by the narrow imprint of the missing frame Little Belle's face dreamed with that quality of sweet chair-oscuro. Communicated to the cardboard by some quality of the light or perhaps by some infinitesimal movement of his hands, his own breathing, the face appeared to breathe in his palms in a shallow bath of highlight, beneath the slow, smoke-like tongues of invisible honeysuckle. Almost palpable enough to be seen, the scent filled the room and the small face seemed to swoon in a voluptuous languor, blurring still more, fading, leaving upon his eye a soft and fading aftermath of invitation and voluptuous promise and secret affirmation like a scent itself.

Then he knew what that sensation in his stomach meant. He put the photograph down hurriedly and went to the bathroom. He opened the door running and fumbled at the light. But he had not time to find it and he gave over and plunged forward and struck the lavatory and leaned upon his braced arms while the shucks set up a terrific uproar beneath her thighs. Lying with her head lifted slightly, her chin depressed like a figure lifted down from ~~an ancient tomb~~ a crucifix, she watched something black and furious go roaring out of her pale body. She was bound naked on her back on a flat car moving at speed through a black tunnel, the blackness streaming in rigid threads overhead, a roar of iron wheels in her ears. The car shot bodily from the tunnel in a long upward slant, the darkness overhead now shredded with parallel attenuations of living fire, toward a crescendo like a held breath, an interval in which she would swing faintly and lazily in nothingness filled with pale, myriad points of light. Far beneath her she could hear the faint, furious uproar of the shucks.

XIX.

The first time Temple went to the head of the stairs Minnie's eyeballs rolled out of the dusky light beside Miss Reba's door. Leaning once more within her bolted door Temple heard Miss Reba toil up the stairs and knock. Trembling with fury Temple leaned silenly against the door while Miss Reba panted and wheezed beyond it with a mixture of blandishment and threat. She made no sound. After a while Miss Reba went back down the stairs.

Temple turned from the door and stood in the center of the room, beating her hands silently together, her eyes black in her livid face. She wore a street dress, a hat. She removed the hat and hurled it into a corner and went and flung herself face down upon the bed. The bed had not been made. The table beside it was littered with cigarette stubs, the adjacent floor strewn with ashes. The pillow slip on that side was spotted with brown holes. Often in the night she would wake to smell tobacco and to see the single ruby eye where Popeye's mouth would be.

It was midmorning. A thin bar of sunlight fell beneath the drawn shade of the south window, lying upon the sill and then upon the floor in a narrow band. The house was utterly quiet, with that quality as of spent breathing which it had in mid-morning. Now and then a car passed in the street beneath.

Temple turned over on the bed. When she did so she saw one of Popeye's innumerable black suits lying across a chair. She lay looking at it for a while, then she rose and snatched the garments up and hurled them into the corner where the hat was. In another corner was a closet improvised by a print curtain. It contained dresses of all sorts and all new. She ripped them down in furious wads and flung them after the suit, and a row of hats from a shelf. Another of Popeye's suits hung there also. She flung it down. Behind it, hanging from a nail, was an automatic pistol in a holster of oiled silk. She took it down gingerly and removed the pistol and stood with it in her hand. After a moment she went to the bed and hid it beneath the pillow.

The dressing-table was cluttered with toilet-things ---brushes and mirrors, also new; with flasks and jars of delicate and bizarre shapes, bearing French labels. One by one she gathered them up and hurled them into the corner in thuds and splintering crashes. Among them lay a platinum bag: a delicate webbing of metal upon the smug orange gleam of banknotes. This followed the other things into the corner and she returned to the bed and lay again on her face in a slow thickening of expensive scent.

At noon Minnie tapped at the door. "Here yo dinner." Temple didn't move. "I ghy leave it here by the door. You can git it when you wants it." Her feet went away. Temple did not move.

Slowly the bar of sunlight shifted across the floor; the western side of the window-frame was now in shadow. Temple sat up, her head turned aside as though she were listening, fingering with deft habitude at her hair. She rose quietly and went to the door and listened again. Then she opened it. The tray sat on the floor. She stepped over it and went to the stairs and peered over the rail. After a while she made Minnie out, sitting in a chair in the hall.

"Minnie," she said. Minnie's head jerked up; again he eyes rolled whitely. "Bring me a drink," Temple said. She returned to her room. She waited fifteen minutes. She banged the door and was tramping furiously down the stairs when Minnie appeared in the hall.

"Yessum," Minnie said, "Miss Reba say------We aint got no-------" Miss Reba's door opened. Without looking up at Temple she spoke to Minnie. Minnie lifted her voice again. "Yessum; all right. I bring it up in just a minute."

"You'd better," Temple said. She returned and stood just inside the door until she heard Minnie mount the stairs. Temple opened the door, holding it just ajar.

"Aint you going to eat no dinner?" Minnie said, thrusting at the door with her knee. Temple held it to.

"Where is it?" she said.

"I aint straightened your room up this mawnin," Minnie said.

"Give it here," Temple said, reaching her hand through the crack. She took the glass from the tray.

"You better make that un last," Minnie said. "Miss Reba say you aint gwy git no more.......What you want to treat him this-a-way, fer? Way he spend his money on you, you ought to be ashamed. He a right pretty little man, even if he aint no John Gilbert, and way he spendin his money-------" Temple shut the door and shot the bolt. She drank the gin and drew a chair up to the bed and lit a cigarette and sat down with her feet on the bed. After a while she moved the chair to the window and lifted the shade a little so she could see the street beneath. She lit another cigarette.

At five oclock she saw Miss Reba emerge, in the black silk and flowered hat, and go down the street. She sprang up and dug the hat from the mass of clothes in the corner and put it on. At the door she turned and went back to the corner and exhumed the platinum purse and descended the stairs. Minnie was in the hall.

"I'll give you ten dollars," Temple said. "I wont be gone ten minutes."

"I caint do it, Miss Temple. Hit be worth my job if Miss Reba find it out, and my th'oat too, if Mist Popeye do."

"I swear I'll be back in ten minutes. I swear I will. Twenty dollars." She put the bill in Minnie's hand.

"You better come back," Minnie said, opening the door.

"If you aint back here in ten minutes, I aint going to be neither."

Temple opened the lattice and peered out. The street was empty save for a taxi at the curb across the way, and a man in a cap standing in a door beyond it. She went down the street, walking swiftly. At the corner a cab overtook her, slowXing, the driver looking at her interrogatively. She turned into the drug store at the corner and went back to the telephone booth. Then she returned to the house. As she turned the corner she met the man in the cap who had been leaning in the door. She entered the lattice. Minnie opened the door.

"Thank goodness," Minnie said. "When that cab over there started up, I got ready to pack up too. If you aint ghy say nothing about it, I git you a drink."

When Minnie fetched the gin Temple started to drink it. Her hand was trembling and there was a sort of elation in her face as she stood again just inside the door, listening, the glass in her hand. I'll need it later, she said. I'll need more than that. She covered the glass with a saucer and hid it carefully. Then she dig into the mass of garments in the corner and found a dancing-frock and shook it out and hung it back in the closet. She looked at the other things a moment, but/s she returned to the bed and lay down again. At once she rose and drew the chair up and sat down, her feet on the unmade bed. While daylight died slowly in the room she sat smoking cigarette after cigarette, listening to every sound on the stairs.

St half-past six Minnie brought her supper up. On the tray was another glass of gin. "Miss Reba sont this un," she said. "She say, how you feelin?"

"Tell her, all right," Temple said. "I'm going to have a bath and then go to bed, ~~later on~~ tell her."

When Minnie was gone Temple poured the two drinks into a tumbler and gloated over it, the glass shaking in her hands. She set it carefully away and covered it and ate her supper from the bed. When she finished she lit a cigarette. Her movements were jerky; she smoked swiftly, moving about the room. She stood for a moment at the window, the shade lifted aside, then she dropped it and turned into the room again, spying herself in the mirror. She turned before it, studying herself, puffing at the cigarette.

She snapped it behind her, toward the fireplace, and went to the mirror and combed her hair. She ripped the curtain aside and took the dress down and laid it on the bed and returned and drew out a drawer in the dresser and took a garment out. She paused with the garment in her hand, then she replaced it and closed the drawer and caught up the frock swiftly and hung it back in the closet. A moment later she found herself walking up and down the room, another cigarette burning in her hand, without any recollection of having lit it. She flung it away and went to the table and looked at her watch and propped it against the pack of cigarettes so she could see it from the bed, and lay down. When she did so she felt the pistol through the pillow. She slipped it out and looked at it, then she slid itunder her flank and lay motionless, her legs straight, her hands behind her head, her eyes focussing into black pinheads at every sound on the stairs.

At nine she rose. She picked up the pistol again; after a moment she thrust it beneath the mattress and undressed and in a spurious Chinese robe splotched with gold dragons and jade and scarlet flowers she left the room. When she returned her hair curled damply about her face. She went to the washstand and took up the tumbler, holding it in her hands, but she set it down again.

She dressed, retrieving the bottles and jars from the corner. Her motions before the glass were furious yet painstaking. She went to the washastand and took up the glass, but again she paused and went to the corner and got her coat and put it on and put the platinum bag in the pocket and leaned once more to the mirror. Then she went and took up the glass and gulped the gin and left the room, walking swiftly.

A single light burned in the hall. It was empty. She could hear voices in Miss Reba's room, but the lower hall was deserted. She descended swiftly and silently and gained the door. She believed that it would be at the door that they would stop her and she thought of the pistol with acute regret, almost pausing, knowing that she would use it without any compunction whatever, with a kind of pleasure. She sprang to the door and pawed at the ~~door~~ bolt, her head turned over her shoulder.

It opened. She sprang out and out the lattice door and ran down the walk and out the gate. As she did so a car, moving slowly along the curb, stopped opposite her. Popeye sat at the wheel. Without any apparent movement from him the door swung open. He made no movement, spoke no word. He just sat there, the straw hat slanted a little aside.

"I wont!" Temple said. "I wont!"

He made no movement, no sound. She came to the car.

"I wont, I tell you!" Then she cried wildly: "You're scared of him! You're scared to!"

"I'm giving him his chance," he said. "Will you go back in that house, or will you get in this car?"

"You're scared to!"

"I'm giving him his chance," he said, in his cold soft voice. "Come on. Make up your mind."

She leaned forward, putting her hand on his arm. "Popeye," she said; "daddy." His arm felt frail, no larger than a child's, dead and hard and light as a stick.

"I dont care which you do," he said. "But do it. Come on."

She leaned toward him, her hand on his arm. Then she got into the car. "You wont do it. You're afraid to. He's a better man than you are."

He reached across and shut the door. "Where?" he said. "Grotto?"

"He's a better man than you are!" Temple said shrilly. "You're not even a man! He knows it. Who ~~dont~~ does know it if he dont?" The car was in motion. She began to shriek at him. "You, a man, a bold bad man, when you cant even-------When you had to bring a real man in to------And you hanging over the bed, moaning and slobbering like a-------You couldn't fool me but once, could you? No wonder I bled and bluh------" his hand came over her mouth, hard, his nails going into her flesh. With the other hand he drove the car at reckless speed. When they passed beneath lights she could see him watching her as she struggled, tugging at his hand, whipping her head this way and that.

She ceased struggling, but she continued to twist her head from side to side, tugging at his hand. One finger, ringed with a thick ring, held her lips apart, his finger-tips digging into her cheek. With the other hand he whipped the car in and out of traffic, bearing down upon other cars until they slewed aside with brakse squealing, shooting recklessly across intersections. Once a policeman shouted at them, but he did not even look around.

Temple began to whimper, moaning behind his hand, drooling upon his fingers. The ring was like a dentist's instrum ment; she could not close her lips to regurgitate. When he removed it she could feel the imprint of his fingers cold on her jaw. She lifted her hand to it.

"You hurt my mouth," she whimpered. They were approaching the outskirts of the city, the speedometer at fifty miles. His hat slanted above his delicate hooked profile. She nursed her jaw. The houses gave way to broad, dark subdivisions out of which realtors' signs loomed abrupt and ghostly, with a quality of forlorn assurance. Between them low, far lights hung in the cool empty darkness blowing with fireflies. She began to cry quietly, feeling the cooling double drink of gin inside her. "You hurt my mouth," she said in a voice small and faint with self-pity. She nursed her jaw with experimental fingers, pressing harder and harder until she found a twinge. "You'll be sorry for this," she said in a muffled voice. "When I tell Red. Dont you wish you were Red? Dont you? Dont you wish you could do what he can do? Dont you wish ~~you were~~ he was the one watching us instead of you?"

They turned into the Grotto, passing along a closely curtained wall from which a sultry burst of music came. She sprang out while he was locking the car and ran on up the steps. "I gave you your chance," she said. "You brought me here. I didn't ask you to come."

She went to the washroom. In the mirror she examined her face. "Shucks," she said, "it didn't leave a mark, even;" drawing the flesh this way and that. "Little runt," she said, peering at her reflection. She added a phrase, glibly obscene, with a detached parrotlike effect. She painted her mouth again.

Another woman entered. They examined one another's clothes with brief, covert, cold, embracing glances.

Popeye was standing at the door to the dance-hall, a cigarette in his fingers.

"I gave you your chance," Temple said. "You didn't have to come."

"I dont take chances," he said.

"You took one," Temple said. "Are you sorry? Huh?"

"Go on," he said, his hand on her back. She was in the act of stepping over the sill when she turned and looked at him, their eyes almost on a level; then her hand flicked toward his armpit. He caught her wrist; the other hand flicked toward him. He caught that one too in his soft, cold hand. They looked eye to eye, her mouth open and the rouge spots darkening slowly on her face.

"I gave you your chance back there in town," he said. "You took it."

Behind her the music beat, sultry, evocative; filled with movement of feet, the voluptuous hysteria of muscles warming the scent of flesh, of the blood. "Oh,God; oh,God," she said, her lips scarce moving. "I'll go. I'll go back."

"You took it," he said. "Go on."

In his grasp her hands made tenative plucking motions at his coat just out of reach of her finger-tips. Slowly he was turning her toward the door, her head reverted. "You just dare!" she cried. "You just------" His hand closed upon the back of her neck, his fingers like steel, yet cold and light as aluminum. She could hear the vertebrae grating faintly together, and his voice, cold and still.

"Will you?"

She nodded her head. Then they were dancing. She could still feel his hand at her neck. Across his shoulder she looked swiftly about the room, her gaze flicking from face to face among the dancers. Beyond a low arch, in another room, a group stood about the crap-table. She leaned this way and that, trying to see the faces of the group.

Then she saw the four men. They were sitting at a table near the door. One of them was chewing gum; the whole lower part of his face seemed to be cropped with teeth of an unbelievable whiteness and size. When she saw them she swung Popeye around with his back to them, working the two of them toward the door again. Once more her harried ~~face~~ gaze flew from face to face in the crowd.

When she looked again two of the men had risen. They approached. She dragged Popeye into their path, still keeping his back turned to them. The men paused and essayed to go around her; again she backed Popeye into their path. She was trying to say something to him, but her mouth felt cold. It was like trying to pick up a pin with the fingers numb. Suddenly she felt herself lifted bodily aside, Popeye's small arms light and rigid as aluminum. She stumbled back against the wall and watched the two men leave the room. "I'll go back," she said. "I'll go back." She began to laugh shrilly.

"Shut it," Popeye said. "Are you going to shut it?"

"Get me a drink," she said. She felt his hand; her legs felt cold too, like they were not hers. They were sitting at a table. Two tables away the man was still chewing, his elbows on the table. The fourh man sat on his spine, smoking, his coat buttoned across his chest.

She watched hands: a brown one in a white sleeve, ~~, a~~ a soiled white one beneath a dirty cuff, setting bottles on the table. She had a glass in her hand. She drank, gulping; with the glass in her hand she saw Red standing in the door, in a gray suit and a spotted bow tie. He looked like a boy in school, and he looked about the room until he saw her. He looked at the back of Popeye's head, then at her as she sat with the glass in her hand. The two men at the other table had not moved. She could see the faint, steady movement of the one's ears as he chewed. The music started.

She held Popeye's back toward Red. He was still watching her, almost a head taller than anybody else. "Come on," she said in Popeye's ear. "If you're going to dance, dance."

She had another drink. They danced again. Red had disappeared. When the music ceased she had another drink. It did no good. It merely lay hot and hard inside her. "Come on," she said, "dont quit." But he wouldn't get up, and she stood over him, her muscles flinching and jerking with exhaustion and terror. She began to jeer at him. "Call yourself a man, a bold, bad man, and let a girl dance you off your feet." Then her face drained, became small and haggard and sincere; she spoke like a child, with sober despair. "Popeye." He sat with his hands on the table, finicking with a cigarette, the second glass with itsmelting ice before him. She put her hand on his shoulder. "Daddy," she said. Moving to shield them from the room, her hand stole toward his arm pit, touching the butt of the flat pistol. It lay rigid in the light, dead vise of his arm and side. "Give it to me," she whispered. "Daddy. Daddy." She leaned her thigh against his shoulder, caressing his arm with her flank. "Give it to me, daddy," she whispered. Suddenly her hand began to steal down his body in a swift, covert movement; then it snapped away in a movement of revulsion. "I forgot," she whispered; "I didn't mean.... .I didn't......."

One of the men at the other table hissed once through his teeth. "Sit down," Popeye said. She sat down. She filled her glass, watching her hands perform the action. Then she was watching the corner of the gray coat. He's got a broken button, she thought stupidly. Popeye had not moved.

"Dance this?" Red said.

His head was bent but he was not looking at her. He was turned a little, facing the two men at the other table. Still Popeye did not move. He shredded delicately the end of the cigarette, pinching the tobacco off. Then he put in into his mouth.

"I'm not dancing," Temple said through her cold lips.

"Not?" Red said. He said, in a level tone, without moving: "How's the boy?"

"Fine," Popeye said. Temple watched him scrape a match, saw the flame distorted through glass. ~~The glass was em- empty again.~~ "You've had enough," Popeye said. His hand took the glass from her lips. She watched him empty it into the ice bowl. The music started again. She sat looking quietly about the room. A voice began to buzz faintly at her hearing, then Popeye was gripping her wrist, shaking it, and she found that her mouth was open and that she must have been making a noise of some sort with it. "Shut it, now," he said. "You can have one more." He poured the drink ~~for her~~ into the glass.

"I haven't felt it at all," she said. He gave her the glass. She drank. When she set the glass down she realised that she was drunk. She believed that she had been drunk for some time. She thought that perhaps she had passed out and that it had already happened. She could hear herself saying Ihope it has. I hope it has. Then she believed it had and she was overcome by a sense of bereavement and of physical desire. She thought, It will never be again, and she sat in a floating swoon of agonised sorrow and erotic longing, thinking of Red's body, watching her hand holding the empty bottle over the glass.

"You've drunk it all," Popeye said. "Get up, now. Dance it off." They danced again. She moved stiffly and languidly, her eyes open but unseeing; her body following the music without hearing the tune for a time. Then she became aware that the orchestra was playing the same tune as when Red was asking her to dance. If that were so, then it couldn't have happened yet. She felt a wild surge of relief. It was not too late: Red was still alive; she felt long shuddering waves of physical desire going over her, ~~drying the~~ draining the color from her mouth, drawing her eyeballs back into her skull in a shuddering swoon.

They were at the crap table. She could hear herself shouting to the dice. She was rolling them, winning; the counters were piling up in front of her as Popeye drew them in, coaching her, correcting her in his soft, querulous voice.

He had the cup himself. She stood beside him cunningly, feeling the desire going over her in wave after wave, in volved with the music and with the smell of her own flesh. She became quiet. By infinitesimal inches she moved aside until someone slipped into her place. Then she was walking swiftly and carefully across the floor toward the door, the dancers, the music swirling slowly about her in a bright myriad wave. The table where the two men had sat was empty, but she did not even glance at it. She entered the corridor. A waiter met her.

"Room," she said. "Hurry."

The room contained a table and four chairs. The waiter turned on the light and stood in the door. She jerked her hand at him; he went out. She leaned against the table on her braced arms, watching the door, until Red entered.

He came toward her. She did not move. Her eyes began

to grow darker and darker, lifting into her skull above a half moon of white, without focus, with the blank rigidity of a statue's eyes. She began to say Ah-ah-ah-ah in an expiring voice, her body arching slowly backward as though faced by an exquisite torture. When he touched her she sprang like a bow, hurling herself upon him, her mouth gaped and ugly like ~~that/of~~ that of a dying fish as she writhed her loins against him.

He dragged her face free by main strength. With her hips grinding against him, her mouth gaping in straining protrusion, bloodless, she began to speak. "Let's hurry. Anywhere. I've quit him. I told him so. It's not my fault. Is it my fault? You dont need your hat and I dont either. He came here to kill you but I said I gave him his chance. It wasn't my fault. And now it'll just be us. Without him there watching. Come on. What're you waiting for?" She strained her mouth toward him, ~~dragge~~ dragging his head down, making a whimpering moan. He held his face~~/ree~~ free. "I told him I was. I said if you bring me here. I gave you your chance I said. And now he's got them there to bump you off. But you're not afriad. Are you?"

"Did you know that when you telephoned me?" he said.

"What? He said I wasn't to see you again. He said he'd kill you. But he had me followed when I telephoned. I saw him. But you're not afraid. He's not even a man, but you are. You're a man. You're a man." She began to grind against him, dragging at his head, murmuring to him in parrotlike underworld epithet, the saliva running pale over her bloodless lips. "Are you afraid?"

"Of that dopey bastard?" Lifting her bodily he turned so that he faced the door, and slipped his right hand free. She did not seem to be aware that he had moved.

"Please. Please. Please. Please. Dont make me wait. I'm burning up."

"All right. You go on back. You wait till I give you the sign. Will you go on back?"

"I cant wait. You've got to. I'm on fire, I tell you." She clung to him. Together they blundered across the room toward the door, he holding her clear of his right side; she in a voluptuous swoon, unaware that they were moving, straingaing at him as though she were trying to touch him with all of her body-surface at once. He freed himself and thrust her into the passage.

"Go on," he said. "I'll be there in a minute."

"You wont be long? I'm on fire. I'm dying, I tell you."

"No. Not long. Go on, now."

The music was playing. She moved up the corridor, staggering a little. She thought that she was leaning against the wall, when she found that she was dancing again; then that she was dancing with two men at once; then she found that she was not dancing but that she was moving toward the door between the man with the chewing gum and the one with the buttoned coat. She tried to stop, but they had her under the arms; she opened her mouth to scream, taking one last despairing look about the swirling room.

"~~Yell~~ "Yell," the man with the buttoned coat said. "Just try it once."

Red was at the crap table. She saw his head turned, the cup in his lifted hand. With it he made her a short, cheery salute. He watched her disappear through the door, between the two men. Then he looked briefly about the room. His face was bold and calm, but there were two white lines at the base of his nostrils and his forehead was damp. He rattled the cup and threw the dice steadily.

"Eleven," the dealer said.

"Let it lay," Red said. "I'll pass a million times tonight."

They helped Temple into the car. The man in the buttoned coat took the wheel. Where the drive joined the lane that led to the highroad a long touring car was parked. ~~Temple saw,~~ When they passed it Temple saw, leaning to a cupped match, Popeye's delicate hooked profile beneath the slanted hat as he lit the cigarette. The match flipped outward like a ~~small~~ dying star in miniature, sucked with the profile into darkness by the rush of their passing.

XX.

The tables had been moved to one end of the dance floor. On each one was a black table-cloth. The curtains were still drawn; a thick, salmon-colored light fell through them. Just beneath the orchestra platform the coffin sat. It was an expensive one: black, with silver fittings, the trestles hidden by a mass of flowers. In wreathes and crosses and other shapes of ceremonial mortality, the mass appeared to break in a symbolical wave over the bier and on upon the platform and the piano, the scent of them thickly oppressive.

The proprietor of the place moved about among the tables, speaking to the arrivals as they entered and found seats. The negro waiters, in black shirts beneath their starched jackets, were already moving in and out with glasses and bottles of ginger ale. They moved with swaggering and decorous repression; already the scene was vivid, with a hushed, macabre air a little febrile.

The archway to the dice-room was draped in black. A black pall lay upon the crap table, upon which the overflow of floral shapes was beginning to accumulate. People entered steadily, the men in dark suits of decorous restraint, others in the light, bright shades of spring, increasing the atmosphere of macabre paradox. The women---the younger ones---wore bright colors also, in hats and scarves; the older ones in sober gray and black and navy blue, and glittering with diamonds: matronly figures resembling housewives on a Sunday afternoon excursion.

The room began to hum with shrill, hushed talk. The waiters moved here and there with high, precarious trays, their white jackets and black shirts resembling photograph negatives. The proprietor went from table to table with his bald head, a huge diamond in his black cravat, followed by the bouncer, a thick, muscle-bound, bullet-headed man who appeared to be on the point of bursting out of his dinner-jacket.

In a private dining-room, on a table draped in black, sat a huge bowl of punch floating with ice and sliced fruit. Beside it leaned a fat man in a shapeless greenish suit, from the sleeves of which dirty cuffs fell upon hands rimmed with black nails. The soiled collar was wilted about his neck in limp folds, knotted by a greasy black tie with an imitation ruby stud. His face gleamed with moisture and he adjured the throng about the bowl in a harsh voice:

"Come on, folks. It's on Gene. It dont cost you nothing. Step up and drink. There wasn't never a better boy walked than him." They drank and fell back, replaced by others with extended cups. From time to time a waiter entered with ice and fruit and dumped them into the bowl; from a suitcase under the table Gene drew fresh bottles and decanted them into the bowl; then, proprietorial, adjurant, sweating, he resumed his harsh monologue, mopping his face on his sleeve. "Come on, folks. It's all on Gene. I aint nothing but a bootlegger, but he never had a better friend than me. Step up and drink, folks. There's more where that come from."

From the dance hall came a strain of music. The/ people entered and found seats. On the platform was the orchestra from a downtown hotel, in dinner coats. The proprietor and a second man were conferring with the leader.

"Let them play jazz," the second man said. "Never nobody liked dancing no better than Red."

"No, no," the proprietor said. "Time Gene gets them all ginned up on free whisky, they'll start dancing. IT'll look bad."

"How about the Blue Danube?" the leader said.

"No, no; dont play no blues, I tell you," the proprietor said. "There's a dead man in that bier."

"That's not blues," the leader said.

"What is it?" the second man said.

"A waltz. Strauss."

"A wop?" the second man said. "Like hell. Red was an American. You may not be, but he was. Dont you know anything American? Play I Cant Give You Anything but Love. He always liked that."

"And geth them all to dancing?" the proprietor said. He glanced nack at the tables, where the women were beginning to talk a little shrilly. "You better start off with Nearer, My God, To Thee," he said, "and sober them up some/. I told Gene it was risky about that punch, starting it so soon. My suggestion was to wait until we started back to town. But I might have knowed somebody'd have to turn it into a carnival. Better start off solemn and keep it up until I give you the sign."

"Red wouldn't like it solemn," the second man said. "And you know it."

"Let him go somewheres else, then," the proprietor said. "I just done this as an accomodation. I aint running no funeral parlor."

The orchestra played Nearer, My God, To Thee. The audience grew quiet. A woman in a red dress came in the door unsteadily. "Whoopee," she said, "so long, Red. He'll be in hell before I could even get to Little Rock."

"Shhhhhhhh!" voices said. She fell into a seat. Gene came to the door and stood there until the music stopped.

"Come on, folks," he shouted, jerking his arms in a fat, sweeping gesture, "come and get it. It's on Gene. I dont a dry throat or eye in this place in ten minutes." Those at the rear moved toward the door. The proprietor sprang to his feet and jerked his hand at the orchestra. The cornetist rose and played In That Haven of Rest in solo, but the crowd at the back of the room continued to dwindle through the door where Gene stood waving his arm. Two middle-aged women were weeping quietly beneath flowered hats.

They surged and clamored about the diminishing bowl. From the dance hall came the rich blare of the cornet, Two soiled young men worked their way toward the table, shouting "Gangway.

Gangway" monotonously, carrying suitcases. They opened them and set bottles on the table, while Gene, frankly weeping now, opened them and decanted them into the bowl. "Come up, folks. I couldn't a loved him no better if he'd a been my own son," he shouted hoarsely, dragging his sleeve across his face.

A waiter edged up to the table with a bowl of ice and fruit and went to put them into the punch bowl. "What the hell you doing?" Gene said, "putting that slop in there? Get to hell away from here."

"Ra-a-a-a-y-y-y-y!" they shouted, clashing their cups, drwoning all save the pantomime as Gene knocked the bowl of fruit from the waiter's hand and fell again to dumping raw liquor into the bowl, sploshing in into and upon the extended hands and cups. The two youths opened bottles furiously.

As though swept there upon a brassy blare of music the proprietor appeared in the door, his face harried, waving his arms. "Come on, folks," he shouted, "let's finish the musical program. It's costing us money."

"Hell with it," they shouted.

"Costing who money?"

"Who cares?"

"Costing who money?"

"Who begrudges it? I'll pay it. By God, I'll buy him two funerals."

"Folks! Folks!" the proprietor shouted. "Dont you realise there's a bier in that room?"

"Costing who money?"

"Beer?" Gene said. "Beer?" he said in a broken voice. "Is anybody here trying to insult me by--------"

"He begridges Red the money."

"Who does?"

"Joe does, the cheap son of a bitch."

"Is somebody here trying to insult me-------"

"Let's move the funeral, then. This is not the only place in town."

"Let's move Joe."

"Put the son of a bitch in a coffin. Let's have two funerals."

"Beer? Beer? Is somebody------"

"Put the son of a bitch in a coffin. See how he likes it."

"Put the son of a bitch in a coffin," the woman in red shrieked. They rushed toward the door, where the proprietor stood waving his hands above his head, his voice shrieking out of the uproar before he turned and fled.

In the main room a male quartet engaged from a vaudeville house was singing. They were singing mother songs in close harmony; they sang Sonny Boy. The weeping was general among the older women. Waiters were now carrying cups of punch in to them and they sat holding the cups in their fat, ringed hands, crying.

The orchestra played again. The woman in red staggered into the room. "Come on, Joe," she shouted, "open the game. Get that damn stiff out of here and open the game." A man tried to hold her; she turned upon him with a burst of filthy language and went and on to the shrouded crap table and hurled a wreath to the fllor. The proprietor rushed toward her, followed by the bouncer. The proprietor grasped the woman as she lifted another floral piece. The man who had tried to hold her intervened, the woman cursing shrilly and striking at both of them impartially with the wreath. The bouncer caught the man's arm; he whirled and struck at the bouncer, who knocked him halfway across the room. Three more men entered. The fourth rose from the floor and all four of them rushed at the bouncer.

He felled the first and whirled and sprang with unbelievable celerity, into the main room. The orchestra was playing. It was immediately drowned in a sudden pandemonium of chairs and screams. The bouncer whirled again and met the rush of the four men. They mingled; a second man flew out and skittered along the floor on his back; the bouncer sprang free. Then he whirled and rushed them and in a whirling plunge they bore down upon the bier and crashed into it. The orchestra had ceased and were now climbing onto their chairs, with their instruments. The floral offerings flew; the coffin teetered. "Catch it!" a voice shouted. They sprang forward, but the coffin crashed heavily to the floor, coming open. The corpse tumbled slowly and sedately out and came to rest with its face in the center of a wreath.

"Play something!" the proprietor bawled, waving his arms; "play! Play!"

When they raised the corpse the wreath came too, attached to him by a hidden end of wire driven into his cheek. He had worn a cap which, tumbling off, exposed a small blue hole in the center of his forehead. It had been neatly plugged with wax and was painted, but the wax had been jarred out and lost. They couldn't find it, but by unfastening the snap in the ~~peak of the cap, they could pull it down to his eyes.~~ peak, they could draw the cap down to his eyes.

XXI.

As the cortege neared the downtown section more cars joined it. The hearse was followed by six Packard touring cars with the tops back, driven by liveried chauffeurs and filled with flowers. They looked exactly alike and were of the type rented by the hour by the better class agencies. Next came a nondescript line of taxis, roadsters, sedans, which increased as the procession moved slowly through the restricted district where faces peered from beneath lowered shades, toward the main artery that led back out of town, toward the cemetary.

On the avenue the hearse increased its speed, the procession stretching out at swift intervals. Presently the private cars and the cabs began to drop out. At each intersection they would turn this way or that, until at last only the hears and the six Packards were left, each carrying no occupant save the liveried driver. The street was broad and now infrequent, with a white line down the senter that diminished on ahead into the smooth. ~~alp~~ asphalt emptiness. Soon the hearse was making forty miles and hour and then forty-five and then fifty.

One of the cabs drew up at Miss Reba's door. She get out, followed by a thin woman in sober, severe clothes and gold nose-glasses, and a short plump woman in a plumed hat, her face hidden by a handkerchief, and a small bullet-headed boy of five or six. The woman with the handkerchief continued to sob in snuffy gasps as they went up the walk and entered the lattice. Beyond the house door the dogs set up a falsetto uproar. When Minnie opened the door they surged about Miss Reba's feet. She kicked them aside. Again they assailed her with snapping eagerness; again she flung them back against the wall in muted thuds.

"Come ø in, come in," she said, her hand to her breast. Once inside the house the woman with the handkerchief began to weep aloud.

"Didn't he look sweet?" she wailed. "Didn't he look sweet!"

"Now, now," Miss Reba said, leading the way to her room, "come in and have some beer. You'll feel better. Minnie!" They entered the room with the decorated dresser, the safe, the screen, the draped portrait. "Sit down, sit down," she panted, shoving the chairs forward. She lowered herself into one and stooped terrifically toward her feet.

"Uncle Bud, honey," the weeping woman said, dabbing at her eyes, "come and unlace Miss Reba's shoes."

They boy knelt and removed Miss Reba's shoes. "And if you'll just reach me them house slippers under the bed there, honey," Miss Reba said. The boy fetched the slippers. Minnie entered, followed by the dogs. They rushed at Miss Reba and began to worry the shoes she had just removed.

"Scat!" the boy said, striking at them with his hand.

The dog's head snapped around, its teeth clicking, its half-hidden eyes bright and malevolent. The boy recoiled. "You bite me, you thon bitch," he said.

"Uncle Bud!" the fat woman said, her round face, ridged in fatty folds and streaked with tears, turned upon the boy in shocked suprise, the plumes nodding precariously above it. Uncle Bud's head was quite round, his nose bridged with freckles like splotches of huge summer rain on a sidewalk. The other woman sat primly erect, in gold nose-glasses on a gold chain. and neat iron-gray hair. She looked like a school-teacher. "The very idea!" the fat woman said. "How in the world he can learn such words on a Arkansaw farm, I dont know."

"They'll learn meanness anywhere," Miss Reba said. Minnie leaned down a tray bearing three frosted tankards. Uncle Bud watched with round cornflower eyes as they took one each. The fat woman began to cry again.

"He looked so sweet!" she wailed.

"We all got to suffer it," Miss Reba said. "Well, ~~any~~ may it be a long day," lifting her tankard. They drank, bowing formally to one another. The fat woman dried her eyes; the two guests wiped their lips with prim decorum. The thin one coughed delicately aside, behind her hand.

"Such good beer," she said.

"Aint it?" the fat one said. "I always say it's the greatest pleasure I have to call on Miss Reba."

They began to talk politely, in decorous half-completed

sentences, with little gasps of agreement. The boy had moved aimlessly to the window, peering beneath the lifted shade.

"How long's he going to be with you, Miss Myrtle?" Miss Reba said.

"Just till Sat'dy," the ~~dat~~ fat woman said. "Then he'll go back home. It makes a right nice little change for him, with me for a week or two. And I enjoy having him."

"Children are such a comfort to a body," the thin one said.

"Yes," Miss Myrtle said. "Is them two nice young fellows still with you, Miss Reba?"

"Yes," Miss Reba said. "I think I got to get shut of them, though. I aint specially tender-hearted, but after all it aint no use in helping young folks to learn this world's meanness until they have too. I already had to stop the girls running around the house without no clothes on, and they dont like it."

They drank again, decorously, handling the tankards delicately, save Miss Reba who grasped hers as though it were a weapon, her other hand lost in her breast. She set her tankard down empty. "I get so dry, seems like," she said. "Wont you ladies have another?" they murmured, ceremoniously. "Minnie!" Miss Reba shouted.

Minnie came and filled the tankards again. "Reely, I'm right ashamed," Miss Myrtle said. "But Miss Reba has such good beer. And then we've all had a ~~light/trying/afternoon/kind~~

kind of upsetting afternoon."

"I'm just surprised it wasn't upset no more," Miss Reba said. "Giving away all that free liquor like Gene done."

"It must have cost a good piece of jack," the thin woman said.

"I believe you," Miss Reba said. "And who got anything out of it? Tell me that. Except the privilege of having his place hell-full of folks not spending a cent." She had set her tankard on the table beside her chair. Suddenly she turned her head sharply and looked at it. Uncle Bud was now behind her cjair, leaning against the table. "You aint been into my beer, have you, boy?" she said.

"You, Uncle Bud," Miss Myrtle said. "Aint you ashamed? I declare, it's getting so I dont dare take him nowhere. I never see such a boy for snitching beer in my life. You come out here and play, now. Come on."

"Yessum," Uncle Bud said. He moved, in no particular direction. Miss Reba drank and set the tankard back on the table and rose.

"Since we all been kind of tore up," she said, "maybe I can prevail on you ladies to have a little sup of gin?"

"No; reely," Miss Myrtle said.

"Miss Reba's the perfect hostess," the thin one said. "How many times you heard me say that, Miss Myrtle?"

"I wouldn't undertake to say, dearie," Miss Myrtle said.

Miss Reba vanished behind the screen.

"Did you ever see it so warm for June, Miss Lorraine?" Miss Myrtle said.

"I never did," the thin woman said. Miss Myrtle's face began to crinkle again. Setting her tankard down ahe began to fumble for her handkerchief.

"It just comes over me like this," she said, 2and them singing that Sonny Boy and all. He looked so sweet," she wailed.

"Now, now," Miss Lorraine said. "Drink a little beer. You'll feel better. Miss Myrtle's took again," she said, raising her voice.

"I got too tender a heart," Miss Myrtle said. She snuffled behind the handkerchief, groping for her tankard. She groped for a moment, then it touched her hand. She looked quickly up. "You, Uncle Bud!" she said. "Didn't I tell you to come out from behind there and play? Would you believe it? The other afternoon when we left here I was so mortified I didn't know what to do. I was ashamed to be seen on the street with a drunk boy like you."

Miss Reba emerged from behind the screen with three glasses of gin. "This'll put some heart into us," she said. "We(re setting here like three old sick cats." They bowed formally and drank, patting their lips. Then they began to talk. They were all talking at once, again in half-completed sentences, but without pauses for agreement or affirmation.

"It's us girls," Miss Myrtle said. "Men just cant seem

to take us and leave us for what we are. They make us what we are, then they expect us to be different. Expect us not to never look at another man, while they come and go as they please."

"A woman that wants to fool with more than one man at a time is a fool," Miss Reba said. "They're all trouble, and why do you want to double your trouble? And the woman that ~~dit~~ cant stay true to a good man when she gets him, a free-hearted spender that never give her a hour's uneasiness or a hard word........" looking at them, her eyes began to fill with a sad, unutterable expression, of baffled and patient despair.

"Now, now," Miss Myrtle said. She leaned forward and patted Miss Reba's huge hand. Miss Lorraine made a faint clucking sound with her tongue. "You'll get yourself started."

"He was such a good man," Miss Reba said. "We was like two doves. For eleven years we was like two doves."

"Now, dearie; now, dearie," Miss Myrtle said.

"It's when it comes over me like this," Miss Reba said. "Seeing that boy laying there under them flowers."

"He never had no more than Mr Binford, had," Miss Myrtle said. "Now, now. Drink a little beer."

Miss Reba brushed her sleeve across her eyes. She drank some beer.

"He ought to known better than to take a chance with Popeye's girl," Miss Lorraine said.

"Men dont never learn better than that, dearie," Miss

Myrtle said. "~~What you reckon~~ "Where you reckon they went, Miss Reba?"

"I dont know and I dont care," Miss Reba said. "And how soon they catch him and burn him for killing that boy, I dont care neither."

"He goes all the way to Pensacola every summer to see his mother," Miss Myrtle said. "A man that'll do that cant be all bad."

"I dont know how bad you like them, then," Miss Reba said. "Me trying to run a respectable house, that's been running a shooting-gallery for twenty years, and him trying to turn it into a peep-show."

"It's us poor girls," Miss Myrtle said," causes all the trouble and gets ~~all the suffering~~ all the suffering."

"I heard two years ago he wasn't no good that way," Miss Lorraine said.

"I knew it all the time," Miss Reba said. "A young man spending his money like water on girls and not never going to bed with one. It's against nature. All the girls thought it was because he had a little woman out in town somewhere, but I says mark my words, there's something funny about him. There's a funny business somewhere."

"He was a free spender, all right," Miss Lorraine said.

"The clothes and jewelry that girl bought, it was a shame," Miss Reba said. "There was a Chinee robe she paid a hundred dollars for---imported, it was---and perfume at ten dollars an ounce; and next morning when I went up there, they was all wadded in the corner and the perfume and rouge busted all over them like a cyclone. That's what she'd do when she got mad at him, when he'd beat her. After he shut her up and wouldn't let her leave the house. Having the front of my house watched like it was a........." She raised the tankard from the table to her lips. Then she halted it, blinking. "Where's my------"

"Uncle Bud!" Miss Myrtle said. She grasped the boy by the arm and snatched him out from behind Miss Reba's chair and shook him, his round head bobbing on his shoulders with an expression of equable idiocy. "Aint you ashamed? Aint you ashamed? Why cant you stay out of these ladies' beer? I'm a good mind to take that dollar back and make you buy Miss Reba a can of beer, I am for a fact. Now, you go over there by that window and stay there, you hear?"

"Nonsense," Miss Reba said. "There wasn't much left. You ladies are about ready too, aint you? Minnie!"

Miss Lorraine touched her mouth with her handkerchief. Behind her glasses her eyes rolled aside in a veiled, secret look. She laid the other hand to her flat spinster's breast.

"We forgot about your heart, honey," Miss Myrtle said. "Dont you reckon you better take gin this time?"

"Reely, I-- ---" Miss Lorraine said.

"Yes; do," Miss Reba said. She rose heavily and fetched three more glasses of gin from behind the screen. Minnie entered and refilled the tankards. They drank, patting their lips.

"That's what was going on, was it?" Miss Lorraine said.

"First I knowed was when Minnie told me there was something funny going on," Miss Reba said. "How he wasn't here hardly at all, gone about every other night, and that when he was here, there wasn't no signs at all the next morning when she cleaned up. She'd hear them quarrelling, and she said it was her wanting to get out and he wouldn't let her. With all them clothes he was buying her, mind, he didn't want her to leave the house, and she'd get mad and lock the door and wouldn't even let him in."

"Maybe he went off and got fixed up with one of these glands, these monkey glands, and it quit on him," Miss Myrtle said.

"Then one morning he come in with Red and took him up there. They stayed about an hour and left, and Popeye didn't show up again until next morning. Then him and Red come back and stayed up there about an hour. When they left, Minnie come and told me what was going on, so next day I waited for them. I called him in here and I says 'Look here, you son of a buh----' " She ceased. For an instant the three of them sat motionless, a little forward. Then slowly their heads turned and they looked at the boy leaning against the table.

"Uncle Bud, honey," Miss Myrtle said," dont you want to go and play in the yard with Reba and Mr Binford?"

"Yessum," the boy said. He went toward the door. They

watched him until the door closed upon him. Miss Lorraine drew her chair up; they leaned together.

"And that's what they was doing?" Miss Myrtle said.

"I says 'I been running a house for twenty years, but this is the first time I ever had anything like this going on in it. If you want to turn a stud in to your girl' I says 'go somewhere else to do it. I aint going to have my house turned into no French joint.' "

"The son of a bitch," Miss Lorraine said.

"He'd ought to've had a sense enough to got a old ugly man," Miss Myrtle said. "Tempting us poor girls like that."

"Men always expects us to resist temptation," Miss Lorraine said. "The lousy son of a bitch."

"Except what they offers themselves," Miss Reba said. "Then watch them......Every morning for four days that was going on, then they didn't come back. For a week Popeye didn't show up at all, and that girl wild as a young mare. I thought he was out of town on business maybe, until Minnie told me he wasn't and that he give her five dollars a day not to let that girl out of the house nor use the telephone. And me trying to get word to him to come and take her out of my house because I didn't want nuttin like that going on in it. Yes, sir, Minnie said the two of them would be nekkid as two snakes, and Popeye hanging over the foot of the bed without even his hat took off, making a kind of whinnying sound."

"Maybe he was cheering for them," Miss Lorraine said. "The lousy son of a bitch."

Feet came up the hall; they could hear Minnie's voice

lifted in adjuration. The door opened. She entered, holding Uncle Bud erect by one hand. Limp-kneed he dangled, his face fixed in an expression of glassy idiocy. "Miss Reba," Minnie said, "this boy done broke in the icebox and drunk a whole bottle of beer~~,~~. You, boy!" she said, shaking him, "stan up!" Limply he dangled, his face rigid in a slobbering grin. Then upon it came an expression of concern, ~~constre~~ consternation; Minnie swung him sharply away from her as he began to vomit.

XXII.

It was just five oclock when he put Belle's letter into the postoffice. The sun was just about to show. But it would be two hours yet before he could get breakfast even, so he walked quietly about the town, watching it rose and wake into the increasing immaculate morning, making his plans to go abroad. He thought of Belle, then he was thinking of the three of them. He saw Belle and Narcissa and the woman with the child on her lap, all sitting on the cot in the jail, and himself like one of those furious and aimless bugs that dart with sporadic and unbelievable speed upon the surface of stagnant water as though in furious escape from the very substance that spawned them, as he strove with subterfuge and evasion and stubbornness and injustice, with that fundamental abhorrence of truth which is in mankind.

I'll go to Europe, he said. I'm sick. I'm sick to death. Lookimg about him he saw his life isolated in all its ludicrous and optimistic frustration; looking ahead he could see it diminishing into a amall frenzied dust where he strove with the subterfuge and prejudice and lying, to no end. What did it matter who killed the man? what became of Goodwin, of her, of a fool little girl, of himself? All that matters is to accomplish what is in hand, clean up the mess he had got himself into, then be forever afterward as fearful as any buck of the scent or sight or sound of collective man.

The first thing would be to clean up the mess. He would sub-poena Temple; he thought in a paroxysm of raging pleasure of flinging her into the court-room, of stripping her: This is what a man has killed another over. This, the offspring of respectable people: let them blush for shame, since he could never blush for anything again. Stripping her, backgraound, environment, all. Not that it mattered whether they hung Goodwin or not, any more than it mattered whether or not Tommy was dead. Telling the jur$ What ever you do will be as stupid as what has been done, but just do something, because he was sick to death. Then suddenly, passi|g a house, he smelled coffee. and he knew he could not do that. He went to the hotel and with knife and fork he dug himself back into that world he had vomited himself out of for a time, i| which he must follow a certain ordered proceedure about which he had neither volition nor will.

After breakfast he felt better. It might not be necessary to use Temple at all. He need only arrange to procure her if things went wrong. Whatever he did, the evidence against Goodwin was not strong enough to convict him as it was now, and so when he saw Senator Snopes on the street he was almost civil to him. Snopes was sitting before the hotel, a bag at his feet.

"Going down to Jackson for a couple of days," he said. "Too bad I missed you the other night. I could have took you to a place most folks dont know about, where a man can do anything he's big enough to do. I reckon there'll be another time, though. And dont you be uneasy none. I aint no talker. When I'm in Jefferson I'm one thing; when I'm up town aint nobody's business but mine. And I expect to treat everbody the same way."

That day he met his sister on the street. They talked for a few minutes, then parted. She went on and turned and mounted a narrow stairway between two stores. The day Horace moved back to town, when Miss Jenny came down Narcissa said:

"He's gone back to town. He thinks he ought to be nearer his client."

"I gathered that from the way he went to bed last night," Miss Jenny said. "Why dont you let him alone until he gets done with his case? He'll go on home then."

"I know it," Narcissa said. "Who is the District Attorney?"

"You've known him all your life. Eustace Graham. Dont you remember reading about it in the paper when he got elected last winter?"

"No, I dont remember."

"What do you think about while you are reading the paper, then?"

"Eustace Graham," Narcissa said. "Yes. I know him."

He had a club foot. As usual, the deformity had invested him in the eyes of the town with that sentimental illusion of deserving worth. That boy'll get somewhere, they said, simply because he drove a grocery wagon and then a truck with a club foot ---the one in which the foot could be neither help nor hindrance, the other in which it was an asset. He got as far as the state university, where he played poker each Saturday night in the office of a livery stable. When he graduated in law he left an anecdote bhind him.

It was in the poker game. The bet came to him. He looked across at the proprietor, who was his only remaining opponent.

"How much have you got there, Mr Harris?" he said.

"Forty-two dollars, Eustace," the proprietor said. Eustace ~~counted~~ shoved some chips into the pot. "How much is that?" the proprietor said.

"Forty-two dollars, Mr Harris."

"Hmmm," the proprietor said. He examined his hand. "How many cards did you draw, Eustace?"

"Three, Mr Harris."

"Hmmm. Who dealt the cards, Eustace?"

"I did, Mr Harris."

"I pass, Eustace."

He had been District Attorney but a short time, yet already he had ~~had~~ let it be known that he would announce for Congress on his record of convictions, so when he found himself facing Narcissa across the desk in his dingy office, his expression was like that when he had put the forty-two dollars into the pot.

"I only wish it were your brother," he said. "I hate to see a brother-in-arms, you might say, with a bad case." She was watching him with a blank, envelbping look. "After all, we've got to protect society, even when it does seem......."

"Are you sure he cant win?" she said.

"Well, the first principle of law is, God alone knows what the jury will do. Of course, you cant expect-------"

"But you dont think he will."

"Naturally, I-------"

"You have good reason to think he cant. I suppose you know things about it that he doesn't."

He looked at her briefly. Then he picked up a pen from his desk and began to scrape at the point with a paper cutter. "This is purely confidential. I am violating my oath of office; I wont have to tell you that. But it may save you worry to know that he hasn't a chance in the world. I know what the disappointment will be to him, but that cant be helped. We happen to know that the man is guilty. So if there's any way you know of to get your brother out of the case, I'd advise you to do it. A losing lawyer is like a losing anything else, ballplayer or merchant or doctor: his business is to-------"

"~~It would be better if the~~ "So the quicker he loses, the better it would be, wouldn't it?" she said. "If they hung the man and got it over with." His hands became perfectly still. He did not look up. She said, her tone cold and level: "I have reasons for wanting Horace out of this case. The sooner the better. Three nights ago that Snopes, the one in the legislature, telephoned out home, trying to find him. The next day he went to Memphis. I dont know what for. You'll have to find that out yourself. I just want Horace out of this business as soon as possible."

She rose and moved toward the door. He hobbled over to open it; again/ she put that cold, still, unfathomable gaze upon him as though he were a dog or a cow and she waited for it to get out of her path. Then she was gone. He closed the door and struck a clumsy clog-step, snapping his fingers just as the door opened again; he snapped his hands toward his tie and looked at her in the door, holding it open.

"What day do you think it will be over with?" she said.

"Why, I cuh----Court opens the twentieth," he said. "It will be the first case. Say..... Two days. Or three at the most, with your kind assistance. And I need not assure you that this will be held in strictest confidence between us......." He moved toward her, but her blank calculating gaze was like a wall, surrounding him.

"That will be the twenty-fourth." Then she was looking at him again. "Thank you," she said, and closed the door.

That night / she wrote Belle that Horace would be home on the twenty-fourth. She telephoned Horace and asked for Belle's address.

"Why?" Horace said.

"I'm going to write her a letter," she said, her voice tranquil, without threat. Dammit, Horace thought, holding the dead wire in his hand, How can I be expected to combat people who will not even employ subterfuge. But soon he forgot it, forgot that she had called. He did not see her again before the trial opened.

Two days before it opened Snopes emerged from a dentist's office and stood at the curb, spitting. He took a gold-wrapped cigar from his pocket and removed the foil and put the cigar gingerly between his teeth. He had a black eye, and the bridge of his nose was ~~t~~ bound in soiled adhesive tape. "Got hit by a car in Jackson," he told them in the barbershop. "But dont think I never made the bastard pay," he said, showing a sheaf of ywllow bills. He put them into a notecase and stowed it away. "I'm an American," he said. "I dont brag about it, because I was born one. And I been a decent Baptist all my life, too. Oh, I aint no preacher and I aint no old maid; I been around with the boys now and then, but I reckon I aint no worse than lots of folks that pretends to sing loud in church. But the lowest, cheapest thing on this earth aint a nigger: it's a jew. We need laws against them. Drastic laws. When a durn lowlife jew can come to a free country like this and just because he's got a law degree, it's time to put a stop to things. A jew is the lowest thing on this creation. And the lowest kind of jew is a jew lawyer. And the lowest kind of jew lawyer is a Memphis jew lawyer. When a jew lawyer can hold up an American, a white man, and not give him but ten dollars for something that two Americans already give him ten times that much for something exactly like it, we need a law. I been a liberal spender all my life; whatever I had has always been my friends', but when a durn,/ stinking, lowlife--------"

"Why'd you sell it to him, then?" a barber said.

"What?" Snopes said. "......Have a cigar?"

XXIII.

The trial opened on the twentieth of June. On the table lay the sparse objects which the District Attorney had offered in evidence: the bullet from Tommy's skull, a ~~potonewar~~ stoneware jug half full of corn whisky.

Horace had not summoned Temple. Twice he had telephoned Miss Reba, the second time two days before the trial opened.

"They aint here no more," Miss Reba said. "I dont know nuttin about them and I dont want to know nuttin."

"But cant you find where she went to, in case I need her?"

"I dont know nuttin and I dont want to," Miss Reba said. Thank God," Horace said, thank God. He realised now that it was too late, that he could not have summoned her; realised again that furious homogeneity of the middle classes when opposed to the proletariat from which it so recently sprung and by which it is so often threatened. Better that he should hang, he thought, than to expose.......than to expose........ I cannot even face the picture, he told himself.

"I will call Mrs Goodwin to the stand," he said. He did not look around, but he felt Goodwin's eyes come to rest quickly upon him. He could feel them as he helped the woman into the chair and while she was being sworn. With the child on her lap she began her testimony, repeating the story as she had told it to him in the hotel that morning the child was ill. Twice Goodwin tried to interrupt and was silenced. Horace could feel the cold fury of his gaze, but he would not look around.

The woman finished her story. She sat erect in the chair, in her neat, worn gray dress and hat with the darned veil, the purple ornament on her shoulder. The child lay on her lap, its eyes closed in that drugged immobility. For a while her hand hovered about its face, performing those needless maternal acyions as though unawares.

Horace went and sat down. Then only did he look at Goodwin. But the other sat quietly now, his arms folded and his head bent a little, but Horace could see that his nostrils were waxy white against his dark face with rage. He leaned toward him and whispered, but Goodwin did not move.

The District Attorney now faced the woman.

"Mrs Goodwin," he said, "what was the date of your marriage to Mr Goodwin?"

"I object!" Horace said, on his feet.

"Can the prosecution show how this question is relevant?" the Court said.

"I waive, your Honor," the District Attorney said, glancing at the jury. Damn! Horace thought. He took me, then.

When court adjourned for the day Goodwin said bitterly: "Well, you've said you would kill me someday, but I didn't think you meant it."

"Dont be a fool," Horace said. "Dont you see your

case is won? That they are reduced to trying to impugn ~~of~~ the character of your witness?" But when they left the jail he found the woman still watching him from some deep reserve of foreboding. "You mustn't worry at all, I tell you. You may know more about making whisky or love than I do, but I know more about criminal proceedure than you, remember."

"You dont think I made a mistake?"

"I know you didn't. Dont you see how that explodes their case? The best they can hope for now is a hung jury. And the chances of that are not one in fifty. I tell you, he'll walk out of that jail tomorrow a free man."

"Then I guess it's time to think about paying you."

"Yes," Horace said, "all right. I'll come out tonight."

"Tonight?"

"Yes. He may call you back to the stand tomorrow. We'd better prepare for it, anyway."

At eight oclock he entered the mad woman's yard. A single light burned in the crazy depths of the house, like a firefly caught in a brier patch, but the woman did not appear when he called. He went to the door and knocked. A shrill voice shouted something; he waited a moment. He was about to knock again when he heard the voice again, shrill and wild and faint,as though from a distance, like a reedy pipe buried by an avalanche. He circled the house in the rank, waist-high weeds. The kitchen door was open. The lamp was there, dim in a smutty chimney, filling the room---a jumble of looming shapes rank with old foul female flesh---not with light but with shadow. White eyeballs rolled in a high, tight bullet head in brown gleams above a torn singlet strapped into overalls. Beyond the negro the mad woman turned in an open cupboard, brushing her lank hair back with her forearm.

"Your bitch has gone to jail," she said. "Go on with her."

"Jail?" Horace said.

"That's what I said. Where the good folks live. When you get a husband, keep him in jail where he cant bother you." She turned to the negro, a small flask in her hand. "Come on, dearie. Give me a dollar for it. You got plenty money."

Horace returned to the front, breathing deep to clear his lungs and his nostrils. He returned to town, to the jail. They admitted him. He mounted the stairs; the jailer locked a door behind him. Through the barred window of the general room he could see the windows in the hotel wall, thinking of that fatality which may be engendered by a conviction of disaster.

The woman admitted him to the cell. The child lay on the cot. Goodwin sat beside it, his arms crossed, his legs extended in the attitude of a man in the last stage of physical exhaustion.

"Why are you sitting there, in front of that slit?" Horace said. "Why not get into the corner, and we'll put the mattress over you."

"You come to see it done, did you?" Goodwin said.

"Well, that's nor more than right. It's your job. You promised I wouldn't hang, didn't you?"

"You've got an hour yet," Horace said. "The Memphis train doesn't get here until eight-thirty. He's surely got better sense than to come here in that canary-colored car." He turned to the woman. "But you. I thought better of you. I know that he and I are fools, but I expected better of you."

"You're doing her a favor," Goodwin said. "She might have hung on with me until she was too old to hustle a good man. If you'll just promise to get the kid a newspaper grift when he's old enough to make change, I'll be easy in my mind."

The woman had returned to the cot. She lifted the child onto her lap. Horace went to her. He said: "You come on, now. Nothing's going to happen. He'll be all right here. He knows it. You've got to go home and get some sleep, because you'll both be leaving here tomorrow. Come, now."

"I reckon I better stay," she said.

"Damn it, dont you know that putting yourself in the position is the surest way in the world to bring it about? Hasn't your own experience shown you that? Lee knows it. Lee, make her stop this."

"Go on, Ruby," Goodwin said. "Go home and go to bed."

"I reckon I better stay," she said.

Horace stood over them. The woman mused above the child, her face bent and her whole body motionless. Goodwin leaned back against the wall, his brown wrists folded into the faded sleeves of his shirt. "You're a man now," Horace said. "Aren't you? I wish that jury could see you now, locked up in a ~~ssll~~ concrete cell, scaring women and children with fifth grade ghost stories. They'd know you never had the guts to kill anybody."

"You better go on and go to bed yourself," Goodwin said. "We could sleep here, if there wasn't so much noise going on."

"No; that's too sensible for us to do," Horace said. He left the cell. The jailer unlocked the door for him and he quitted the building. In tenminutes he returned, with a parcel. Goodwin had not moved. The woman watched him open the package. It contained a bottle of milk, a box of candy, a box of cigars. He gave Goodwin one of the cigars/ and took one himself. "You brought his bottle, didn't you?"

The woman produced the bottle from a bundle beneath the cot. "It's got some in it," she said. She filled it from the bottle. Horace lit his and Goodwin's cigars. When he looked again the bottle was gone.

"Not time to feed him yet?" he said.

"I'm warming it," the woman said.

"Oh," Horace said. He tilted the chair against the wall, across the cell from the cot.

"Here's room on the bed," the woman said. "It's softer./ Some."

"Not enough to change, though," Horace said.

"Look here," Goodwin said, "you go on home. No use in you doing this."

"We've got a little work to do," Horace said. "That lawyer'll call her again in the morning. That's his only chance: to invalidate her testimony someway. You might try to get some sleep while we go over it."

"All right," Goodwin said.

Horace began to ~~r~~construct the scene, coaching the woman, pausing now and then to tramp back and forth upon the narrow floor. Goodwin finished his cigar and sat motionless again, his arms folded and his head bent. The clock above the square struck nine and then ten. The child whimpered, stirred. The woman stopped and changed it and took the bottle from beneath her flank and fed it. Then she leaned forward carefully and looked into Goodwin's face. "He's asleep," she whispered.

"Shall we lay him down?" Horace whispered.

"No. Let him stay there." Moving quietly she laid the child on the cot and moved herself to the other end of it. Horace carried the chair over beside her. They spoke in whispers.

The clock struck eleven. Still Horace drilled her, going over and over the imaginary scene, trying to anticipate every eventuality. At last he said: "I think that's all. Can you remember it, now? If he should ask you anything you cant answer in the exact words you've learned tonight, just say nothing for a moment. I'll attend to the rest. Can you remember, now?"

"Yes," she whispered. He reached across and took the box of candy from the cot and opened it, the glazed paper crackling faintly. She took a piece. Goodwin had not moved. She looked at him, then at the narrow slit of window.

"Stop that," Horace whispered. "He couldn't reach him through that window with a hat-pin, let alone a bullet. Dont you know that?"

"Yes," she said. She held the bon-bon in her hand. She was not looking at him. "I know what you're thinking," she whispered.

"What?"

"When you got to the house and I wasn't there. I know what you're thinking." Horace watched her, her averted face. "You said tonight was the time to start paying you."

For a while longer he looked at her. "Ah-h-h," he said. "O tempora! O mores! O hell! Can you stupid mammals never believe that any man, every man-- - -----" he began to flap his hands in a faint repressed gesture. "You thought that was what I was coming for? You thought that if I had intended to, I'd have waited this long?"

She looked at him briefly. "It wouldn't have done you any good if you hadn't waited."

"What?" He blinked. "Oh. Well. But you would have tonight?"

"I thought that was what--------"

"You would now, then?" She looked around at Goodwin. He was snoring a little. "Oh, I dont mean right this minute," he whispered. "But you'll pay on demand."

"I thought that was what you meant. I told you we didn't have--------"

"Oh, Lord; oh,Lord; oh, Lord," Horace whispered.

"If that aint enough pay, I dont know that I blame you."

"It's not that. You know it's not that. But cant you see that perhaps a man might do something just because he knew it was right, necessary to the harmony of things that it be done?"

The woman turned the bon-bon slowly in her hand. "I thought you were mad about him."

"Lee?"

"No. Him." She touched the child. "Because I'd have to bring him with us."

"You mean, with him at the foot of the bed, maybe? perhaps you holding him by the leg all the time, so he wouldn't fall off?"

She looked at him, her eyes grave and blank and contemplative, and they looked at one another across that old barrier composed on the one hand of a quixotic folly which she knows serenely will soon be completely lost in the recrudescent fury of the flesh; on the other hand of a cold despair which he knows sorrowfully that the immemorial magic of the flesh will anneal. Outside the clock struck twelve.

"Good God," he whispered. "What kind of men have you known?"

"I got him out of jail once that way. Out of Leavenworth, too. When they knew he was guilty."

"You did?" Horace said. "Here. Take another piece. That one's about worn out." She looked down at her chocolate-stained fingers and the shapeless bon-bon. She dropped it behind the cot. Horace extended his handkerchief.

"It'll soil it," she said. "Wait." She wiped her fingers on the child's discarded garment and sat again, her hands clapped in her lap. Goodwin was snoring regularly. "When he went to the Philippines he left me in San Francisco. I got a job and I lived in a hall room, cooking over a gas-jet, because I told him I would. I didn't know how long he'd be gone, but I promised him I would and he knew I would. When he killed that other soldier over that nigger, I didn't even know it. I didn't get a letter from him for five months. It was just when I happened to see an old newspaper I was spreading on a closet shelf in the place where I worked that I saw the regiment was coming home, and when I looked at the calender it was that day. I'd been good all that time. I'd had good chances; ~~with~~ everyday I had them with the men coming in the restaurant.

"They wouldn't let me off~~, so I had to quit~~ to go and meet the ship, so I had to quit. Then they wouldn't let me see him, wouldn't even let me on the ship. I stood there while they came marching off of it, watching for him and asking the ones that passed if they knew where he was and them kidding me ~~and~~ if I had a date that night, telling me they never heard of him or that he was dead or he had run off to Japan with the colonel's wife. I tried to get on the ship again, but they wouldn't let me. So that night I dressed up and went to the cabarets until I found one and let him pick me up, and he told me. It was like I had died. I sat there with the music playing and all, and that drunk soldier pawing at me, and me wondering why I didn't let go, go on with him, get drunk and never sober up again and me thinking And this is the sort of animal I wasted a year over. I guess that was why I didn't.

"Anyway, I didn't. I went back to my room and the next day I started looking for him. I kept on, with them telling me lies and trying to make me, until I found he was in Leavenworth. I didn't have enough money for a ticket, so I had to get another job. It took two months to get enough money. Then I went to Leavenworth. I got another job as waitress, in Childs', nightshifts, so I could see Lee every other Sunday afternoon. We decided to get a lawyer. We didn't know that a lawyer couldn't do anything for a federal prisoner. The lawyer didn't tell me, and I hadn't told Lee how I was getting the lawyer. He thought I had saved some money. I lived with the lawyer two months before I found it out.

"Then the war came and they let Lee out ~~to~~ and sent him to France. I went to New York and got a job in a munitions plant. I stayed straight too, with the cities full of soldiers with money to spend, and even the little ratty girls wearing silk. But I stayed straight. Then he came home. I was at the ship to meet him. He got off under arrest and they sent him back to Leavenworth for killing that soldier ~~two~~ three years ago. Then I got a lawyer to get a Congressman to get him out. I gave him all the money I had saved too. So when Lee got out, we had nothing. He said we'd get married, but we couldn't afford to. And when I told him about the lawyer, he beat me."

Again she dropped a shapeless piece of candy behind the cot and wiped her hands on the garment. She chose another piece from the ~~bo~~ box and ate it. Chewing, she looked at Horace, turning upon him a blank, musing gaze for an unhurried moment. Through the slotted window the darkness came chill and dead.

Goodwin ceased snoring. He stirred and sat up.

"What time is it?" he said.

"What?" Horace said. He looked at his watch. "Half-past two."

"He must have had a puncture," Goodwin said.

Toward dawn Horace himself slept, sitting in the chair. When he waked a narrow rosy pencil of sunlight fell level through the window. Goodwin and the woman were talking quietly on the cot. Goodwin looked at him bleakly.

"Morning," he said.

"I hope you slept off that nightmare of yours," Horace said.

"If I did, it's the last one I'll have. They say you

dont dream there."

"You've certainly done enough not to miss it," Horace said. "I suppose you'll believe us, after this."

"Believe, hell," Goodwin said, who had sat so quiet, so contained, with his saturnine face, negligent in his overalls and blue shirt; "do you think for one minute that man is going to let me walk out of that door and up the street and into that courthouse, after yesterday? What sort of men have you lived with all your life? In a nursery? I wouldn't do that, myself."

"If he does, he has sprung his own trap," Horace said.

"What good will that do me? Let me tell-------"

"Lee," the woman said.

"------you something: the next time you want to play dice with a man's neck------"

"Lee," she said. She was stroking her hand slowly on his head, back and forth. She began to smooth his hair into a part, patting his collarless shirt smooth. Horace watched them.

"Would you like to stay here today?" he said quietly. "I can fix it."

"No," Goodwin said. "I'm sick of it. I'm going to get it over with. Just tell that goddamned deputy not to walk too close to me. You and her better go and eat breakfast."

"I'm not hungry," the woman said.

"You go on like I told you," Goodwin said.

"Lee."

"Come," Horace said. "You can come back afterward."

Outside, in the fresh morning, he began to breathe deeply. "Fill your lungs," he said. "A night in that place would give anyone the jim-jams. The idea of three grown people.. ... My Lord, sometimes I believe that we are all children, except children themselves. But today will be the last. By noon he'll walk out of there a free man: do you realise ~~it~~ that?"

~~"I dont know how youll get paid~~ They walked on in the fresh sunlight, beneath the high, soft sky. To them both it seemed now that last night had been the crux, the crisis; high against the blue fat little clouds blew up from the south-west, and the cool steady breeze shivered and twinkled in the locusts where the blooms had long since fallen.

"I dont know how you'll get paid," she said.

"Forget it. I've been paid. You wont understand it, but my soul has served an apprenticeship that has lasted for forty-three years. Forty-three years. Half again as long as you have lived. So you see that folly, as well as poverty, cares for its own."

"And you know that he-----that-------"

"Stop it, now. We dreamed that away, too. God is foolish at times, but at least He's a gentleman. Dont you know that?"

"I always thought of Him as a man," the woman said.

The bell was already ringing when he crossed the square toward the courthouse. Already the square was filled with wagons and cars, and the overalls and khaki thronged slowly beneath the gothic entrance of the building. Overhead the clock was striking nine as he mounted the stairs.

The broad double doors at the head of the cramped stair were open. From beyond them came a steady preliminary stir of people settling themselves. Above the seat-backs Horace could see their heads---bald heads, gray heads, shaggy heads and heads trimmed to recent feather-edge above sun-baked necks, ~~oiled heads~~ oiled heads above urban collars and here and there a ~~a~~ sunbonnet or a flowered hat.

The hum of their voices and movements came back upon the steady draft which blew through the door. The air entered the open windows and blew over the heads and back to Horace in the door, laden with smells of tobacco and stale sweat and the earth and with that unmistakable odor of courtrooms; that musty odor of spent lusts and greeds and bickerings and bitterness, and withal a certain clumsy stability in lieu of anything better. The windows gave upon balconies close under the arched porticoes. The breeze drew through them, bearing the chirp and coo of sparrows and pigeons that nested in the eaves, and now and then the sound of a motor horn from the square below, rising out of and sinking back into a hollow rumble of feet in the corridor below and on the stairs.

The Bench was empty. At one side, at the long table, he could see Goodwin's ~~head~~ black head and gaunt brown face, and the woman's gray hat. At the other end of the table sat a man picking his teeth. His skull was capped closely by tightly-curled black hair thinning upon a bald spot. He had a long, pale nose. He wore a tan palm beach suit; upon the table near him lay a smart leather brief-case and a straw hat with a red-and-tan band, and he gazed lazily out a window above the ranked heads, picking his teeth. Horace stopped, motionless. A jew, he said. A jew lawyer, his glance flicking away, darting this way and that about the adjacent heads. For seconds before he saw Temple he knew what he was going to find.

Once when he was a boy he had two possums in a barrel. A negro told him to put a cat in with them if he wanted to see something, and he had done so. When he could move at all he ran to his mother in a passion of crying that sent him staggering and vomiting toward the house. All that night he lay beneath an ice-pack in a lighted room, tearing himself now and then by main strength out of a writhing coil of cat-entrails, toward the thin, shawled figure of his mother sitting beside the bed.

"Mr Benbow," the Court was saying, "this is your witness?"

"It is, your Honor."

"You wish her sworn?"

"Yes, your Honor," he heard himself saying, while all the time it seemed to him that he still heard the bell ringing and the bailiff's voice on the balcony beneath the eaves where the pigeons preened and crooned:

"The honorable Circuit Court of Yoknapatawpha County is now open according to law..........."

XXIV.

The District Attorner faced the jury. "I offer as evidence this object which was found at the scene of the crime." He held in his hand a corn-cob. It appeared to have been dipped in dark brownish paint. "The reason this was not offered sooner is that its bearing on the case was not made clear until the testimony of the defendant's wife which I have just caused to be read aloud to you gentlemen from the record.

"You have just heard the testimony of the chemist and the gynicologist---who is, as you gentlemen know, an authority on the physical affairs of that most sacred thing in life: womanhood---who says that this is no longer a matter for the hangman, but for a bonfire of gasoline---------"

"I object!" Horace said. "The prosecution is attempting to sway--------"

"Sustained," the Court said. "Strike out the phrase beginning 'who says that', mister clerk. You may instruct the jury to disregard it, Mr Benbow. Keep to the matter in hand, Mr District Attorney."

The District Attorney bowed. He turned to the witness stand, where Temple sat. From beneath her black hat her hair escaped in tight red curls like clots of resin. The hat bore a rhinestone ornament. Upon her black satin lap lay a platinum bag.

Her pale tan coat was open upon a shoulder knot of pirple. Her hands lay motionless, palm-up on her lap. Her long blonde legs slanted, lax-ankled, her two motionless slippers with their glittering buckles lay on their sides as though empty. Above the ranked intent faces white and pallid as the floating bellies of dead fish, she sat in an attitude at once detached and cringing, her gaze fixed on something at the back of the room. Her face was quite pale, the two spots of rouge like paper discs pasted on her cheek bones, her mouth painted into a savage and perfect bow, also like something both symbolical and cryptic cut carefully from purple paper and pasted there.

The District Attorney stood before her.

"What is your name?" She did not answer. She moved her head slightly, as though he had obstructed her view, gazing at something in the back of the room. "What is your name?" he repeated, moving also, into the line of her vision again. Her mouth moved. "Louder," he said. "Speak out. No one will hurt you. Let these good men, these fathers and husbands, hear what you have to say and right your wrong for you."

The Court glanced at Horace, his eyebrows raised. But Horace made no move. He sat with his head bent a little, his hands clutched in his lap.

"Temple Drake," Temple said.

"Your age?"

"Eighteen."

"Where is your home?"

"Memphis," she said in a scarce distinguishable voice.

"Speak a little louder. These men will not hurt you. They are here to right the wrong you have suffered. Where did you live before you went to Memphis?"

"In Jackson."

"Have you relations there?"

"Yes."

"Come. Tell these good men-------"

"My father."

"Your mother is dead?"

"Yes."

"Have you any sisters?"

"No."

"You are your father's only daughter?"

Again the Court looked at Horace; again he made no move.

"Yes."

"Where have you been living since May twelfth of this year?" Her head moved faintly, as though she would see beyond him. He moved into her line of vision, holding her eyes. She stared at him again, giving her parrotlike answers.

"Did your father know you were there?"

"No."

"Where did he think you were?"

"He thought I was in school."

"You were in hiding, then, because something had happened to you and you ~~were~~ dared not--------"

"I object!" Horace said. "The question is lead------"

"Sustained," the Court said. "I have been on the point of warning you for some time, Mr Attorney, but defendant would not take exception, for some reason."

The District Attorney bowed toward the Benck. He turned to the witness and held her eyes again.

"Where were you on Sunday morning, May twelfth?"

"I was in the crib."

The room sighed, its collective breath hissing in the musty silence. Some newcomers entered, but they stopped at the rear of the room in a clump and stood there. Temple's head had moved again. He caught her gaze and held it. He half turned and pointed at Goodwin.

"Did you ever see that man before?" She gazed at the District Attorney, her face quite rigid, empty. From a short distance her eyes, the two spots of rouge and her mouth were like five meaningless objects in a small heart-shaped dish. "Look where I am pointing."

"Yes."

"Where did you see him?"

"In the crib."

"What were you doing in the crib?"

"I was hiding."

"Who were you hiding from?"

"From him."

"That man there? Look where I am pointing."

"Yes."

"But he found you."

"Yes."

"Was anyone else there?"

"Tommy was. He said------"

"Was he inside the crib or outside?"

"He was outside by the door. He was watching. He said he wouldn't let------"

"Just a minute. Did you ask him not to let anyone in?"

"Yes."

"And he locked the door on the outside?"

"Yes."

"But Goodwin came in."

"Yes."

"Did he have anything in his hand?"

"He had the pistol."

"Did Tommy try to stop him?"

"Yes. He said he--------"

"Wait. What did he do to Tommy?"

She gazed at him.

"He had the pistol in his hand. ~~What did he do to Tom~~ What did he do then?"

"He shot him." The District Attorney stepped aside. At once the girl's gaze went to the back of the room and became fixed there. The District Attorney returned, stepped into her line of vision. She moved her head; he caught her gaze and held it and lifted the stained corn-cob before her eyes. The room sighed, a long hissing breath.

"Did you ever see this before?"

"Yes."

The District Attorney turned away. "Your honor and gentlemen, you have listened this horrible, this unbelievable, story which this young girl has told; you have seen the evidence and heard the doctor's testimony: I shall no longer subject this ~~/////~~ ~~///////////~~ ruined, defenseless child to the agony of------" he ceased; the heads turned as one and watched a man come stalking up the aisle toward the Bench. He walked steadily, paced and followed by a slow gaping of the small white faces, a slow hissing of collars. He had ~~/~~ neat white hair and a clipped moustache like a bar of ~~//////~~ hammered silver against his dark skin. His eyes were pouched a little. A small paunch was buttoned snugly into his immaculate linen suit. He carried a panama hat in one hand and a slender black stick in the other. He walked steadily up the ~~/~~ aisle in a slow expulsion of silence like a prolonged sigh, looking to neither side. He passed the witness stand without a glance at the witness, who still gazed at something in the back of the room, walking right through her line of vision like a runner crossing a tape, and stopped before the bar above which the Court had half-risen, his arms on the desk.

"Your Honor," the old man said, "is the Court ~~///~~ done with this witness?"

"Yes, sir, Judge," the Court said; "yes, sir. Defenddant, do you waive ---------"

The old man turned slowly, erect above the held breaths, the little white faces, and looked down at the six people at the counsel table. Behind him the witness had not moved. She sat in her attitude of childish immobility, gazing like a drugged person above the faces, toward the rear of the room. The old man turned to her and extended his hand. She did not move. The room expelled its breath, sucked it quickly in and held it again. The old man touched her arm. She turned her head toward him, her eyes blank and all pupil above the three savage spots of rouge. She put her hand in his and rose, the platinum bag slipping from her lap to the floor with a thin clash, gazing again at the back of the room. With the toe of his small gleaming shoe the old man flipped the bag into the corner where the jury-box joined the Bench, where a spittoon sat, and steadied the girl down from the dais. The room breathed again as they moved on down the aisle.

Half way down the aisle the girl stopped again, slender in her smart open coat, her blank face rigid, then she moved on, her hand in the old man's. They returned down the aisle, the old man erect beside her, looking to neither side, paced by that slow whisper of collars. Again the girl stopped. She began to cringe back, her body arching slowly, her arm tautening in the old man's grasp. He bet toward her, speaking; she moved again, in that shrinking and rapt abasement. Four younger men were standing stiffly erect near the exit. They stood like soldiers, staring straight ahead until the old man and the girl reached them. Then they moved and surrounded the other two, and in a close body, the girl hidden among them, they moved toward the door. Here they stopped again; the girl could be seen shrunk against the wall just inside the door, her body arched again. She appeared to be clinging there, then the five bodies hid her again and again in a close body the group passed through the door and disappeared. The ro m sighed: a buzzing sound like a wind getting up. It moved forward with a slow increasing rush, on above the long table where the prisoner and the woman with the child and Horace and the District Attorney and the Memphis lawyer sat, and across the jury and against the Bench in a long sigh. The Memphis lawyer was sitting on his spine, gazing dreamily out the window. The child make a fretful sound, whimpering.

"Hush," the woman said. "Shhhhhhhh."

XXV.

"June 23.

"Dear Narcissa----

"I ran. Once I had not the sourage to admit it; now I have not the courage to deny it. I found more reality than I could stomach, I suppose. Call it that, anyway. I dont seem to care. Only I wish Belle had stayed in Kentucky. At least, that's out of the whole damned state wher such things can happen.

"She was at home. When Jones---you remember him: the one who says he used to lead Kinston society; now he drives it---put me down at the corner, I saw her shade up and the rosy light, and I thought of that unfailing aptitude of women for coinciding with the emotional periphery of a man at the exact moment when it reaches top dead center, at the exact moment when the fates have prized his jaws for the regurgitated bit. Thus (your own words) like a nigger I left her; like a nigger I returned (via the kitchen) ; entered the house and stood in the door while she laid her magazine down and watched me from her pink nest while I shed the ultimate cockleburr of errant itch and the final mudflake of the high pastures where the air had been a little too ardent and a little too stark, and so into the old barn and the warm twilight and the old stall fitting again to the honorable trace-galls, and, ay, the old manger lipped satin-smooth by the old unfailing oats.

"Little Belle is not at home. Thank God: at what age does man cease to believe he must support a certain figure before his women-folks? She is at a house-party. Where, Belle did not say, other than it divulging to be in the exact center of bad telephone connections. Thank God she is no flesh and blood of mine. I thank God that no bone and flesh of mine has taken that form which, rife with its inherent folly, knells and bequeaths its own disaster, untouched. Untouched, mind you. That's what hurts. Not that there is evil in the world; evil belongs in the world: it is the mortar in which the bricks are set. It's that they can be so impervious to the mire which they reveal and teach us to abhor; can wallow without tarnishment in the very stuff in the comparison with which their bright, tragic, fleeting magic lies. Cling to it. Not through fear; merely through some innate instinct of female economy, as they will employ any wiles whatever to haggle a butcher out of a penny. Thank God I have not and will never have a child ---and for that reason I have assailed not only a long distance, but a rural, line at eleven P.M. in order to hear a cool, polite, faintly surprised young voice on an unsatisfactory wire; a voice that, between polite inanities in response to inanities, carried on a verbal skirmishing with another one---not feminine---without even doing me the compliment of trying to conceal the fact that she had been squired to the telephone; needs must project over the dead wire to me, whose hair she has watched thinning for ten years, that young mammalian rifeness which she discovered herself less long ago than I the fact that,to anyone less than twenty-five years old, I am worse than dead..

"I ran. I dont try to palliate it. But I want to rectify it as far as possible. I know this will be distasteful to you, but it will be the last time, I promise that: next time I may not even have the courage to return. I want you to find that woman yourself; tell her that I must give up the case because I do not think I am good enough, and that I am putting it in the hands of the best criminal lawyer I can find, for an appeal, and that she is not to worry. Do this, my dear. You will have no trouble finding her. She's there now, in front of the jail with that child, standing where he can see ~~her~~ them from the window: have I not seen her there a thousand times? God, if he were the only one who had to see her there now.

"Horace."

XXVI.

"June 29.

"Dear Horace----

"I received your letter. Your message to that woman I cut off and mailed to her at the jail. I imagine she got it. They took the man away the day after you left. They were getting ready to lynch him, Isom said. So Jefferson is spared that at least. Why they should want to I cant see, since they are going to hang him anyway. So you can save hiring another lawyer.

"Bory has been quite sick. Sundy will let him eat green fruit. A nigger is the ruin of any white child. I dont know what to do. I cant say anything, because Miss Jenny is so foolish about the darkies. She is as usual. She sends love.

"I am glad to hear you have decided to stay at home after this. I think that is wise. Belle is only thirty-eight. She might not be there when you come back, next time.

"Love,

"Narcissa."

XXVII.

While on his way to Pensacola to ~~see/his/mother/~~ visit his mother, Popeye was arrested in Birmingham for the murder of a policeman in a small Alabama town on the night of June 17, 1929. At that time he had ~~been~~ was sitting in a parked touring car near a Memphis road-house, and he said "For Christ's sake", looking about the cell in the county jail, his free hand finicking a cigarette from his coat.

"Let him send for his lawyer," the said, "and get that off his chest. You want to wire?"

"Nah," he said, his cold, soft eyes touching briefly the cot, the high small window, the grated door through which the light fell. They removed the handcuff; Popeye's hand appeared to flick a small flame out of thin air. He lit the cigarette and snapped the match toward the door. "What do I want with a lawyer? I never was in------ What's the name of this dump?"

/They told him. "You forgot, have you?"

"He wont forget it no more," another said.

"Except he'll remember his lawyer's name by morning," the first said.

They left him smoking on the cot. He heard doors clash. Now and then he heard voices from the other cells; somewhere down the corridor a negro was singing. Popeye lay on the cot, his feet crossed in small, gleaming black shoes. "For Christ's sake," he said.

The next morning the judge asked him if he wanted a lawyer.

"What for?" he said. "I told them last night I never was here before in my life. I dont like your twon well enough to bring a stranger here for nothing."

The judge and the bailiff conferred aside.

"You'd better get your lawyer," the judge said.

"All right," Popeye said. He turned and spoke generally into the room: "Any of you ginneys want a one-day job?"

The judge rapped on the table. Popeye turned back, his tight shoulders lifted in a faint shrug, his hand moving toward the pocket where he carried his cigarettes. The judge appointed him counsel, a young man just out of law school.

"And I wont bother about being sprung," Popeye said. "Get it over with all at once."

"You wouldn't get any bail from me, anyway,"the judge told him.

"Yeuh?" Popeye said. "All right, Jack," he told his lawyer, "get going. I'm due in Pensacola right now."

"Take the prisoner back to jail," the judge said.

His lawyer had an ugly, eager, earnest face. He rattled on with a kind of gaunt enthusiasm while Popeye lay on the cot, smoking, his hat over his eyes, motionless as a basking snake save for the periodical movement of the hand that held the cigarette.

At last he said: "Here. I aint the judge. Tell him all this."

"But I've got-------"

"Sure. Tell it to them. I dont know nothing about it. I wasn't even there. Get out and walk it off."

The trial lasted one day. While a fellow policeman, a cigar-clerk, a telephone girl testified, while his own lawyer rebutted in a gaunt mixture of uncouth enthusiasm and earnest ill-judgment, Popeye lounged in his chair, looking out the window above the ~~judge's head~~ jury's heads. Now and then he yawned; his hand moved to the pocket where his cigarettes lay, then refrained and rested idle against the black cloth of his suit, in the waxy lifelessness of shape and size like the hand of a doll.

The jury was out eight minutes. They stood and looked at him and said he was guilty. Motionless, his position unchanged, he looked back at them in a slow silence for several moments, "Well, for Christ's sake," he said.

The judge rapped sharply with his gavel; the officer touched his arm.

"I'll appeal," the lawyer babbled, plunging along beside him. "I'll fight them through every court---------"

"Sure," Popeye said, lying on the cot and lighting a cigarette; "but not in here. Beat it, now. Go take a pill."

The District Attorney was already making his plans for the appeal. "It was too easy," he said. "He took it-----Did you see how he took it? like he might be listening to a song he was too lazy to either like or dislike, and the Court telling him on what day they were going to break his neck. Probably got a Memphis lawyer already there outside the supreme court door now, waiting for a wire. I know them. It's them thugs like that that have made justice a laughing-stock, until even when we get a conviction, everbody knows it wont hold."

Popeye sent for the turnkey and gave him a hundred dollar bill. He wanted a shaving-kit and cigarettes. "Keep the change and let me know when it's smoked up," he said.

"I reckon you wont be smoking with me much longer," the turnkey said. "You'll get a good lawyer, this time."

"Dont forget that lotion," Popeye said. "Ed Pinaud." He called it "Py-nawd."

It had been a gray summer, a little cool. Little daylight ever reached the cell, and a light burned in the corridor all the time, falling into the cell in a broad pale mosaic, reaching the cot where his feet lay. The turnkey gave him a chair. He used it for a table; upon it the dollar watch lay, and a carton of cigarettes and a cracked soup bowl of stubs, and he lay on the cot, smoking and contemplating his feet while day after day passed. The gleam of his shoes grew duller, and his clothes needed pressing, because he lay in them all the time, since it was cool in the stone cell.

One day the turnkey said: "There's folks here says that deppity invited killing. He done two-three mean things folks knows about." Popeye smoked, his hat over his face. The turnkey said: "They might mot a sent your telegram. You want me to send another one for you?" Leaning against the grating he could see Popeye's feet, his thin, black legs motionless, merging into the delicate bulk of his prone body and the hat slanted across his averted face, the cigarette in one small hand. His feet were in shadow, in the shadow of the turnkey's body where it blotted out the grating. After a while the turnkey went away quietly.

/When he had six days left the turnkey offered to bring him magazines, a deck of cards.

"What for?"Popeye said. For the first time he looked at the turnkey, his head lifted, in his smooth, pallid face his eyes round and soft as those prehensile tips on a child's ~~aro/ arrows~~ toy arrows. Then he lay back again. After that each morning the turmkey thrust a rolled newspaper through the door. They fell to the floor and lay there, accumulating, unrolling and flattening slowly of their own weight in diurnal progression.

When he had three days left a Memphis lawyer arrived. Unbidden,,he rushed up to the cell. All that morning the turnkey heard his voice raised in pleading and anger and expostulation; by noon he was hoarse, his voice not much louder than a whisper.

"Are you just going to lie here and let------"

"I'm~~/~~ all right," Popeye said. "I didn't send for you. Keep your nose out."

"Do you want to hang? Is that it? Are you trying to commit suicide? Are you so tired of dragging down jack that......

You, the smartest---------"

"I told you once. I've got enough on you."

"You, to have it hung on you by a small-time j.p.! When I go back to Memphis and tell them, they wont believe it."

"Dont tell them, then." He lay for a ~~xxxxe~~ time while the lawyer looked at him in baffled and raging unbelief. "Them durn hicks," Popeye said. "Jesus Christ./........Beat it, now," he said. "I told you. I'm all right."

On the night before, a minister came in.

"Will you let me pray with you?" he said.

"Sure," Popeye said; "go ahead. Dont mind me."

The minister knelt beside the cot where Popeye lay smoking. After a while the minister heard him~~xxxe~~ rise and cross the floor, then return to the cot. When he rose Popeye was lying on the cot, smoking. The minister looked behind him, where he had heard Popeye moving and saw twelve marks at spaced intervals along the base of the wall, as though marked there with burned matches. Two of the spaces were filled with cigarette stubs laid in neat rows. In the thrid space were two stubs. Before he departed he watched Popeye rise and go there and crush out two more stubs and lay them carefully beside the others.

Just after five oclock the minister returned. All the spaces were filled save the twelfth one. It was three quarters complete. Popeye was lying on the cot. "Ready to go?" he said.

"Not yet," the minister said. "Try to pray," he said. "Try."

"Sure," Popeye said; "go ahead." The minister knelt again. He heard Popeye rise once and cross the floor and then return.

At five-thirty the turnkey came. "I brought-----" he said. He held his closed fist dumbly through the grating. "Here's your change from that hundred you never------ I brought........ It's forty-eight dollars," he said. "Wait; I'll count it again; I dont know exactly, but I can give you a list-------them tickets.........."

"Keep it," Popeye said, without moving. "Buy yourself a hoop."

They came for him at six. The minister went with him, his hand under Popeye's elbow, and he stood beneath the scaffold praying, while they adjusted the rope, dragging it over Popeye's sleek, oiled head, breaking his hair loose. His hands were tied, so he began to jerk his head, flipping his hair back each time it fell forward again, while the minister prayed, the others motionless at their posts with bowed heads.

Popeye began to jerk his neck forward in little jerks. "Psssst!" he said, the sound cutting sharp into the drone of the minister's voice; "pssssst!" The sheriff looked at him; he //////////The/sheri quit jerking his neck and stood rigid, as though he had an egg balanced on his head. "Fix my hair, Jack," he said.

It had been a gray day, a gray summer, a gray year.

On the street old men wore overcoats, and in the Luxembourg Gardens as Temple and her father passed the women sat knitting in shawls and even the men playing croquet played in coats and capes, and in the sad gloom of the chestnut trees the dry click of balls, the random shouts of children, had that quality of autumn, gallant and evanescent and forlorn. Beyond the circle with its spurious Greek balustrade, clotted with movement, filled with a gray light of the same color and texture as the water which the fountain played into the pool, came a steady crash of music. They went on, passed the pool where the children and an old man or so sailed toy boats, and entered the trees again and found seats. ~~//////~~ Immediately an old woman came with decrepit promptitude and collected four sous.

In the pavilion a band in the horizon blue of the army played Massanet and Scriabine, and Berlioz like a thin coating of tortured Tschaikovsky on a slice of stale bread, while the twilight dissolved in wet gleams from the branches, onto the pavilion and the sombre toadstools of umbrellas. Rich and resonant the brasses crashed and died in the thick green twilight, rolling over them in rich ~~/////~~ sad waves. Temple yawned behind her hand, then she took out a compact and opened it upon a face in miniature sullen and discontented and sad. Beside her her father sat, his hands crossed on the head of his stick, the rigid bar of his moustache beaded with moisture like frosted silver. She closed the compact and from beneath her smart new hat she seemed to follow with her eyes the waves of music, to dissolve into the dying brasses, across the pool and the opposite semicircle of trees where at sombre intervals the dead tranquil queens in stained marbe mused, and on into the sky lying prone and vanquished in the embrace of the season of rain and death.

Sure, the sheriff said, I'll fix it for you; springing the trap.

Oxfd. Miss.
25 May. 1929

This book was written 3 years ago. ~~At that time I was without money a house painter. I had also written 4 novels.~~ It is a ~~bad book, a cheap book.~~ cheap book, deliberately manufactured. idea, a ~~cheap idea~~. It was written to ~~make money~~ sell, to make money. At the time I ~~happened to~~ was a be a house painter. I had written my guts into one book in particular "The Sound and the Fury." Meanwhile I had the mss of another novel which had been refused by all the publishers which I knew.

This book was written 3 years ago. To me it is a cheap idea, because it was deliberately conceived to make money. I had been writing books for about 5 years, which got published and not bought. But that was all right. I was young then, and hard-bellied. I had never lived among nor known people who wrote novels and stories, and I suppose I did not know that people got money for them. I was not very much annoyed when publishers refused the mss. now and then. Because I was hard-gutted then. I could do a lot of things that could earn what little money I needed, thanks to my father's unfailing kindness which supplied me with bread at need despite the outrage to his principles at having been of a bum progenitive.

Then I began to get a little soft. I could still paint houses and do carpenter work, but I got soft. I began to think about making money by writing. I began to be concerned when magazine editors turned down short stories; enough to tell them that they would buy these stories later anyway, and hence why not now. Meanwhile, with one novel completed and consistently refused for 2 years, I had just written my guts into "The Sound and the Fury" though I was not aware until the book was published that I had done so, because I had done it for pleasure. I believed then that I would never be published again. I had stopped thinking of myself in publishers' terms.

But when the third mss. was taken by a publisher and (he having refused "The Sound and the Fury") it was taken by still another publisher, who warned me at the time that it would not sell, I began to think of myself again as a printed object. I began to think of books in terms of possible money. I decided I might just as well make some of it myself. I took a little time out and speculated what a person in Miss. would believe to be current trends, ~~and then I invented~~ I ~~decided~~ chose what I thought was the right answer and so I invented the most horrific tale I could imagine and ~~sent~~ wrote it in about 3 weeks and sent it to Smith, who had done The Sound and the Fury" and who wrote me immediately "Good God, I can't publish this. We'd both be in jail."

So I told Faulkner, "You're damned. You'll have to work now and then for the rest of your life." That was in the summer of 1929. I got a job in the power plant, on the night shift, from 6 p.m. to 6 a.m. ~~About 11 the boilers would begin to go off~~ as a coal passer. I shovelled coal from the bunker into a ~~sheet~~ wheel barrow and wheeled it in ~~and~~ and dumped it where the fireman could put it into the boiler. About 11 oclock the ~~lights~~ people would be gone to bed, and so it did not take so much steam. Then we could rest, the fireman and I. He would sit in a chair and doze. I had made a ~~chair~~ table in a wheelbarrow in the coal bunker, just ~~over~~ beyond a wall from where a dynamo ran. It made a deep ~~humming noise~~ constant hum noise. There was no more work to do until about 4 a.m., when we would have to clean the fires and get up steam again. On these nights between 12 and 4 I wrote "As I Lay Dying" in 6 weeks, without changing a word. I sent it to Smith and wrote him that by it I would stand or fall.

I think I had forgot about "Sanctuary", just as you might forget about anything made for an immediate purpose, which did not come off. "As I Lay Dying" was published, and I didn't remember the mss of "Sanctuary" until Smith sent me the galleys. Then I saw that it was so terrible that there was but 2 things to do. Tear it up or rewrite it. I thought again, "It might sell. Maybe 10,000 of them will buy it." So I tore the galleys down and rewrote the book. It had been already set up, so I had to pay for the privilege of rewriting it, trying to make out of it something which would not shame "The Sound and the Fury" and "As I Lay Dying" too much. And I made a fair job and I hope you will buy it and tell your friends. And I hope they buy it, too.

Let's abolish the preface altogether in new printing. This will make the old prints which have it more valuable. New print dont need it.

SANCTUARY

page - line

p.vi, 13 — it was taken / The "it" probably refers to <u>Sound and Fury</u>, which, however, is in the parenthesis. Shouldn't this passage read: "...<u>Sartoris</u>, was taken by a publisher who had refused <u>The Sound and the Fury</u>, which was taken by still another..."

But see note elsewhere on whether to drop introduction altogether, or only from new trade edition

✓ 40, 16 — <u>Negro</u> - cap throughout, as in all your recent books. Yes

correct this one.

✓ 64, 25 — govenor / governor? as in same speech 3 lines below

This to me has two meanings: "Do you want any more soup?" "I dont love you anymore."

71, 23 — anymore / any more (throughout)

✓ 92, 9-10 — ...the door beyond which Temple lay and where Gowan snored. / The "where" has no function and must have slipped in. OK to delete? Delete

✓ 101, 20 — ~~And coming back with a car~~. And come back with another car to get here. I'll decide... Something went wrong here. Will simple change of period to comma fix it?

✓ 128, 23 — ...to learn that, if a woman dont... better without comma? Yes. delete(s)

✓ 136, 21-22 — I aint going say / I aint going to say? Yes. The "to" must have been lost by printer, because this is not characteristic of Goodwin's speech. OK to restore? Yes

✓ 143, 6 — ...ruined house twelve miles from town... <u>Hamlet</u> (p.3) and <u>Town</u> (p.5) establish distance from Jefferson to Frenchman's Bend as 20 miles. On map in <u>Absalom</u>, the Old Frenchman place is beyond the hamlet itself. So 12 miles must be wrong unless Jefferson has grown to be as big as Memphis in the years from 1910 to 1929. Make it 20 miles from town.

Want to change here? Or ignore? Please indicate wishes on p. 143.

✓ 149, 18 — passerby / The context seems to call for plural (boys, men). OK to make it passersby? Yes

✓ 155, 22 — ...was to be hung / To be strictly correct, this should be hanged. Change? Yes

✓ 170, 1 — negress / Negro woman? as in <u>Reivers</u> Yes. They dont like negress.

SANCTUARY -2-

page - line

173, 17 ...was hael / This seems not to be even a correct old form of wassail, which in Old English is wes hal; in Middle English, waes hail or wes hail; and by Shakespeare's time, wassel. Use this one

Why not simply wassail here? Indicate preference on p. 173.

174, 22 A Negro maid... / shouldn't this be The Negro maid, as already identified, middle of p. 170? Yes

207, 20 ...the sleek crowns / This might be right, but I wonder if it should be crowds. Please indicate. Crowds Yes

209, 16 Should "at" be inserted before "an express truck"--to conform with other two "ats" in the series? delete other "at" (margin)

209, 19 ...gone restfully against the wall / This is probably right, but maybe something got lost. Is it OK as set? OK as set. "gone" equals "relaxed"

230, 15 ...almost seven oclock / This pretty clearly should be almost six oclock. On p. 229, they reach the front of the house at five-thirty, walk around block to the back, then come back around to front.

OK to make it six on p. 230? O.K. But they probably took that hour & 1/2 going around the block. I think it's funnier to leave it 7 o'clock.

265,17-18 ...how that were the only solution / ? that was the Which should it be? Horace would have thought "were".

300, 9-10 The street was broad and now infrequent... Something must have gotten fouled up here, or something left out. Or is it simply that the street is "now unfrequented"? Make it "almost empty" if you like.

312, 12 Is "stan up!" OK? or a typo? It's dialect, like "runnin".

316, 21 were your brother / this has to be "weren't" Yes

336, 21 High against the blue, fat little clouds...

A comma after blue will keep it from seeming to modify clouds. OK to put? Yes

see 215 (cf Note 71,23)
250

Time discrepancies between The Reivers (1905) and Sanctuary (1929 or 1930) (page and line references are Sanctuary)

185, 1-11 "landlord here eleven years until he die bout two years ago. Next day Miss Reba get these dawgs,..."

Miss Reba seems to have been in business about five years in 1905; so by now it is roughly 30 years. Mr Binford cannot have died too long ago, because she got the dogs "next day"--and they are not only still alive but still active. If passage read: "landlord here twenty-five years until he die bout five years ago..." I think everything would match up. all right.

306, 28-29 "For eleven years we was like two doves." Change to conform with whatever arithmetic is adopted on 185. Yes

307, 25-26 "running a shooting-gallery for twenty years..." / thirty years ? Yes

311, 3-4 "running a house for twenty years..." / thirty years ? Yes